Celebration in Postwar American Fiction

Celebration in Postwar American Fiction 1945-1967

By RICHARD H. RUPP

UNIVERSITY OF MIAMI PRESS

Coral Gables, Florida

PS
379
.R8

Designed by Bernard Lipsky

Manufactured in the United States of America

For Elizabeth and Christopher,
who like stories

Contents

Preface

THIS BOOK is a study of celebration in ten of the best American writers of fiction since the end of the Second World War. Although the concept of celebration is developed more fully in the Introduction, I might say here that it is not so much a theme, like alienation or the absurd, as it is an experience, like singing or jumping. The motive for jumping and celebrating is the same—an acceptance, a joyful approval of life expressed in a physical action. Fiction presents us with experiences like jumping, after all, and not ideas like alienation. Or more bluntly, the experience is in the fiction and the alienation is in the criticism.

This reading of contemporary fiction takes an Emersonian view: "We ought to celebrate this hour by expressions of manly joy. . . . When all is said and done, the rapt saint is found the only logician. Not exhortation, not argument becomes our lips, but paeons of joy and praise." [1] In developing a theory of festivity I have relied on a little book by the German Thomist Josef Pieper, *In Tune with the World*. Current trends in criticism, stressing existentialism, despair, and desperate affirmation, tend to distort the fiction they explicate. No theory, really, whether it be Emerson's, Pieper's, or Sartre's, can represent an esthetic experience.

Nevertheless, some perspective is necessary for the reader and inevitable for the critic. The one in this book is affirmative, festive, and ultimately liturgical. For, as Pieper points out, the ultimate celebration is worship.

Criticism is a game of a high and serious sort, played by its own rules; the first rule is to know how far to stretch the basic metaphor. This book then is a study in the limits of a metaphor. Celebration is a significant act, especially in contemporary fiction. But it is not the only significant act. I have tried to keep a proper perspective here, remembering Frost's dictum that freedom is being easy in harness. The books are what matter, not the theory.

There are other rules. I have referred to paperback editions throughout, with one or two exceptions, on the grounds that they are more accessible. All these works were available in paperback as of January 1, 1968. Another rule: I have kept plot summaries to a minimum, thinking them unnecessary. Again, I have tried to give each novel equal time, so to speak, although the chapter on Ellison confines itself largely to a single work. Furthermore, I have dwelt on the most important work of each writer, rather than restrict myself to novels alone. The best work of Eudora Welty and Flannery O'Connor, for instance, is in the short story. Similarly, the essays of James Baldwin are at least as important as his fiction and offer a perspective on it. The groundrule here has been to pay greatest attention to the most significant work of the writer under review.

I have not felt compelled to assess the critical views currently available on these writers. Unlike scholarship, which conveys or retrieves information for its own sake, criticism conveys a point of view and records the interaction between the work and the sensibility. One ought, it seems to me, to be both a critic and a scholar, but not at the same time. At any rate, to record critical interpretations is to misapply scholarly method. What we learn from criticism is a way of looking at books, and ways of looking do not lend themselves to documentation. I must admit a practical difficulty, too; I cannot synthesize all the critical comments on these ten writers—there is simply too much to account for.

Selecting from among the many talented writers working today is difficult. One could make as strong a case for Mailer (especially Mailer), McCullers, Styron, Warren, Barth, Nabokov, Roth, Porter, Morris, and Powers as I make for these ten. I happen to like my choices better—hopefully because they are indeed significant writers (but I would not say more significant). Their context is more thoroughly traditional, too, and offers a more fruitful basis for comparison. I have chosen to write about Agee and Cheever because I think they have been unduly neglected; I have chosen Salinger and Baldwin because they illustrate a relationship between formal problems and a failure of festivity; the other six are obvious choices, I think.

The chapters are arranged in pairs. Cheever and Updike work in the middle-class Protestant tradition, Welty and O'Connor in the southern tradition, Baldwin and Ellison in the Negro tradition, Malamud and Bellow in the Jewish tradition. A substantive pairing is also possible here: Cheever and Updike share an approach through ceremonial style; Welty and O'Connor share a rural setting; Agee and Salinger have similar views toward innocence; Baldwin and Ellison demonstrate by contrast a sense of celebration lost and found; Malamud and Bellow demonstrate, respectively, a sense of isolated celebration founded on past tradition and a sense of contemporary, pluralistic celebration. But scheme and theme are not ends in themselves here; the observant reader will find many satisfying loose ends.

In summary then this book stresses traditional rather than existential values. Celebration is fundamentally a religious act—an acceptance of order, hierarchy, and authority in life. In this sense my perspective is also optimistic and conservative.

A much shorter version of the O'Connor chapter appeared in *Commonweal* for December 3, 1963; a substantially similar version of the Updike chapter appeared in the *Sewanee Review* for Autumn, 1967 (Copyright © 1967, by the Sewanee Review). I wish to acknowledge the editors' permission to reprint these chapters in their final form.

I wish to thank Georgetown University for a research grant that gave me time to write a substantial portion of this book in the summer of 1967; Ray Reno and Tom Walsh for their careful reading and comments on portions of the manuscript; Roger Slakey for raising some fundamental questions and pushing me to find answers for them; Gerhard Joseph, Peter McNamara, John McKenna, and Cosmo Tassone for help on various points; and my students and colleagues at Georgetown, who have listened patiently to these chapters in various versions. My debt to my wife is best left unspecified.

Coral Gables, Florida
January, 1970

Acknowledgements

Letters of James Agee to Father Flye by James Agee; © by George Braziller, Inc. Excerpts are reprinted by permission of the publisher, George Braziller, Inc.

From books copyrighted by James Baldwin selections are used by permission of the publisher, The Dial Press, Inc. *Another Country* © 1960, 1962. *The Fire Next Time* © 1962, 1963. *Giovanni's Room* © 1956. *Going to Meet the Man* © 1948, 1951, 1957, 1958, 1960, 1965. *Go Tell It On The Mountain* © 1952, 1953. *Nobody Knows My Name* © 1954, 1956, 1958, 1959, 1960, 1961.

The following books by Bernard Malamud are copyrighted by Bernard Malamud. Excerpts are reprinted by permission of Farrar, Straus and Giroux, Inc. *The Assistant* © 1961. *The Fixer* © 1966. *Idiots First* © 1950, 1959, 1961, 1962, 1963. *The Magic Barrel* © 1950, 1951, 1952, 1953, 1954, 1955, 1956, 1958. *The Natural* © 1952. *A New Life* © 1961.

Excerpts from the following books by Flannery O'Connor are reprinted by permission of the publisher, Farrar, Straus and Giroux, Inc. *Everything That Rises Must Converge* © 1956, 1957, 1958, 1960, 1961, 1962, 1964, 1965 by the Estate of Mary Flannery O'Connor. *Wise Blood* © 1949, 1952, 1962 by Flannery O'Connor. *The Violent Bear It Away* © 1955, 1960 by Flannery O'Connor. Selections from "The Role of the Catholic Novelist" by Flannery O'Connor are reprinted from *Mystery and Manners* by Flannery O'Connor. Selected and edited by Sally and Robert Fitzgerald and © 1957, 1969 by the Estate of Mary Flannery O'Connor.

A Death in the Family by James Agee; © 1957 by the James Agee Trust. Excerpts are reprinted by permission of the publisher, Grosset and Dunlap, Inc.

A Good Man Is Hard to Find © 1953, 1954, 1955 by Flannery O'Connor. Excerpts are reprinted by permission of the publisher, Harcourt, Brace & World, Inc.

In Tune With the World by Josef Pieper; © 1963, 1965 by Harcourt, Brace and World, Inc.

14 *Acknowledgements*

The following books by Eudora Welty are copyrighted by Eudora Welty and excerpts are used by permission of the publisher, Harcourt, Brace and World, Inc. *Delta Wedding* © 1945, 1946. *The Golden Apples* © 1947, 1948, 1949. *The Ponder Heart* © 1953, 1954. *The Robber Bridegroom* © 1942. *Thirteen Stories* © 1937, 1938, 1939, 1940, 1942, 1949, 1951, 1965.

The Wapshot Chronicle by John Cheever; © 1954, 1956, 1957 by John Cheever. *The Wapshot Scandal* by John Cheever; © 1959, 1961, 1962, 1963, 1964 by John Cheever. Excerpts are reprinted by permission of Harper and Row, Inc.

"John Cheever and the Charms of Innocence" by George Garrett; © 1964 by *The Hollins Critic*. Selections are reprinted by permission of *The Hollins Critic*.

"Birches" from *Complete Poems of Robert Frost;* © 1916 by Holt, Rinehart and Winston, Inc.; © 1944 by Robert Frost. Excerpt reprinted by permission of Holt, Rinehart and Winston, Inc.

Let Us Now Praise Famous Men by James Agee; © 1939, 1940 by James Agee; © 1941 by James Agee and Walker Evans. © 1960 by Walker Evans. *The Morning Watch* by James Agee; © 1950 by James Agee. Selections reprinted by permission of the publisher, Houghton Mifflin, Inc.

"The House of Pain: Emerson and the Tragic Sense" by Newton Arvin. Excerpts reprinted by permission from *The Hudson Review*, Vol. XII, No. 1 (Spring, 1959); © 1959 by The Hudson Review, Inc.

A World Elsewhere by Richard Poirier; © 1966 by Richard Poirier. Excerpt reprinted with the permission of the author.

Invisible Man by Ralph Ellison; © 1947, 1948, 1952 by Ralph Ellison. *Shadow and Act* by Ralph Ellison; © 1953, 1964 by Ralph Ellison. Excerpts reprinted by permission of the publisher, Random House, Inc., and Alfred A. Knopf, Inc.

"Sunday Morning" from *The Collected Poems of Wallace Stevens.* © 1923, 1954 by Wallace Stevens. Excerpt reprinted by permission of the publisher, Random House, Inc., and Alfred A. Knopf, Inc.

Excerpts from the following books copyrighted by John Updike are reprinted with the permission of the publisher, Random House, Inc., and Alfred A. Knopf, Inc. *Assorted Prose* © 1955, 1956, 1957, 1958, 1959, 1960, 1961, 1962, 1963, 1964, 1965. *The Centaur* © 1962, 1963. *Couples* © 1968. *Of the Farm* © 1965. *Pigeon Feathers* © 1959, 1960, 1961, 1962. *The Poorhouse Fair* © 1958. *Rabbit, Run* © 1960. *The Same Door* © 1954, 1955, 1956, 1957, 1958, 1959.

The Great Gatsby by F. Scott Fitzgerald; © 1925 by Charles Scribner's Sons, Inc.; © 1953 by Frances Scott Fitzgerald Lanahan. Selections reprinted by permission of the publisher, Charles Scribner's Sons, Inc.

Dangling Man by Saul Bellow; © 1944 by The Vanguard Press, Inc. *The Victim* by Saul Bellow; © 1947 by Saul Bellow. Excerpts reprinted by permission of the publisher, Vanguard Press, Inc.

The following books are copyrighted by Saul Bellow and excerpts are reprinted with the permission of the publisher, The Viking Press, Inc. *The Adventures of Augie March* © 1949, 1951, 1952, 1953. *Herzog* © 1961, 1963, 1964. *Seize the Day* © 1956.

Celebration in Postwar American Fiction

"It may not be too much to affirm, on the whole, (the people being then in the first stages of joyless deportment, and the offspring of sires who had known how to be merry, in their day,) that they would compare favorably, in point of holiday keeping, with their descendants, even at so long an interval as ourselves. Their immediate posterity, the generation next to the early emigrants, wore the blackest shade of Puritanism, and so darkened the national visage with it, that all the subsequent years have not sufficed to clear it up. We have yet to learn again the forgotten art of gayety."

—NATHANIEL HAWTHORNE, *The Scarlet Letter*

1 ❧ Living in the Present: American Fiction Since 1945

SINCE 1945 a whole generation has been born, grown to maturity, and moved out into the complexities of the modern world. Perhaps the principal characteristic of that world is confusion: confusion of purpose, uncertain identity, and the widespread abdication of authority. This confusion extends to the arts and to literature in a special way. The contemporary novel seems to offer us unintelligible pictures of an unintelligible world. One of John Cheever's characters, describing a scene she is reading, complains aptly: " 'The things you read about in these paper books,' the maid said. 'I don't know. I been married three times but right here in this book they're doing something and I don't know what it is. I mean I don't know what they're doing.' "

We might ask the same question of our contemporary novelists: what are they doing? The critic's answer is to establish a common theme and to work it out from there. Ihab Hassan sees Radical Innocence at the root of the postwar novel; Jonathan Baumbach sees the Landscape of Nightmare; Marcus Klein sees Accommodation after Alienation.[1]

However one chooses to look at contemporary American fiction, the problems reduce themselves to those of form and feeling. Society itself seems formless, fluid, without the comforting assurances of stability and order. The novel seems to reflect the basic unintelligibility of the present by rejecting fictional form as irrelevant. As for feeling, no response to life is proscribed. Sexual perversion, for instance, is a viable option in the novel of our day—at least in reflecting the general pain of loving in a loveless world. To live is to witness the chaos of personal and social relationships in that world; to write is to show that chaos.

Our problem, as I see it, is a general inability to celebrate reality. Hawthorne noted it as long ago as 1850; by now it is a national trait. Successive generations have never reversed his indictment in *The Scarlet Letter*; our novelists can scarcely project a festive world that does not exist outside of Broadway musicals. If genuine celebration is rare in contemporary life, it is also rare in contemporary fiction. Nevertheless, the best of our novelists seem to move *toward* celebration, although that move is tentative, groping, and fleeting. Our most responsible fiction manifests an assent to reality, a willingness to live. Upon these things is celebration founded.

Celebration is ultimately a religious act, though it has many secular manifestations. It is an act of praise, a ritual sacrifice expressing an assent to reality in corporate action—an action founded on love and leading to individual renewal. In his excellent book on the subject, Josef Pieper puts it this way: "*To celebrate a festival means: to live out, for some special occasion and in an uncommon manner, the universal assent to the world as a whole.*" [2]

Pieper goes on to note several further characteristics of celebration. It is ordinarily expressed in ceremonies of praise; at its best it is a ritual festivity; the most ruthless destruction of festivity is the refusal of ritual praise.

[The] conclusion is divisible into several parts. *First:* there can be no more radical assent to the world than the praise of God, the lauding of the Creator of this same world. One cannot conceive a more intense, more unconditional affirmation of being. If the heart of festivity consists in men's physically expressing their agreement with everything that is, then—*secondly*—the ritual festival is the most festive form that festivity can possibly take. The other side of the coin is that—*thirdly*—there can be no deadlier, more ruthless destruction of festivity than refusal of ritual praise. Any such Nay tramples out the spark from which the flickering flame of festivity might have been kindled anew. (p. 24)

Pieper suggests that festivity is a continuum from the secular to the sacred: "Wherever festivity can freely vent itself in all its possible forms, an event is produced that leaves no zones of life, worldly or spiritual, untouched"; (p. 26) and that the basis for celebration as well as for art is love: *"C'est l'amour qui chante;* only the lover sings; without love we cannot expect song. 'Song' here stands not only for poetry and, of course, music, but also for the utterances and works of all the fine arts taken together. Elegy, too, is song" (p. 41).

Such a bald summary does an injustice to *In Tune with the World;* I refer the interested reader to the book itself. For our purposes, Pieper's concept of celebration seems appropriate to describe the festive moments in contemporary American fiction. Whatever form they take—meals, weddings, funerals, holidays; love-making, race riots, morning swims, trading a car; elegies and laments, the prayers of a drunken minister; Negro spirituals, blues, jazz, and eulogies—whatever the form, all these actions share at some level in the universal assent to the world as a whole. The cause for celebration is reality itself.

Now, good fiction is not written to formula, even so worthy a formula as Pieper suggests. Nor is the best fiction of our time overtly religious. But at some point in the continuum of human experience, the assent to reality becomes an act of faith. I do not wish to isolate such points in fiction—merely to suggest what is often implicit in apparently hopeless situations. As works of art, our novels and stories must stand on their own merits, neither the better nor the worse for their religious content. But the need to celebrate reality in the face of the apocalyptic present is primary in contemporary fiction.

The modern novel, of course, has other subjects. Recently critics have called attention to style as a prime concern of the practicing writer. Richard Poirier's *A World Elsewhere* posits that language creates its own world, an environment radically different from economic, political, and social systems, one livable and lasting. He concludes his study with a commitment to that other world, a world made new by style:

In Faulkner and Fitzgerald, in Nabokov and Mailer is a resurgence of the Emersonian dream of possibly "building" a world out of the self in a style that is that self. The effort in *Lolita* to preserve "an intangible island of entranced time" succeeds no more than did the efforts in *The Crater,* over a hundred years before, to preserve an island paradise from the contaminations of modern democratic America. But such efforts are celebrated by these and by the other

American writers perhaps because success *is* forbidden them by realities other than style, by exigencies of time and space. The effort is celebrated because even out of the perverse design of Nabokov's hero there emerges those marvels of human ingenuity, those exuberances of imagination, those extravagances of yearning that create the objects they yearn for—these are the evidences still in American literature of the continuing struggle of consciousness toward some further created being and some other world.[3]

Perhaps no period more than our own has so emphasized style as an index of the quality of life. The desire for a distinctive style reflects the desire for an authentic voice.

For John Cheever, style is a way of looking at life. The characteristic qualities of his style reveal his essentially conservative outlook. Wryly humorous, nostalgic, and hyperbolic, Cheever's approach to living (as opposed to modern life) is joyful and affirmative. For him living is a reactionary activity, opposed in every way to the flattened perspectives and dehumanized values of contemporary life. Cheever's comic style projects a sense of the self and of human values that are not only traditional but historical: honor, self-reliance, individualism, strong family loyalties, and the strenuous life.

Cheever's approach to our problems is at once deflationary and reassuring. It manifests style in the broad sense—as a way around things if not through them. He evokes a rich life, fully felt. For Cheever life is an affirmative activity and not a prison sentence. Like Thoreau he finds himself the center of a teeming world.

John Updike is probably the finest stylist writing fiction today. He has tight control not only of the sentence and the paragraph but also of the eye and ear. Updike's style reflects the disciplined imagination at work on the riddling surface of sense experience, probing for a way inside. Fidelity to the multiple small sensations of modern living is John Updike's first achievement.

But like Cheever, Updike is at heart a conservative and a ceremonialist. His sense of social order is founded on a pervasive concern for the rituals of daily living. More often than not he plays the devil's advocate with them. In *Rabbit, Run* and *Of the Farm* he demonstrates the emotional squalor of life without social forms, of life without style. Both he and Cheever find an approach to the present and a way of living through ceremonial style.

Another concern, of great prominence in the work of Faulkner and Warren, is the agrarian theme. *I'll Take My Stand* (1930) offered a social and economic platform, but the results have been chiefly literary. John Crowe Ransom, Allen Tate, and Andrew Lytle have been conscious exemplars of Agrarianism in their work. Although manifesting similar values, Eudora Welty and Flannery O'Connor are more concerned with the festive elements in the rural South. Although Miss Welty's mode is fantasy and Miss O'Connor's is an intense realism, both celebrate the mystery of life in their native setting. Protected perhaps by their cultural isolation from the urban crush of contemporary life, they probe the connections between man and nature. It is significant, for instance, that the title of Miss O'Connor's final collection of stories is taken from Teilhard de Chardin. The rising convergence of all natural and human activity is intensely festive for Flannery O'Connor.

In a way quite unlike that of their male contemporaries, Flannery O'Connor and Eudora Welty are contemplatives. One is struck by the stillness and the physical distances in their work. "A Still Moment" and "Revelation" are perhaps the best examples of what I mean. Each story reveals a quiet sense of wonder at reality and at the connections which tie man to the animals, the natural world, and the stars.

Their expression of rural festivity, however, takes quite different forms. In Miss Welty the essential feast is the unique and incommunicable richness of individual experience. This has its dark side of course—consider stories like "Clytie," "The Whistle," and "Petrified Man." I would not wish to misrepresent her as a Louisa May Alcott in a Delta Eden. But once her stories have witnessed pain, death, deformity, and mental aberration, they go on in spite of these things to an affirmation of a festive reality.

In Flannery O'Connor celebration is hidden beneath the surface of the countryside. She demonstrates the tension between surface and depth, between fact and mystery. Violence and grotesquerie allow her to plumb the depths of the heart and to find there the awful depths of God. For her writing was an act of religious faith, and the essential mark of faith is its unknowability. Appropriately the ultimate feast is hidden from human eyes, visible only to the eyes of faith.

Thus if we can read Cheever and Updike as Protestant writers working in the mainstream of American culture, we can also read them as conscious stylists, casting that tradition into new forms and shapes. Similarly, if we can read Welty and O'Connor as southern writers, revealing the interpermeation of character and setting, we can see Miss O'Connor and James Agee using the materials of Catholic tradition. But also important for Agee and for Salinger as well are the rites of innocence. Of all these writers, Agee and Salinger are most intensely concerned with childhood and the effect of death and evil on a child's awareness. Their values and their vision are deeply ingrained in childhood.

Among these ten writers Agee draws most heavily on the institutions of his boyhood: the Episcopal church, the boarding school, and the fatherless family. Through the eyes of children he reveals the difficulties of integrating a coherent past based on love with an incoherent future. His attempt does not quite succeed. His two novels reconstruct the individual past of Richard and of Rufus, but they develop that past only to a point. Beyond the dawning awareness of the self they will not go. Both novels are reflexive, so to speak; both freeze awareness amidst the protections of childhood. Childhood is Agee's subject and innocence his preference. The two novels seem to reject the implications of adulthood. They give the reader a sense of Agee's profound distrust of his own mature, urban, sexual experience; their note is continually elegiac.

With Salinger the case is somewhat different. The central fact in his fictional canon is Seymour's suicide. As the Glass stories develop, that suicide becomes sacrificial and meritorious for his brothers and sisters. Seymour rises to the stature of a dead saint for them, enshrined on their private, exclusive altars. Thus the sacrifice of Seymour is only an elaborate rejection of reality. Holden Caulfield, on the other hand, attempts to return to society with most if not all of his faculties intact. He preserves his integrity while preserving his innocence, sexual and otherwise. *The Catcher in the Rye* is a brilliant example of having it both ways—innocence *and* experience. Through humor, irreverence, physical movement, and dialogue, Salinger here succeeds in fronting a hostile world; Agee does not.

James Baldwin and Ralph Ellison are most obviously Negro novelists, with the special authority over their social scene that the fact implies. But categories are misleading. Baldwin and Salinger, for instance, have reached a similar impasse. They have made love a leap to an ethereal plane and an escape from sordid human emotions. Unable to find a sufficiently pure relationship in reality, their protagonists destroy themselves. Nevertheless, both Baldwin and Ellison are concerned with Negro identity, cultural assimilation, and the blues. Their differences are exemplified in their use of celebration: for Baldwin the search for it is unavailing; for Ellison it is abundantly present, in bizarre forms.

Belying appearances, Baldwin is not even a militant Negro. His essays reveal a longing for racial and personal peace founded on an almost transcendental view of American possibilities. His novels, on the other hand, reveal the chaos of a society devouring itself—but they only reflect the inversion of his hopes. The split between essays and fiction reveals a fictive self at odds with its own experience and on the verge of denying it altogether. The suicide of Rufus Scott in *Another Country* is symptomatic of the self destroyed in Baldwin's fiction. Significantly the close-knit festive world of *Go Tell It on the Mountain* disintegrates in *Another Country* to a few snatches of song, brief moments of assent amidst a general rejection of reality.

In Ellison's *Invisible Man* the assent to reality is expressed in ironic laughter. Society, at least as far as the Negro is concerned, is a gigantic confidence game. But even in the process of being skinned, Ellison's ginger-colored hero learns to play the game and to love it. At the end of the novel society lies in ruins over his head and awaits the rebirth of the only man who can save it—the ginger-colored hero with a socially responsible role to play.

If Baldwin and Ellison are Negro novelists who project a celebration lost and found, Malamud and Bellow are Jewish novelists projecting celebration past and present. One can exaggerate the ethnic contribution, of course—Salinger reveals no evidence of Jewish tradition in his work and Philip Roth uses it for primarily comic effects—but one cannot deny it entirely. Celebration in Malamud and Bellow is largely a social problem: how is one to find a festive community in the diaspora?

Malamud takes a conservative stance. Through myth, irony, burlesque, and comedy, he shows the fallibility of contemporary life and the basic integrity of his heroes. But these heroes never really integrate with their society; they distrust it too much, and with good reason. The forward movement in a Malamud novel is largely an illusion. Roy Hobbs, star centerfielder, is really a knight pursuing the Grail and a lady-love; Frankie Alpine discovers a personal future in Jewish tradition; S. Levin finds the future in an older wife, an older car, and the older, eastern regions of the country (if he finds it at all); Yakov Bok goes all the way back to the Old Testament prophets to find an adequate analogy for his experience. For Malamud the reconstruction of the past is a defensive maneuver; the assent to reality is highly qualified and limited to a narrow personal experience.

Saul Bellow is more at home in the world at large; like Ellison he has a zest for life in the raw. His work begins with a sense of personal imprisonment and develops through a gigantic appetite for experience to a final meditation on the role of the individual in society. Herzog is to some extent a recapitulation of that progression from imprisonment through release to a more profound social commitment. Herzog's pause in Ludeyville at the end of the novel is like the Invisible Man's temporary exile to a coal cellar. Each is preparing for a more deliberate entry into the communal present.

Obviously then these cross and re-cross the lines of demarcation I have laid out for them. But each begins within a context of values—Protestant, Catholic, southern, Negro, or Jewish—and works outward to the community at large. The important point is that these are ten of our best contemporary writers by any classification. In their various feasts they reveal the livability of modern American life, not only to ourselves but to readers around the world. The fiction of the past quarter-century is rich and varied and makes a serious attempt to find coherence in modern life. If we have no literary giants writing at present, we do have many fine and sensitive writers—more than any one book can treat adequately.

The work of these ten treats the special strains of contemporary living: the attempt to find meaning in a cluttered and trivial world; the effort to feel truly, rejecting both callousness and sentimentality; the failure of belief; and the perennial problem of freedom and identity in the flux of existence. One cannot claim that any of these writers have answered the question of how to live in the present, but we can look for the direction in which their art is

moving. The American novel since 1945, it seems, is moving toward celebration—hesitantly, in fits and starts, but honestly. It
suggests that fleeting yet eternal chant of Wallace Stevens' ring of
pagans in "Sunday Morning":

> Supple and turbulent, a ring of men
> Shall chant in orgy on a summer morn
> Their boistrous devotion to the sun,
> Not as a god, but as a god might be,
> Naked among them, like a savage source.
> Their chant shall be a chant of paradise,
> Out of their blood, returning to the sky;
> And in their chant shall enter, voice by voice,
> The windy lake wherein their lord delights,
> The trees, like seraphin, and echoing hills,
> That choir among themselves long afterward.
> They shall know well the heavenly fellowship
> Of men that perish and of summer morn.
> And whence they come and whither they shall go
> The dew upon their feet shall manifest.[4]

2 ล*John Cheever: The Upshot of Wapshot

REGULAR READERS of *The New Yorker* are accustomed to seeing John Cheever stories appear there with the regularity of Cutty Sark advertisements. The stories themselves are whimsical, nostalgic fables for the Connecticut commuter—sometimes slight, but always skillfully done. The first thing to note about Cheever is his clear professionalism. Like the stories, his two novels, *The Wapshot Chronicle* (1957) and *The Wapshot Scandal* (1963), project character and setting briefly and sharply. (*Bullet Park*, 1969, is outside the chronological limits of this study.)

Unfortunately the plots of the two Wapshot novels wander as bizarrely as their characters. The abiding quality is not plot then but the Cheever style. We may properly call it a ceremonial style: the significant action, as exuberant and vital as it is, works itself out in formal, ritualized gestures. Indeed, Cheever's sense of ceremony is his most important organizing principle. A consideration of ceremony in the Wapshot novels brings us close to an understanding of their significance.

Cheever expresses his attitude through the mind of Leander Wapshot, early in the *Chronicle*: "He would like them [his sons] to grasp that the unobserved ceremoniousness of his life was a gesture or sacrament toward the excellence and continuousness of things. . . . The coat he wore at dinner, the grace he said at table, the fishing trip he took each spring, the bourbon he drank at dark and the flower in his buttonhole were all forms that he hoped his sons might understand and perhaps copy." [1]

Ceremony, then, is a formal principle for life. It organizes patterns of private and public behavior in conformity to an image of personal and corporate identity. That image is firmly grounded on unquestioned values, values that the two novels project with great clarity: one should be a good Episcopalian, a good sailor, a lover of the world and of gentle women. Within these limits, any conduct is permissible. And Cheever's ceremonial style embraces wide differences in the conduct of life as evidence for the wisdom and the viability of his approach to it.

The Wapshot Chronicle abounds in ceremony. The novel begins with a Fourth of July parade, continues with a biblical genealogy of Wapshots from Ezekiel, who arrived on the *Arbella* in 1630 (Cheever's own ancestor Ezekiel arrived in Boston in 1633), to Leander, who begat Coverly and Moses. The novel develops through a series of ceremonies, each designed to reinforce the bond between a man and his past. The last of them is Leander's funeral, where ceremony is piled on ceremony: after the service, Honora has Coverly recite Prospero's farewell to his art. In between we note assorted ceremonies: Cousin Honora's odyssey to town and back; Leander's spring fishing trip, morning bath (cold), and nightly bourbon; Moses' and Coverly's ritual leave-taking; Moses' nightly trips across a castle roof to his beloved; above all, the ceremonial chronicling of life in Leander's journal. That journal is the most accurate record of Leander's life and of his assent to the world as a whole.

The final entry is a legacy to his sons: ". . . Bathe in cold water every morning. Painful but exhilirating. Also reduces horniness. Have haircut once a week. Wear dark clothes after 6 P.M. Eat fresh fish for breakfast when available. Avoid kneeling in unheated stone churches. Ecclesiastical dampness causes prematurely gray hair. Fear tastes like a rusty knife and do not let her into your house. Courage tastes of blood. Stand up straight. Admire the world. Relish the love of a gentle woman. Trust in the Lord" (p. 310).

Against the flow of this sometimes sentimental affirmation, Cheever sets the counterflow of technique. He tries to limit the inherent sentimentality of his subject with a fistful of devices: bizarre sexual situations, eccentric characters, incongruous juxtapositions, comic catastrophes, catalogues of sensory detail, constant shifts in setting, desultory dialogue, episodic plot, and shifting point of view. The effect is a tour de force that inverts the cliches of middle-class values and elaborates Cheever's conservative values without disguising them.

Most important among Cheever's stylistic devices is the shifting point of view. Part One ends with a triple departure. Rosalie, a confused and nubile young lady nursed back to life after an auto wreck by Sarah Wapshot, returns to her parents. Moses, the elder son, sets out for Washington. Coverly, the younger son, decamps for New York. Thereafter Cheever switches from Leander to Coverly to Moses. Seven of the chapters in Part Two are Leander's, five belong to Moses, three to Coverly. In Leander's seven chapters, the chronicle-journal is most important. Cheever uses technical point of view to reinforce moral point of view. He stands behind Leander all the way. Thus Leander's is a chronicle within the *Chronicle*. Both author and character are moral historians of the ceremonial life.

In the journal entries Leander tries to accommodate self-confidence and a clean life to a fallen world. After some hard knocks he comes to embrace that world wholeheartedly and to insist upon the rituals that preserve the heart from emotional squalor. Leander is a master teacher of his two sons. Ultimately the teacher is only half-successful, however; Coverly learns the importance of filial piety, but Moses fails as a son and a man. The important point is that both sons operate within the ceremonial context.

Throughout his life, Leander's chief problem has been the deprivation of love. As a young man he was forced to marry a girl impregnated by his employer, J. B. Whittier. He grows to love her, but the girl drowns herself in the Charles after delivery. Leander's comment is characteristically spare and self-denying: "Had no wish to dwell on sordid matters, sorrows, etc. Bestiality of grief. Times in life when we can count only on brute will to live. Forget. Forget" (p. 154). As life develops, the pattern continues; no one returns Leander's love.

By comparison, Coverly and Moses suffer from love's corruption. Coverly's wife Betsey leaves him (unintentionally) to the advances of a homosexual scientist at the missile base. Moses' wife

Melissa leads him through the enchantments of a suburban castle. The simple absence of love in the past gives way to its corruption in the present.

Coverly's test of strength involves him closely with his father. Tormented by fears of his own latent homosexuality, Coverly sees all existence drenched with it: invitations on toilet walls, pictures from a scholar's book bag, the very air of the plains. For a reprieve Coverly flies to Moses, escaping Pancras; enroute he envisions himself in a school of love, conducted by devotees of Venus. "It would be a hard time for Coverly, he knew, and he would be on probation most of the time, but he would graduate."

Coverly's recovery is dual. He meets the Venus-like Melissa and his masculine reactions are restored. More important, he receives a letter from Leander, in which his father recounts his own experience with an earlier Pancras. Only a violent rejection saved him then:

> Opened door of commode. Removed lid of chamberpot. Ample supply of ammunition. Carried same to window and let figure in yard have both barrels. Finis.
> Man is not simple. Hobgoblin company of love always with us. Those who hang their barebums out of street-front windows. Masturbate in YMCA showers. Knights, poets, wits in this love's flotsam. Drapers. Small tradesmen. Docile. Cleanly. Soft-voiced. Mild of wit. Flavorless. Yearn for the high-school boy who cuts the grass. Die for the embraces of the tree surgeon. Life has worse trouble. Sinking ships. Houses struck by lightning. Death of innocent children. War. Famine. Runaway horses. Cheer up my son. You think you have trouble. Crack your skull before you weep. All in love is not larky and fractious. Remember." (pp. 262–263)

After Coverly it is Moses' turn. He and Melissa are imprisoned in a Spenserian castle ruled by the sinister Justina. Moses' test is more sinister even than Coverly's: Melissa tries to destroy his sexual impulses. She assumes protean shapes to escape the domination of his desire—unhappy spinster, psychoanalyist, laundrywoman, invalid. On the brink of impotence, Moses wanders into the castle kitchen, where he meets the cook, Mrs. Reilly. She restores his confidence with tales of her husband's indefatigable prowess.

The initiation of Moses and Coverly tests their manhood—fantastically and comically, but just as undeniably as the bear hunt tests Ike McCaslin's. Both sons must learn sexual love. Through love they will find their place in society. Once restored to their estranged wives (a simultaneous happening), they take their rightful places among the Wapshots—merchant princes, sea-captains, and missionaries. All of them celebrate Venus.

Part Four of *The Wapshot Chronicle* is very short. Leander disappears one morning into the sea. "Then he began to swim—a sidestroke with his face half in the water, throwing his right arm up like the spar of a windmill—and he was never seen again." Leander, the high priest of Venus, performs the ultimate ceremony of self-immolation. His sacrifice is the most notable mythical action in a novel whose milieu is myth, fantasy, and grotesquerie.

The final chapter of *Chronicle* is a mosaic of ceremonies. First comes the funeral; Christ Church is packed with Leander's many friends. Immediately there follows a Fourth of July parade to close the book, as another one opened it. Next Coverly brings his son, the male heir, to meet the matriarchal Honora, who in turn has gone to celebrate the Red Sox ("Sacrifice, you booby, *sacrifice!*"). In a thunderstorm Leander's grounded boat undergoes a metamorphosis from Sarah's floating gift shop into a ship once more, while Coverly discovers his father's legacy in the family Shakespeare.

Life, Cheever seems to be saying, is a familial enterprise, a social enterprise. Past and present are one in every Wapshot's future. Only by recovering the past can each new generation of Wapshots live in the present; the means of recovery are ceremonial. The apparent disunity of *The Wapshot Chronicle* resolves itself in this common recovery. A greater difficulty is Cheever's sentimentality. He elicits sympathy from his reader by appealing to his nostalgia for a simpler life. To this end he uses commentary, guiding the reader's reactions and molding his beliefs in the traditions of New England small town life.

Cheever's wry narrator adapts himself admirably to the non-realistic technique. But he uses eccentric characters, myths, and enchanted castles as a substitute, an evasion even, of the real world. And here perhaps is the heart of our problem: Cheever refuses to take modern life seriously. If the reader can join him in foregoing a serious treatment of modern existence, he can emerge from the novel with the same sense of victory over circumstance. If the reader cannot submit, he will dismiss Cheever as a writer of whimsical illusions, a raffish Prospero on an idyllic island.

But Cheever is frivolous in the same way as Fielding. And he offers the same virtues that the reading of Fielding offers. One of them is his high regard for the bracing pleasures of a full sense life: the smells of the harbor, "the long, foolish, brine-smelling summer days." A passage from the opening chapter is a case in point. Cheever gives us our first view of Leander, outward bound on the *Topaze*.

> But the voyage seemed to Leander, from his place at the helm, glorious and sad. The timbers of the old launch seemed held together by the brilliance and transitoriness of summer and she smelled of summery refuse—sneakers, towels, bathing suits and the cheap fragrant matchboard of old bathhouses. Down the bay she went over water that was sometimes the violet color of an eye to where the land wind brought aboard the music of the merry-go-round and where you could see the distant shore of Nangasakit— the scrim of nonsensical rides, paper lanterns, fried food and music that breasted the Atlantic in such a fragile jumble that it seemed like the rim of flotsam, the starfish and orange skins that came up on the waves. "Tie me to the mast, Perimedes," Leander used to shout when he heard the merry-go-round. He did not mind missing his wife's appearance in the parade. (p. 6)

In such passages Cheever overwhelms the reader with sensory detail. Note the olfactory appeal of sneakers and old bathhouses; the gustatory appeal of carnival fried food; the auditory appeal of the merry-go-round and Leander's shout—the style reinforces the ceremonial attitude of praise for the goodness of life.

The two catalogues, one describing the old launch, the other describing Nangasakit, reflect a way of life. Finally, Cheever's light punctuation increases the pace of the paragraph (. . . Brilliance and transitoriness of summer and she smelled . . . paper lanterns, fried food and music that breasted. . . ."), building a world in increments of detail—a summer world, transitory, delicate; a sea-world; an old, innocent world; a lost world.

Cheever is writing romance here, not fiction. Atmosphere is more important than sustained plot development. Nevertheless, *The Wapshot Chronicle* is sentimental, though Cheever gets value for his money. No other novel since the war has quite captured this sense of a full, idealized place. In effect it most resembles *Under Milk Wood*. St. Botolphs, like Thomas' Welsh fishing village, is better than we deserve, as George Garrett observed in *The Hollins Critic*.

What we deserve is *The Wapshot Scandal*. Here is St. Botolphs brought up to date, a world with no bottom. That pillar of St. Botolphs society, Honora Wapshot, has never paid her income tax. Time takes its revenge in public scandal; the Internal Revenue Service is only its tool. The private scandal is even more disruptive; Melissa Wapshot, the Venus-figure of *Chronicle*, has taken the grocery boy for a lover. The public scandal only echoes the private one.

Cheever enlarges the woman's role in *The Wapshot Scandal*, with appropriate results for a masculine novelist. Women are fragile vessels, unfit for ceremony. Leander's robust vigor gives way to helpless feminine flutterings. As a result the men have less control over their lives than heretofore. Consider Moses, whose conquest of Melissa in *Chronicle* established the supremacy of Venus. He is now in danger of losing Melissa altogether. "The volcanic area [sex] that Moses shared with Melissa was immense, but it was the only one. They agreed on almost nothing else. They drank different brands of whisky, read different books and papers. Outside the dark circle of love they seemed almost like strangers, and glimpsing Melissa down a long dinner table he had once wondered who was that pretty woman with light hair" (p. 41). In fact, Melissa's infidelity destroys him; sex alone cannot give shape to life.

Coverly survives somewhat better. His *pietas* saves him from the apocalypse around him. Like his father, Coverly has been the less-favored son, the Jacob who had to trick himself out for his father's blessing. Returning to St. Botolphs from Talifer, another missile base, he spends a night in the old farmhouse, where he feels Leander's presence in the dark—"Oh, Father, Father, Father, why have you come back?" The memory of his father is a motif for Coverly, enabling him to reject the monstrous present, to flatten the burly neighbor who stole his metal garbage can, to run a word count of Keats' poetry through Talifer's computers—ultimately, to assume the familial obligations of host at Honora's Christmas dinner. One forgets his origins, Cheever seems to be saying, at the expense of his life. Without a sense of the past, the ceremonies of the present are a hideous sacrilege.

For the present does have ceremonies, whether we like them or not. Once the old gods fail, society lusts after strange ones. The new rites are perversions of natural ceremony: Melissa encounters an ardent lesbian at a cocktail party; Emile conducts the rites of love with a cheerful tomato at a drive-in movie; Cameron, the missile scientist, lusts for his Italian doxie while his imbecile son, starved for affection, rots away in a mental hospital; Melissa buys Emile back at a flesh auction on the isle of Ladros. "The times were venereal."

Technology is only partly at fault—it has brutalized the humans at Talifer, destroying any communal sense they might otherwise have had. Rootlessness is another cause of the modern ailment: people fly and sail about in the novel restlessly, guiltily. But most of all, Cheever laments the loss of faith, the vitiation of ultimate ceremonies. Technology, rootlessness, and infidelity are the three marks of the unfestive modern world.

To take these three marks in order: Cameron, the master technologist, is the apotheosis of the power world. Cheever uses the naïve Coverly to show the man's inhumanity. Before Coverly, Cameron lies about his skiing prowess, conspires with missile-minded Arabs, and reveals his monstrous fatherhood. Cameron is thus the inversion of Leander.

In counterpoint to Cameron's power world—a world of uncontrollable lust, uncontrollable anger, and cheerful inhumanity—is the world of St. Botolphs. Coverly represents the nostalgic past, brought to witness the sterility of the present. To bolster Coverly's position, Cheever's narrator underlines the discrepancy between technological power and self-control. The scientists at Talifer "were men born of women and subject to all the ravening caprices of the flesh. They could destroy a great city inexpensively, but had they made any progress in solving the clash between night and day, between the head and the groin? Were the persuasions of lust, anger and pain any less in their case? Were they spared toothaches, nagging erections and fatigue?" (p. 141).

Cheever's technique allows him to develop the technology motif with great variety. Sometimes through commentary and sometimes through the reflections of his characters, Cheever reveals the ills of our age: pornographic novels, southern grotesquerie, drive-ins, interstate highways, wash'n wear shirts, advertising, third-rate hotels, lugubrious folk singers, inept repairmen, homosexuals, avaricious housewives, philandering doctors, fox-trotting psychoanalysts, and TV-loving ministers. Cheever manipulates his narrator and his varying spokesmen to demonstrate that everything breaks down.

The most direct clash between the power world and the human one occurs at the senate investigation of Cameron. An antebellum senator can only remind the present of its lost past: " 'We possess Promethean powers, but don't we lack the awe, the humility, that primitive man brought to the sacred fire? Isn't this a time for uncommon awe, supreme humility? If I should have to make some final statement, and I shall very soon for I am nearing the end of my journey, it would be in the nature of a thanksgiving for stouthearted friends, lovely women, blue skies, the bread and wine of life. Please don't destroy the earth, Dr. Cameron,' he sobbed. 'Oh, please, please don't destroy the earth' " (pp. 170–171). Thanksgiving is an inherently human, ceremonial act. But the technological world is incapable of giving thanks and will perish as a result.

The second mark of the present age is rootlessness. *The Wapshot Scandal* suggests a profound disorientation from tradition and a usable past. Cheever's characters wander aimlessly from husband to lovers, from party to party, from country to country. Cheever's shifts in physical scene do much to underline this contrast between traditional past and rootless present. St. Botolphs is the scene for chapters 1, 2, 3, 6, and 8 in Part One; in Part Two the village never appears; in Part Three it is the setting for the final chapters, 31 and 32. Thus Cheever opens and closes the novel with St. Botolphs, furnishing his readers with a vision of the world they have lost. Significantly, Cheever's commenting narrator appears at greatest length in these final chapters.

The early contrasts between St. Botolphs and the other two towns establish Cheever's value scheme. Coverly flies from his father's ghost to Talifer, where he immediately fights with his next-door neighbor; to Talifer, where Betsey sees a man fall from his window to die and fails to call an ambulance; to Talifer, where the Wapshots have a party to which no one comes. "They aren't very friendly" runs like a refrain through chapter four, counterpointing Coverly's "Father, Father, why have you come back?" Talifer is anti-communal; this community values isolation. Similarly, Moses' home, Proxmire Manor, is a place "that was known up and down the suburban railroad line as the place where the lady got arrested," i.e., a place where nothing ever happens.

In contrast, St. Botolphs is full of eccentrics: the drunken minister, Mr. Applegate; the exhibitionist, Uncle Pee-Pee; old Mr. Spofford, who tries to drown a sack of kittens on Christmas Eve and drowns himself instead. In further contrast, ancient Honora acts decisively; modern Melissa drifts in the current of her lust. Yet Cheever always preserves his comic perspective. Even when the story trembles on the brink of tragedy, when Honora tries to hang herself from an attic rafter, Cheever brings her back. Rope in hand, Honora pauses before suicide to look through an old trunk. She finds Leander's forgotten journal and reads an account of his affair with a Victorian actress of insatiable appetites.

Leander recalls the merry sequence of events leading up to the end of the affair. "Tour included Worcester, Springfield, Albany, Rochester, Buffalo, Syracuse, Jamestown, Ashtabula, Cleveland, Columbus and Zanesville. Suspected Lottie of concupiscence in Jamestown. Found naked stranger in clothes closet in Ashtabula. Caught red-handed in Cleveland. Sold gold cuff-links and returned to Boston via steamcars on March 18. No hard feelings. Laugh and the world laughs with you. Weep and you weep alone" (p. 70).

One recalls the indefatigable Reilly, the cook's husband in *Chronicle*. Just as the example of his sexual vigor saved Moses, so Leander's fortitude saves Honora. On the one hand Cheever's innocent ribaldries celebrate a vital reality, a cheerful grossness in the service of love. On the other the journal celebrates endurance, the ability to assent to the real despite all difficulties. Honora takes up the burden of love, which ultimately redeems her; Melissa, given the same choice, does not.

George Garrett points up a distinction which *The Wapshot Chronicle* failed to make, the distinction between love and lust: "Venus has been ubiquitous in this book, too, but here she is clearly the old Venus *in malo*, whose rewards are folly and degradation, who is the first handmaiden of Dame Fortune who gives all who serve her a spin on the wheel. . . . In *Scandal* John Cheever makes a firm and definite distinction between false love [*cupiditas*] and the love that moves the stars [*caritas*]. And he ends on the note we are now familiar with, for there is no other song or burden for our times, that 'we must love one another or die.' " [2]

The distinction between *cupiditas* and *caritas* is reflected in that between Melissa and Honora. Driven to Rome by Moses' discovery of her affair, Melissa abandons herself to Emile—who, appropriately, is always hungry. St. Botolphs and Rome are polar extremes here. For Cheever Rome symbolizes rootlessness (though he himself loves it). Both Honora and Melissa fly to Rome, but Honora regains her identity there while Melissa loses it altogether. She and Emile drift further and further from society. *Cupiditas* is suicidal; we can love one another *and* die.

The third and most profound mark of the modern age is the loss of faith. The contrast between the first and the last chapters of the novel emphasizes this loss. Though both are set in the village, they contrast Christmas past with Christmas present. In chapter one the local eccentrics found a momentary unity in the rituals of Christmas Eve. They carol from door to door, forgetting their human absurdities; "the moment they began to sing they were transformed." While the music lasts, even Mr. Applegate, the drunken curate of Christ Church, feels his faith renewed. Human frailty transcends itself in the ceremonies of Christmas.

In chapter 32, years later, Mr. Applegate is still drunk, but the church is now empty. He flounders through the Christmas Eve service in despair. Only Coverly remains after the flight of the scandalized village matrons, and he hears a prayer for our times: " 'Let us pray for all those killed or cruelly wounded on thruways, expressways, freeways, and turnpikes. Let us pray for those burned to death in faulty plane-landings, mid-air collisions and mountainside crashes. Let us pray for all those wounded by rotary lawn mowers, chain saws, electric hedge clippers and other power tools. Let us pray for all alcoholics measuring out the days that the Lord has made in ounces, pints and fifths.' Here he sobbed loudly. 'Let us pray for the lecherous and the impure. . . .' " (p. 238).

Like Honora, Coverly is saved by his faith and by his love. He emerges from the Christmas Eve service feeling community with the dead and the living. Specifically he feels his kinship with the dead Honora, who has returned to face the Internal Revenue Service only to die of malnutrition first. But she has made Coverly promise to host her Christmas Eve dinner for the blind. Thus Coverly goes from the empty church to the crowded table, from religious to secular ceremonies.

Enroute he tries to rescue Moses from the debauchery that Melissa's infidelity has led him to. Moses is drunk upstairs at the Viaduct House with the widow Willston: "He lay athwart her, his cheek against the carpet, which had a pleasant, dusty smell like the wood in autumn. Oh, where was his dog, his gun, his simple joy in life! She, still lying in a heap, was the first to speak. She spoke without anger or impatience. She smiled. 'Let's have another drink,' she said. Then Coverly opened the door. 'Come home, Moses,' he said. 'Come home, brother. It's Christmas Eve' " (p. 239).

The reprieve is only temporary, however: "The brilliance of light, the birth of Christ, all seemed to him like some fatuous shell game invented to dupe a fool like his brother while he saw straight through into the nothingness of things." Moses has lost faith in life itself—and this is the basic infidelity of our times. Coverly keeps faith with Honora and their blind guests.

The fleeting community on Christmas Day demonstrates the thread of ceremony that can alone preserve the race from self-destruction. But this act of faith is free. Coverly can make it; Moses and Melissa cannot. The result for them is chaos. Melissa wanders with a sad heart at the Roman-American supermarket; Moses sinks back into oblivion.

Cheever's narrator concludes the novel with a moving meditation on the corrosion of time and the transcendence of faith. In the light of the first, one must insist on the second. Man must come to grips with the mystery behind reality. In the best Protestant fashion, Cheever shows that the individual must affirm his own existence in a leap of faith. The narrator finds the possibility for that leap in the example of Coverly and in the words of Leander: "Let us consider that the soul of a man is immortal, able to endure every sort of good and every sort of evil."

The final paragraph balances Leander's act of faith against the narrator's need to move on, but the note of sadness casts a doubt on the possibilities for future ceremony. Cheever's narrator bids farewell to the lost world of St. Botolphs, admitting as Thomas Wolfe did before him that you can't go home again.

The two Wapshot stories reveal John Cheever's growth as a novelist. The first of them dwells at length on the natural ceremonies of a coherent, traditional past. The style has only to recall them in order to reveal their value. But the style in *The Wapshot Chronicle* is too often merely winsome and nostalgic. Like Henry Adams' *Mont St. Michel and Chartres*, *The Wapshot Chronicle* indulges the wish for a coherent present by idealizing the past.

The ceremonies of *The Wapshot Scandal* are less nostalgic and more relevant. If a Fourth of July parade typifies the first novel, a rocket launching typifies the second. Cheever faces the conflict of past and present in the second book and reveals a crucial paradox: in a time of highly-organized social effort, the individual is more isolated than ever. In order to live he must find significant ceremonies. Mr. Applegate's Christmas prayer is significant, and so is Coverly's Christmas dinner.

Cheever's style reflects the essential need of contemporary life, the need for appropriate forms. For John Cheever, the act of writing is itself a ceremonial act that he invites his reader to share: "the unobserved ceremoniousness of his life is a gesture or sacrament toward the excellence and continuousness of things."

3 &~ John Updike:
Style in Search of a Center

"We in America need ceremonies, is I suppose,
sailor, the point of what I have written."

LIKE CHEEVER, John Updike is concerned with ceremonial style.
Though neither writer can project a sustained festive action, each
man tries to make style carry the burden of a ceremonial attitude
toward life. Updike's ceremony is different from Cheever's, however, in some important ways: first, Cheever's ceremonial style is
founded on social and religious certitudes, whereas Updike's style
is not. Second, Cheever's ceremonies are generally social and light-
hearted, whereas Updike's are solitary and solemn. Compare Updike's George Caldwell and Leander Wapshot, for instance: Caldwell is a master of ceremony, a noble agonist largely detached
from the world around him. Leander is very much involved in the
vicissitudes of life and is more often than not the butt of its jokes.
Third, Updike's style is highly self-conscious, whereas Cheever's
is not. Cheever falls in and out of narrative commentary with
careless ease; Updike's narrator is more solemn. As a result Updike's style circles relentlessly on the circumference of experience,
seeking entry into its center.

I do not wish to imply that Updike is merely superficial. He
simply has no starting point for natural ceremonies, no St. Botolphs. If Cheever's problem is finding a substitute world with a
coherence and a vitality for the world of St. Botolphs, Updike's
problem is believing that such a world can exist. Consequently,

ceremony is dependent on Updike's world of the moment, upon the shifting sensibility of the author. The protagonist in his stories must find restorative ceremonies on his own.

Updike's style bears the double burden of making a world and making it festive. At its worst the feast is merely verbal, an indulgence of poetic epiphanies bursting like Roman candles in the summer sky. At its best, however, in stories like "Packed Dirt," "The Blessed Man of Boston," and *The Centaur*, the private feast becomes a joyful public action, liberating the isolated sensibility in a communal song of love. At such times style finds its center.

The most obvious characteristic of Updike's style is his exhaustive exploration of minute physical detail. Even in his first collection, *The Same Door* (1959), the scene is microscopic. Take the following passage, for instance:

> He was perfect: the medium-short dry-combed hair, the unimpeachable brown suit, the buttonless collar, the genially dragged vowels, the little edges of efficiency bracing the consonants. Some traces of the scholarship-bothered freshman from Hampton (Md.) High School who had come down to the *Quaff* on Candidates' Night with an armful of framed sports cartoons remained—the not smoking, the tucked-in chin and the attendant uplook of the boyishly lucid eyes, and the skin allergy that placed on the flank of each jaw a constellation of red dots.[1]

The cadences fall smoothly. The catalogue of physical traits is complete, down to the shape of the rash on Clayton's jaws. Such catalogues, rhythmic phrasing, proper nouns, and brand names are all marks of Updike's style. But their primary function is to establish the writer's authority: the story itself is secondary. This is a new look at experience, a new voice speaking. We remember the voice far longer than the story.

The narrative voice is largely concerned with ways of feeling. The characters in Updike's first collection of stories are young, sensitive, and intelligent people. More often than not, Updike juxtaposes them against a vaguely hostile urban environment. Obliquely, the stories chronicle integrity, honesty, and the confrontation of experience.

"Toward Evening" tells of a young married man, Rafe, returning home after work with a mobile for his daughter. Half-dreaming, he is aroused by the sight of a beautiful redhead at the back of the bus, then by a mulatto. The bus, the two women, and Rafe's dreams are juxtaposed against his apartment, wife, and baby girl. At the end of the story, Rafe has finished his favorite meal, which, like the clumsy mobile for the baby, is vaguely disappointing. Husband and wife are balanced against each other and against the outside world in a silent struggle to find the right way. Their life is dominated by a huge Spry sign, white and red, blinking through their window from the Jersey shore. In a brisk rondo, Updike explains how the sign got there, and the account is a perfect example of the unfestive, commercialized existence that Rafe can feel but cannot explain to Alice. Without comment, Updike ends the story.

A second story presents a small-town version of this conflict, "Ace in the Hole"—a story that is the germ of *Rabbit, Run*. The setting is Olinger, an eastern Pennsylvania town near the Dutch country. (Olinger is also the setting for *The Centaur* and several of the stories in *Pigeon Feathers*.) Ace Anderson is more boy than man. An ex-basketball star in high school, Ace has just been fired from his job parking cars. He stops at his mother's to pick up his daughter and ponders how to explain the firing to his wife. He doesn't explain, though. Flipping on the radio, he seizes his wife and dances away from his problems, stilling her protests in their dance. "The music ate through his skin and mixed with the nerves and small veins; he seemed to be great again, and all the other kids were around them, in a ring, clapping time" (p. 27).

Ace's escape is an uneasy compromise between athletic pride and responsibility to his wife and daughter. For the moment he has dodged his crisis, but the difficulty remains: Ace has no idea of what to do. Needing contact with others but unable to make it, he plays the radio and the television incessantly. In these stories of conflict between the mechanized present and the family, dancing is only an evasion.

Though brilliant, the stories in *The Same Door* do not show the connection between the periphery of experience and the center. The style catches only the outside of things, the shell of the corporate experience we all have in being twentieth-century Americans. The inside, the characters' capacity to connect feeling and form, is missing. The range of emotional response, furthermore, is quite limited. Updike's self-conscious characters guard themselves from each other, and from the reader. At worst the style leaves only an empty husk. At best it reveals characters who are potentially interesting. One does not remember them by name, only collectively—the young husband, the student abroad, the long-suffering wife.

The second collection of stories, *Pigeon Feathers* (1962), shows some improvements in the attempt to make the internal connection. Most impressive technically is Updike's montage effect, achieved by a juxtaposition of entirely separate scenes in the same story. Hints of such a development have appeared earlier, in "Toward Evening," for example. As Rafe moved from bus to apartment to Spry sign, the overlapping scenes commented silently on each other.

In *Pigeon Feathers*, the montage technique is more evident. Three stories especially demonstrate the effect. The first of them, "Home," portrays Robert's return from England with his wife and child. He plans to spend July with his parents before going to teach mathematics at a girls' college. Robert's father, an amiable Pennsylvania high school teacher—one of many in Updike's fiction—understands almost nothing of modern ways. His simple reactions to situations are open and genuine; they embarrass his sophisticated son.

The first half of the story tells of the many small corruptions involved in this homecoming—corruptions of feeling, loyalty, and speech. Robert's values are always in motion, it seems; but his father gives them substance in an unexpected encounter. The second half of the story recounts his only triumph, that won by default over a belligerent Pennsylvania Dutchman they pass on the highway. The Dutchman pursues them down the road; the father pulls off on the shoulder and stops. The Dutchman also stops, ahead of them, and trots back to them howling obscenities. The father gets out to speak to him, but the Dutchman, suddenly afraid, turns and runs back to his car. Robert's father is ignorant of his triumph: "That man had something to say to me and I wanted to hear what it was." Puzzled, he gets back into the ancient Plymouth and begins to drive on.

The two parts of the story move Robert to a feeling of joy. In the person of his father, home once more becomes real for him.

His father's awkwardness, his hopeless innocence, his openness to the world make him genuine. He symbolizes the ceremonies of the land, the rural Pennsylvania of his son's youth, unchanged by scholarship and sophistication.

Furthermore, the father is a memorable character. He has much in common with the grandmother in "The Blessed Man of Boston, My Grandmother's Thimble, and Fanning Island," and with Mr. Kern, the dying father in "Packed Dirt, Churchgoing, A Dying Cat, A Traded Car." Each story reveals a young man's reaction to his inheritance—a ceremonial reaction. The three older figures, gauche and out of touch, represent tradition and a coherent life. For the young they are a source of strength and self-definition.

"The Blessed Man" juxtaposes three characters: a smiling Chinaman, serene amidst the mob scrambling out of Fenway Park; the narrator's grandmother, who had clung to life tenaciously and left him her only possession, a silver thimble; and a nameless Polynesian, the last of his tribe, writing a journal on Fanning Island. Each character is the custodian of a tradition that is handed down to the narrator and then to us. Writing the story thus celebrates filial piety, a sense of the goodness and continuity of experience. The reader, like the narrator, must make the leap of faith:

> This is the outline; but it would be the days, the evocation of the days . . . the green days. The tasks, the grass, the weather, the shades of sea and air. Just as a piece of turf torn from a meadow becomes a *gloria* when drawn by Dürer. Details. Details are the giant's fingers. He seizes the stick and strips the bark and shows, burning beneath, the moist white wood of joy. For I thought that this story, fully told, would become without my willing it a happy story, a story full of joy; had my powers been greater, we would know. As it is, you, like me, must take it on faith. (p. 167)

Style here serves Updike well: unconnected experiences move the narrator to a leap of affirmation, a commitment to tradition. At the end of "Packed Dirt," for instance, the narrator equates the car he is trading in with his father's death, and it makes him glad:

> Any day now we'll trade it in; we are just waiting for the phone to ring. I know how it will be. My father traded in many cars. It happens so cleanly, before you expect it. He would drive off in the old

car up the dirt road exactly as usual and when he returned the car would be new, and the old was gone, gone, utterly dissolved back into the mineral world from which it was conjured, dismissed without a blessing, a kiss, a testament, or any ceremony of farewell. We in America need ceremonies, is I suppose, sailor, the point of what I have written. (p. 188)

These three stories, probably the best in the collection (though "Pigeon Feathers" and "The Doctor's Wife" are fine and moving), stress a common theme, revealed through a common technique: We need ceremonies, for they keep us in touch with the familial past, the only true source of strength and identity. The montage technique demonstrates the personal reconstruction of experience by the narrator. He finds his center in a past refashioned for present needs, present living.

Other stylistic experiments in *Pigeon Feathers*, however, are not so successful. One story, "Dear Alexandros," uses the epistolary style in a manner reminiscent of "For Esme—With Love and Squalor." But Updike's story lacks the honest feeling of Salinger's. He substitutes situational irony for Salinger's compassion. While Updike avoids sentimentality (which he charges Salinger with elsewhere) [2], he substitutes less feeling altogether. The contrast between the past happiness and the present misery of the now-divorced American father who is answering the letter from an innocent Greek orphan whom he and his wife had sponsored in the early years of their marriage is simply too pat.

Another stylistic dead end is "Archangel," a story told literally from the angelic viewpoint. It too is a ceremonial story, like "Packed Dirt," for it catalogues the various pleasures of angelic life. Heaped up with dazzling metaphors and unusual yokings, the story is too ingenious to manifest a human ceremony—but that may be its point.

Two other stories exemplify what we might call baroque style: "Wife-Wooing" and "Lifeguard." In each story Updike is experimenting with unreliable narrators. Each narrator takes himself and his situation far too seriously, indulging his capacity to formulate sense impressions. The narrator in "Wife-Wooing" defines the import of his experience in a way which is simply silly: "Monday's wan breakfast light bleaches you blotchily, drains the goodness from your thickness, makes the bathrobe a limp stained tube flapping disconsolately, exposing sallow decolletage." These stories are exercises for Updike, self-reminders to avoid the excesses that they portray.

On the whole, the experiments in *Pigeon Feathers* meet with mixed success. Updike writes best of simple people; but in this collection he does not always close the gap between style and emotion, between the outside and the inside.

The four novels (I have considered *Couples* separately, in the Postscript) represent a clearer development in Updike's style. The first of them, *The Poorhouse Fair* (1958), is the simplest. The story takes place in a state house for the aged toward the end of our century. Its subject is freedom; its theme is that freedom is the property of those who preserve their identity amidst the indignities of life.

The poorhouse itself is an anomaly. Those who have power, the administrators, are imprisoned in a struggle for supremacy. The aged residents, on the other hand, are variously free. Certain of themselves, they can ignore the machinations of those in charge. The best of them have a sense of tradition and ceremony based on an ingrained sense of order. Within the walls of an institution supposedly depriving them of their freedom, they find it anew.

Their strength is built on a ceremonial sense of life. Despite a rainstorm, they put up booths. Unflappable, they sit soaking on the porch, waiting for the band to play. The band has always played at the fair; it must play now, and it does. Updike's point, however, is that ceremony is dying with these aged poor. When they go, they will take the ceremonial sense of life with them.

The novel is anti-utopian satire. As a symbol of the welfare state, the poorhouse is a prison; its annual fair is the only sign of a corporate life better than the daily isolation. Thus the fair is a curious relic of the ordered past imbedded in the fabric of the disordered present. For John Updike, as for Edward Albee, the American Dream ends in banalities and obscenities.

Conner, the prefect, is the composite organization man; he accepts the dehumanization of the aged residents with glib sociological formulas. Updike's style, especially when Conner is the subject, becomes gray and bureaucratic:

At any rate there was nothing to do but persevere in his work. He would not, unlike Mendelssohn, be a poorhouse prefect forever. In another year or two, if his progress here continued to look impressive on paper—the two most important statistics were the yield from the farm and the longevity of the inmates—he would be moved up, perhaps into a State Health Service Council. He expected association with scientists to be pleasanter, more suited to his gifts and to the quality of his dedication. Still, he prized a useful over a pleasant life. Wherever I can serve, he told himself. . . . (p. 108)

The other end of the stylistic spectrum is evidenced by Gregg, who leads a hooting mob of aged residents in stoning Conner: "Son of a bitch of a cat-killer, brave bastard run your a. h. off." Conner recovers from the indignity and tries to forget it. But the style indicates the problem: the world of the future vitiates all ceremony, all tradition. In its swing from institutional prose to invective, Updike's style describes a world without proportion, that yardstick of civilized society.

Despite the clean bite of his irony, Updike's lyricism is the dominant quality of the style. He has a fine sense of place in this novel. The pages describing western New Jersey and the poorhouse lawn after a rain are the most poetic in the novel. This is Updike's country; he has found a context for tradition that he will develop more fully and more ambitiously in his later novels.

In a sense *Rabbit, Run* (1960) poses a question which *The Centaur* answers: how does a man love? Implicit in the question is a context for love and for freedom. In *Rabbit, Run* that context is the rootless present, in which family, church, and the individual are sterile. In *The Centaur* that present is richly permeated with the past and its multiple traditions.

Running is the basic metaphor of Updike's second novel. Rabbit Angstrom runs through all the certitudes of his life. He was once a high school basketball star but is now a sometime used-car salesman. He once loved his wife, but in a fit of disgust at her stupidity he leaves her for another girl. One by one, Rabbit's certitudes collapse: belief in God, belief in love, belief in his own beauty.

Rabbit's certitudes are based on feeling. In order to act, he must feel that what he does is right. Right feeling becomes an obsession with Rabbit; he wants everything he does to feel right to him. But as his problems increase, feeling ceases to guide him.

He leaves Ruth, his girl friend, when his wife, Janice, has their second baby: he feels his place is with his wife. He leaves Janice a second time after she refuses him, still tender from the stitches of childbirth: he feels that his marital rights have been abrogated. He flies to Ruth once again, after Janice drunkenly drowns the baby in the bathtub. This time feeling cannot guide him: Ruth is pregnant. He must choose.

> "Please have the baby," he says. "You got to have it."
> "Why? Why do you *care?*"
> "I don't know. I don't know any of these answers. All I know is what feels right. You feel right to me. Sometimes Janice used to. Sometimes nothing does."
> "Who cares? That's the thing. Who cares *what* you feel?"
> "I don't know," he says again. (p. 252)

In truth, Rabbit does not know. He reacts, he moves. Movement has always carried him through, and he hopes it will continue to do so. The novel opens with an alley scrimmage, where Rabbit, six feet three and twenty-six, drives and fakes past the grade school kids. Memories of past successes crowd about him thereafter. The motions of basketball merge in his memory with the motions of sex. In motion he finds victory, upon which he builds his identity.

Two extended motions reflect Rabbit's character. The first, immediately after his initial break with Janice, is a restless all-night drive from Brewer (Reading) to West Virginia and back. Updike's style fits itself around Rabbit's nervous vibrations like a glove here:

> He drives through Frederick, a discouraging town because an hour back he had thought he had reached Frederick when it was really Westminster. He picks up 340. The road unravels with infuriating slowness, its black wall wearilessly rising in front of his headlights no matter how they twist. The tar sucks his tires. . . . He grinds his foot down as if to squash this snake of a road, and nearly loses the car on a curve, as the two right wheels fall captive to the dirt shoulder. He brings them back but keeps the speedometer needle leaning to the right. (p. 32)

Through all this we get a sense of Rabbit's feeling: blind panic guided only by motor reflexes. The style chronicles the exact stimulus and the precise shade of response on Rabbit's part.

Rabbit, Run is a powerful novel, but it overwhelms its hero. Dependent upon appropriate feeling, Rabbit can only respond to his situation—he cannot initiate action. His ceremonies are basketball and sex. He knows his role as celebrant in each area. Once the demands of responsible adulthood impinge upon him, he can no longer be a hero. The age of innocent heroism is past, leaving Rabbit with no role to play. The plot neatly cancels his attempts to feel his way: modern life does not allow feeling. It confronts him with the dilemma of Janice and her dead baby versus a pregnant Ruth. Feeling can carry him no further.

The conclusion gives us the second extended motion, Rabbit's flight from the cemetery. Blindly he stumbles through the undergrowth. Branches catch at him, tearing his shirt. He pauses in his flight only to plead with Ruth to have the baby and then stumbles on, at last alone. "His hands lift of their own and he feels the wind on his ears even before, his heels hitting heavily on the pavement at first but with an effortless gathering out of a kind of sweet panic growing lighter and quicker and quieter, he runs. Ah: runs. Runs" (p. 255).

Updike's style in *Rabbit, Run* projects powerful feelings: innocence, isolation, self-delusion, betrayal. His nostalgia for high school glories and uncomplicated sex comes through clearly, but the very power of such memories isolates him from what is happening to him at the moment. Updike plays the devil's advocate with Rabbit: the activities in which he excels, speed and sex, have no commercial value. As his nickname indicates, Rabbit can only run and breed. He does not know what is happening to him. He has an incorruptible innocence and a belief in his dignity as a person. But circumstances destroy him.

Updike has instilled most of urban man's frustrations into his hapless hero; the book is a kind of extended elegy for the child's view of life. Perhaps Rabbit *is* the representative modern man. But Rabbit is too much an indictment of the inhuman present and too little a character who lives in it.

Rabbit, Run exorcises the demons possessing its author. The style is a kind of weapon in his attack on the present. Religion is a special target of that attack. When Updike describes the impact of religion on Rabbit, who genuinely desires to repent and to believe, he either burlesques the institutions of religion through the insipid Reverend Eccles or else he cranks out a pat symbol of life without God: "Afraid, really afraid, he remembers what once consoled him by seeming to make a hole where he looked through into underlying brightness, and lifts his eyes to the church window. It is, because of church poverty or the late summer nights or just carelessness, unlit, a dark circle in a stone facade" (p. 254).

Our clearest view of Rabbit comes from Ruth, the most realized character in the novel. She sees his vitality, his pride, and his final defeat. Yet she is not the emotional center of the novel— he is. When he runs away from her at the end, he runs toward a self he will never reach, an ideal destroyed by his lust, his guilt, and the spiritual poverty of modern life.

Whatever our reservations about it, *Rabbit, Run* is a considerable advance for Updike. The relationship between Rabbit and the two women is well done. With both, Rabbit feels the need to be a husband and father. Yet he cannot accept his share in the drowning of his daughter. He wants to accept his role as the father of Ruth's baby, but he doesn't know how. *Rabbit, Run* simply inverts the situation of "The Blessed Man" and "Packed Dirt," but the values on which the emotion rests are the same: familial love and a sense of the past. They are simply unavailable for Rabbit Angstrom. Unable to resolve past and present, Rabbit runs.

The Centaur is a ceremonial statement of man's power to love and to order his experience in love. That ability is based on a dual nature. George Caldwell develops a center that Rabbit never found because he is at once a school teacher and a centaur, i.e., he is vitally involved in both past and present and can place present action in the widest possible context. One of the marvels of the novel is Updike's ability to render both natures without contradiction.

A chief means of rendering Caldwell is Updike's handling of point of view. Four chapters (1, 3, 9, and the Epilogue) are told from Chiron's point of view. One chapter, 5, is told by the omniscient narrator and one, 7, by George Caldwell himself.

Second in importance to Caldwell-Chiron is his son Peter. The myth of the novel dramatizes the death of Chiron, who, wounded with a silver arrow, offers himself to Zeus as an expiation for the sin of Prometheus. In his own person, Peter expresses the love of life that his father tried to instill in him, Chiron's only real student. In addition to point of view, the mythological parallels help to unite past and present. Thus we have Peter's girl friend Penny (Pandora); Al Hummel, the garage man (Hephaestus); his promiscuous wife Vera (Venus); Zimmerman, the high school principal (Zeus); Pop Kramer, Caldwell's father-in-law (Kronos), etc. Tongue in cheek, Updike indexes all the parallels at the end of the novel.

One effect of the mythologizing is comedy; *The Centaur* is Updike's only comic novel. In a riotous class on the origins of man, the wounded Caldwell must contend with the seduction of two girls before his eyes, one by Zimmerman. The class meanwhile seethes with a desire to escape. Furiously racing the clock, Chiron-Caldwell ends his account on a note of incorrigible hope: "He opened his mouth; his very blood loathed the story he had told. 'One minute ago, flint-chipping, fire-kindling, death-foreseeing, a tragic animal appeared—' The buzzer rasped; halls rumbled throughout the vast building; faintness swooped at Caldwell but he held himself upright, having vowed to finish. '—called Man' " (p. 40).

Caldwell's task is hopeless. Having met Mim Herzog (Hera) emerging mussed from Zimmerman's office, he expects to be fired. Moreover, he lives in constant knowledge of his coming death. But like Chiron, the wisest and gentlest of the untamed centaurs, Caldwell has a compulsion to teach anyway. Chapter 3 shows him at his best—Chiron now, teaching the sons and daughters of the gods: "Chiron inhaled; air like honey expanded the spaces of his chest; his students completed the centaur. They fleshed his wisdom with expectation. The wintry chaos of information within him, elicited into sunlight, was struck through with the young colors of optimism. Winter turned vernal" (p. 78). This is the past that George Caldwell brings to his biology classes at Olinger High School. Teaching is the ceremonial connection between Greek myth and contemporary life; it is a gesture of piety before God.

Chapter 3 works against chapter 1 in every way. Here Updike gives us the ideal teacher, ideal students, in an idyllic setting. The style itself shows significant changes. "The air like honey" expands in Chiron's breast. Abstract nouns, denoting the qualities of a state of life, abound—"wisdom, wintry chaos, optimism." Setting and character are eternal and transcendent.

Such marked contrasts in style continue throughout the book. At such times Updike celebrates his own liturgy, to use Michael Novak's term.[3] Thus the mythological parallels have a significant purpose in the novel; they posit a belief in the old gods. In the elaborate catechesis with Venus in the girls' locker room, Chiron overcomes his own desire for the beautiful goddess and asserts his belief in the gods. To Chiron, "reality" is the joke. It is a travesty of the world that used to be—and through belief still is.

Technique serves Updike well in this task of reversing our notions of reality. Even-numbered chapters, told by Peter, give us the necessary filter of an awareness removed one degree from experience. Filial piety does not allow frequent access to Caldwell's mind, and never for any length of time. Thus Updike can use Peter as his spokesman and can mythologize the centaur-father. And in keeping the two apart, Updike can dramatize the common bond of nostalgia for a better time and place: Caldwell for Mt. Olympus, Peter for his childhood and his magical father.

More important, however, is the thematic importance of technique. Caldwell's spectacular failure to control the events of his life is a clue to the theme: his life for his son's. At the end we realize that the significance of the story is that Caldwell's love allows Peter to act. Peter realizes the sacrifice that Chiron has made for him, Prometheus. He feels inadequate to recompense his father for what he has done. His chapters are an elegiac tribute to his father's memory: "I am my father's son. In the late afternoons while the day hangs in distending light waiting to be punctured by the darkness that in arrows of shadow rides out from the tall buildings across the grid of streets, I remember my father and even picture—eyes milky with doubts, mustache indecisive and pale—his father before him, whom I never knew. Priest, teacher, artist: the classic degeneration" (p. 201).

The Epilogue indicates that the sacrifice is acceptable: "Zeus had loved his old friend, and lifted him up, and set him among the stars as the constellation Sagittarius. Here, in the Zodiac, now above, now below the horizon, he assists in the regulation of our destinies, though in this latter time few living mortals cast their eyes respectfully toward Heaven, and fewer still sit as students to the stars" (p. 222).

Updike himself is such a student. In *The Centaur* he formulates rituals for connecting son and father, present and past. Like Mark Twain and Henry Adams before him, Updike has found a usable past. No matter that it is the most remote in human memory. It is usable, and offers at last a center, pulling all toward itself.

Throughout these three novels the ceremonies of existence depend upon the protagonist's ability to connect present experience with traditional attitudes and values. Ceremony is always a rite of connection for Updike: The poorhouse with its band, its homemade candy, and its patchwork quilts is a gesture toward the continuity of things; the vitiation of all ceremonies disconnects Rabbit from wife, home, and God; the filial pieties of George Caldwell and his son are a source of life and renewal for them. In each case the ceremonial action, whether anonymous (*The Poorhouse Fair*), inverted (*Rabbit, Run*), or mythical (*The Centaur*), proceeds from an individual belief that the act is possible. The chief significance of Updike's fourth novel, *Of the Farm* (1965), is the doubt that ceremony is still possible.

The plot recounts a weekend visit of Joey Robinson, his second wife Peggy, and her son Richard to the Robinson family farm in the Dutch country of eastern Pennsylvania, where Joey's recently widowed mother awaits them. The occasion for the visit is the need to cut the high weeds that have overrun the farm since Joey's father died. The action of the novel is a complex and continuous assault on Joey's loyalties to new wife, old wife, children, mother, self, and regional past. Peggy and his mother wish to define him, if not to possess him, and he will not even define or possess himself.

Joey is another Rabbit Angstrom, with this vital difference: unlike Rabbit, Joey does not want to feel right about what he does; he simply wants not to feel. His essential activity is the evasion of feeling. With this motive, he sees no ethical dimension to ceremonial activity. Tradition is important only for what he can take from it. Joey refuses to admit the corporate responsibility for his family which a ceremonial attitude requires. The refusal kills the ceremonial connection between self and tradition.

Admittedly, Joey's situation is complex. It is the particularly modern situation of one beset by the contradictory claims of love. Joey is a thirty-five-year-old advertising consultant who must reconcile the conflicting forces of death, inheritance, and sonship with those of profession, remarriage, and divided paternity. Which action is free? Unable to decide, Joey takes refuge in his memories—much as Rabbit did. He muses on his childhood, on his winning Peggy, and on his happy days with Charlie, Ann, and Martha, his children by his first wife.

The weekend visit to the family farm would seem to be another ceremonial gesture, like the selling of the car in "Packed Dirt." But the farm is no home; vainly trying to recover a sense of his old home, Joey goes out to cut the weeds. But it just won't work. Home and tradition are not subject to recall by empty rituals. The ceremonial gesture of cutting the weeds is only an evasion of his duty to accept the responsibilities of love.

Joey's is a failure in moral nerve. In recompense he attempts to be precise in everything he says, but that precision is purely cerebral—confined to the nuances of sense impression, voice, and gesture. Such precision becomes a kind of grand imprecision when they substitute intellection for love. With such a character it is difficult to determine the values implied by the author, and this is the principal difficulty with *Of the Farm*.

Consider a passage where Joey tells his mother that he will bring Charlie, Ann, and Martha to see her in the fall. His mother interprets the statement as a disloyal act to Peggy; furthermore, she says that she does not expect to see Joey or Peggy again, either. Mrs. Robinson is posturing, but Joey either does not realize it or he does not care. Now if we assume that both his mother and his children matter to him, then he must care, and he must decide whether love compels him to arrange the visit. At the very least he must interpret his mother's turnabout to himself. Instead he indulges his sensibility and his penchant for precision:

This window, giving on the most lonely side of the house, where the grass was softest and where Peggy had lain, bore on its sill a toy metropolis of cereal and dogfood and bird-seed boxes, whose city gates were formed by an unused salt-and-pepper set of aqua ceramic I had sent from Cambridge fifteen years ago. It was a window enchanted by the rarity with which I looked from it. Its panes

were strewn with drops that as if by amoebic decision would
abruptly merge and break and jerkily run downward, and the
window screen, like a sampler half-stitched, or a crossword puzzle
invisibly solved, was inlaid erratically with minute, translucent
tesserae of rain. . . . (p. 80)

Does Joey feel anger at his mother? A desire to reassert that he
will bring the children in the fall? Did he make the offer to begin
with merely to assuage her grief? We do not know—and neither,
I suspect, does John Updike. All Joey feels is "ulterior mercy"—
but why? And for whom? And what will he do about it?

The emotional groping and the timid maneuvering of these
three characters are believable enough. But Updike undermines his
characters here. We cannot believe that they have ever loved each
other. All dialogue, all action is defensive. Memory isolates; it does
not reinforce experience. Mrs. Robinson will not relinquish her
dream of the farm as a family saga; Peggy must defend her life
with her first husband, McCabe; Joey must protect himself from
an exclusive definition as son, lover, or father until he is able to
find the right combination for himself. These characters are afraid
of love's responsibilities, of life in the present—yet the epigraph
from Sartre insists upon the need to be free *in* the present.

Perhaps the contrast is the point. But whatever it is, Updike
seems to have abandoned the ceremonial elements that he used so
well in his earlier work. *Of the Farm* seems to be a withdrawal
from the reality that *The Centaur* engaged so wholeheartedly. At
best we can say that the fourth novel is experimental and explora-
tory. In a sense it turns *Rabbit, Run* upside down. Rabbit manifests
a hunger for appropriate feeling; Joey Robinson evades feeling altogether.

Updike seems to use style then to protect the characters from
emotional commitment. He makes them so aware of the process
by which they feel that they are afraid to feel at all. They seem
too conscious of being characters in a novel—which brings us
back to our original problem, John Updike's search for a center.

If *The Centaur* offered him a way to resolve style and feeling,
it was not a permanent way. The father who is so important in
that book (and in most of Updike's fiction) is altogether missing
from *Of the Farm*. The novel gives us a neurotic Peter Caldwell

without George Caldwell; without a father his son can find no viable context for living.

Indeed, *Of the Farm* suggests that the resources of familial and cultural past are running out for John Updike; once back in New York, Joey Robinson faces affluence and anonymity. True, the mode of the novel is ironic, and we can at least project the desirable alternative, the kind of ceremonial connection which Updike would like his hero to make. Yet that connection seems to be an impossibility now. In this fourth novel, John Updike questions the very sources of personal renewal.

The ability to question one's assumptions is a sign of artistic and personal maturity, of course—and it may be that *Of the Farm* marks a transitional state in Updike's artistic growth. Like Cheever's narrator at the end of *The Wapshot Scandal,* Joey Robinson is closing a chapter in his life. He stands in a balancing position, between childhood loyalties to a farm that is becoming a commodity ("when you sell my farm, don't sell it cheap. Get a good price") and an uncertain future ("down the road, along the highway, up the Turnpike"). Perhaps Joey's uncertain position is the only one available to show the complex and contradictory claims of love.

For both Cheever and Updike, at any rate, ceremonial style is only a tentative resolution of the problem with which we began. An entirely ordered and ceremonial fiction would be as formal (and as lifeless) as a minuet. Yet their achievement to date rests largely on their artistic projection of the conflict between the past and the present, the traditional and the new, and on its brief resolution in ceremonial moments. For them both, style is a way of experiencing the pressures of modern life. If style cannot resolve those pressures, it can at least present them as they are.

4 ❧ Eudora Welty:
A Continual Feast

"All the days of the afflicted are evil:
but he that is of a merry heart hath
a continual feast." Proverbs 15:15.

CELEBRATION in Eudora Welty's fiction is so pervasive as to become a problem. When all of her work manifests a festive encounter with reality, how can we identify the essential feast? This at least we can say: Eudora Welty's fiction demonstrates a sense of wonder at the real and a belief in the mystery underlying the banalities of daily life. It affirms personal feeling, the restorative power of art, and the poetry of physical place. In some of her stories, the place *is* the feast.

And yet it is not. For place is an imaginative reconstruction rather than a physical entity here. Miss Welty has never lived in the Delta country, though it is the almost invariable setting for her fiction. Her Delta is a land of myth and dreams, as imaginative a region as Faulkner's Yoknapatawpha. Indeed, the golden, dreamlike quality of her work has often been noted by her critics.[1]

The connection between place and dream is fundamental in Eudora Welty's fiction. A striking disconnection exists, on the other hand, between plot and feeling. The surface action of *The Robber Bridegroom* is abduction and rape; in *Delta Wedding*, it is rescue from a train and estrangement between husband and wife; in *The Golden Apples*, assorted rapes, arsons, and deaths; in *The Ponder Heart*, a murder trial. Clearly the essential action is interior and private. The private sensibility charges public action with a festive spirit.

In *The Robber Bridegroom* (1942) Miss Welty combines fairy tale and folk tale to produce a fantasy that transcends the violence of the story. The book is not her best, and if *she* had not written it, it would quite likely fall into the limbo of juvenile fiction. But the book is redeemed by Miss Welty's appetite for her characters and her setting. The story is a tale *told*—the narrator's controlling hand mutes violence with fable. The violent abduction of Rosamond, for example, becomes an act of fabulous beauty:

> Rosamond's hair lay out behind her, and Jamie's hair was flying too. The horse was the master of everything. He went like an arrow with the distance behind him and the dark wood closing together. On Rosamond's arm was the pail of milk, and yet so smoothly did they travel that not a single drop was spilled. Rosamond's cloak filled with the wind, and then in the one still moment in the middle of a leap, it broke from her shoulder like a big bird, and dropped away below. Red as blood the horse rode the ridge, his mane and tail straight out in the wind, and it was the fastest kidnapping that had ever been in that part of the country.[2]

The ensuing rape occurs in a peaceful setting with plums raining down all around and the river flowing below them slow as sand.

Throughout the fantasy external violence is contained (like Big Harp's head) in a box—Rosamond's love for her unknown bridegroom. The landscape itself is an interior world of love, reflecting mystery and wonder. Though Rosamond profanes that love by cleansing the berry stain from her robber bridegroom's face as he sleeps, her steadfast loyalty to him thereafter regains love, together with a legitimate marriage and motherhood. In her search for Jamie, she passes like a totem through the hands of a sinister dwarf, wild Indians, robbers, an evil stepmother, and Mike Fink.

The fruitful wilderness extends Rosamond's love in a foreshadowing of motherhood. Miss Welty's narrator comments extensively on the symbiosis of Rosamond and the wilderness in the following passage:

> The trees *were golden* under the sky. The grass was *as soft as a dream* and the wind blew *like the long rising and falling breath of Summer when she has just fallen asleep.* One day Jamie did not

ride away with the others, and then the day was night and *the woods were the roof over their heads. The tender flames of the myrtle trees and the green smoke of the cedars* were the fires of their hearth. *In the radiant noon* they found the shade, and ate the grapes from the muscadine vines. *The spice-dreams rising from the fallen brown pine needles floated through their heads* when they stretched their limbs and slept in the woods. The stream lay still *in the golden ravine, the water glowing darkly, the color of fruits and nuts.* (p. 86, italics mine)

Game abounds here; Jamie Lockhart's raven sings in their cave; rich gowns, English silver, and Creek scalps festoon their bower. Thus the setting short-circuits the plot, making private lyric of public violence.

The reader's final impression of *The Robber Bridegroom* is a sense of place, the Delta country that Miss Welty exploits so well in her later work. Like the wilderness of Faulkner's "Was" and "The Bear," place is the real hero of the work. Fantasy serves to affirm the real, not to evade it.

Delta Wedding (1946) is a sustained celebration of a time and place. The time is 1923, chosen because it was the only year in which there had been no "external catastrophe such as a war, a depression, or a flood." [3] The place is not only the Delta, but plantation life there at Shellmound, Marmion, and the Grove. The occasion is the wedding of Troy Flavin, an overseer, and Dabney Fairchild, daughter of a family so close-knit and so magically protected from external evil as to defy death and disorder—at least for the moment.

This book is Miss Welty's only novel. It is simply too long for an exclusive preoccupation with private responses to experience. The work has no plot, no significant character development, no crisis or climax. It is rather an attempt at a sustained lyric moment, revealing Eudora Welty's essential concern with the validity of different ways of seeing.

As a result, the small rituals of a family preparing for a wedding, told from a shifting omniscience, reveal individual rather than group celebration. To use her own terms from "A Still Moment," the novel reveals love and separateness, complementary qualities in any mature vision of the world. The eleven-year-old Laura, the young flapper Shelley, the fiancé Troy, and the bride Dabney are all narrators reaching towards a communal integration greater than their individual isolation. The wedding is that integration.

The characters never lose that individual sense, however; the novel asserts no false solutions to the essential problem of loneliness. Consider for instance the effect of the wedding on Robbie Reid and on Ellen Fairchild, Dabney's mother. The central action of the whole novel is conveyed in a simple sentence: "Mr. Rondo married Dabney and Troy." But the passage immediately prior to this one reflects Robbie's own thoughts on marriage and the one just following, Ellen's.

Robbie Reid is just a store clerk, like Bonny Lee Ponder. But she married the idol of the family, Ellen's brother George. She feels defensive about her position and possessive of George. Just before the ceremony she realizes that no one can have him, and only she can know the inviolable separateness that no love can bridge, the uniqueness of personality.

> He had not yielded up to that family what they really wanted! Or they would not keep after him. But where she herself had expected light, all was still dark too.
> He wanted her so blindly—just to hold. . . .
> But he turned his head a little now and glanced at her with that suddenness—curiosity, not quite hope—that tore her heart, like a stranger inside some house where he wanted to make sure that she too had come, had really come.
> It was all right with her, she wanted him to look at her and see that. She was rising a little on her chair as if she would stand up, while the music swelled—looking over Aunt Tempe's hothouse corsage and meeting the dark look. Somehow it was all right, every minute that they were in the one place. (p. 248)

In Robbie's mind, marriage is an intimate relation of strangers. With that insight she enters into the spirit of the feast.

Married life-wedding-motherhood: the inverted sequence concludes as Ellen retells the comic birth of Shelley, Dabney's sister. Her own mother, Mama, had come from Virginia to be with her for the delivery. Having felled the doctor with a gargantuan breakfast, she had to load him on the bed with Ellen. When he recovered, he "went over and he fiddled with the gas machine and he bent over and took a testing breath and he fell over. Mama just was not able to pick him up a second time, so we just let him alone, and I asked Mama to leave the room, I was shy before her, and I had the baby by myself—the cook came and she knew everything necessary—Partheny it was" (p. 251).

The experience of the two women is identical; only the response differs. If Robbie Reid sees the pathos of separateness, Ellen Fairchild realizes "the comedy of love." [4] Childbirth is anticlimactic; the chance events of life cannot be contained by human action. For Ellen the unattended birth of Shelley reveals both love and separateness. But this is not all: Ellen tells the story at Dabney's wedding, amidst general laughter. Her guests share the anticlimactic experience of love and separateness, celebrating the vagaries of life.

This short section of the novel suggests the cycle of love. The wedding itself occurs in one sentence, a brief moment capable of extension into married life (Robbie Reid's reflections) and further, into childbirth (Ellen's anecdote). The ultimate extension of the wedding ceremony is thus marriage and motherhood, isolation and community, pathos and laughter. The complete experience is what Miss Welty celebrates in *Delta Wedding*.

In a wider sense, celebration involves the whole community in an act of wonder at life. For the briefest of moments, that life is poised between holiday and everyday, the family and the individual, the Delta and the world. The novel itself is a brief moment in their lives, which will shortly resume the banal round.

On the final page, the newlyweds, children, and adults are out singing in the late summer night:

> George, with his left-handed throw, put pebbles in the Yazoo. "We'll keep in touch. . . ."
> One great golden star went through the night falling.
> "Oh!" cried Laura aloud. "Oh, it was beautiful, that star!"
> "I saw it, I saw it!" cried India.
> Dabney reached over and put her arm around her, drew her to her. "Yes. Beautiful!" India smiled faintly, leaning on Dabney's beating heart, the softness of her breast. . . .
> "I saw where it fell," said Laura, bragging and in reassurance.
> She turned again to them, both arms held out to the radiant night. (p. 287)

Though the great golden star falls and the family celebration is about to dissolve, the experience has an infinite extension. The wedding has been only a moment in the flux of life. But that moment, like the falling star, is a festive response to a chance event. In its widest sense, love itself is a chance which one must seize.

The Golden Apples is probably Eudora Welty's finest achievement. The seven connected stories celebrate an almost magical place and the relentless press of time and chance that push people farther and farther from it. *The Golden Apples* is a myth of origins. Its characters are exiled from the land of the sun, condemned to seek it elsewhere forever.

Essentially, the stories are about relation, the influence of one life upon another. King MacLain affects them all; his break from Morgana and his periodic returns mark stages in the action. His wanderings are archetypal foreshadowings of the common fate. The golden apples, then, are both the source and the object of human wandering.

King's two sons reflect this fated wandering in different places. Randall, the son who stayed home, is condemned to a loveless life by his falsehearted Jinny. Ran tells his story as an interior monologue to his absent father. His mother's comments echo throughout, connecting him in temperament and action with the roving King. At the end, Ran is a stranger in his own land, cut off from love by the failure of love—the country girl he seduced shoots herself with his gun.

> How was I to know she would go and hurt herself? She cheated, she cheated too.
> Father, Eugene! What you went and found, was it better than this?
> And where's Jinny? (p. 181)

His brother Eugene experiences a corresponding disappointment in San Francisco. "Music from Spain," the only non-Morgana story, describes the heart's desire for the lyric moment which circumstances forbid. The spirit went out of Eugene's marriage with the death of his daughter. One day, in an effort to revive it, he slaps his wife and walks out. On the street he sees a mysterious Spanish guitarist whom they had heard at a concert the previous night. Eugene saves him from an oncoming car. Though

they eat together and face death together, Eugene and the Spaniard never converse. The music is from Spain, or Morgana, a
timeless place in the imagination. After a day in the city, Eugene
comes home to the banalities of married life, revived by the strange
existence he has shared with the musical wanderer.

Music is an important motif in another of these stories, "June
Recital." The Aengus-figure is neither King MacLain nor the
Spaniard, but Miss Eckhart, a German music teacher. The story
is a struggle between this incommunicative woman, parched for
love, and her prize pupil, Virgie Rainey. Virgie turns her talent
against the teacher and refuses to accept her life, *frei aber einsam.*
After several years Miss Eckhart is caught trying to burn her deserted studio, while Virgie and her sailor sport in the bedroom
above.

The context for the revelation of one's essential strangeness varies
from story to story. Here the revelation comes to neither woman,
but to the onlooker, Cassie Morrison. She reflects on the moment
when the crazy old woman meets her best student before they
take her away: "*Danke schoen.* . . . That much was out in the open.
Gratitude—like rescue—was simply no more. It was not only past;
it was outworn and cast away. Both Miss Eckhart and Virgie
Rainey were human beings terribly at large, roaming on the face
of the earth. And there were others of them—human beings, roaming, like lost beasts" (p. 96).

The context of the essential separateness is love, however. Cassie
remembers Yeats' poem word for word. "All of it passed through
her head, through her body. She slept, but sat up in bed once and
said aloud, '*Because a fire was in my head.*' Then she fell back
unresisting. She did not see except in dreams that a face looked in;
that it was the grave, unappeased, and radiant face, once more and
always, the face that was in the poem" (pp. 96–97). That face is
Miss Eckhart's and Virgie's; Aengus's and King's.

"Moon Lake" tells of Loch Morrison, the next heir of King Mac-
Lain. Like Virgie he is a musician—the camp bugler for the whole
group of orphans. He disdains the girls, but his isolation and his
humble art require their presence. "He played taps for them, invisibly then, and so beautifully they wept together, whole tentfuls
some nights. Off with the whip-poor-wills and the coons and the
owls and the little bobwhites—down where it all sloped away, he

had pitched his tent, and slept there. Then at reveille, how he would spit into that cornet" (p. 113).

At the end of the story, after he has saved Easter from drowning, Loch is observed, just as he himself observed Virgie Rainey and Miss Eckhart in the empty house next door. Mina and Jinny Love crawl down to his tent and peek at the strange hero. "It seemed to them they could still hear in the beating air of night the wild tattoo of pride he must have struck off. His silly, brief, overriding little show they could well imagine there in his tent of separation in the middle of the woods, in the night. Minnowy thing that matched his candle flame, naked as he was with that, he thought he shone forth too. Didn't he?" (p. 156)

Yet for all his splendor, Loch "looked rather at loose ends." The perception of the self is a moment of mystery and wonder, a silent celebration of one's unique identity. But, like the isolation of love in *Delta Wedding*, this one is hedged about with the community. True, Loch wants no part of the gaggle of girls. But their corporate action counterpoints his lone one, restoring the social balance to isolated awareness: "They went up and joined the singing."

"Moon Lake" and "June Recital" are the longest stories in *The Golden Apples* and probably the best of them. Eudora Welty is never better at lyric evocation than she is here; moreover, she enriches the physical scene with allusions to the Eden myth, the myths of Zeus and Perseus, and the myth of Aengus. Celebration in these stories is indirect, the attitude of the implied narrator, whose combination of the celebrants (Virgie and Loch) and the community (the townsfolk and the pubescent girls) makes that vision festive. The hand of the maker resolves the otherwise incomplete elements of the feast.

To a large extent, myth-making itself, *poiesis*, is the subject of *The Golden Apples*. "A Shower of Gold" and "Sir Rabbit" are evidence of the viability of myth—clearly celebrations of the shaping imagination. The comic irony of the first story, for instance, lies in Miss Welty's choice of a narrator: the gossipy, just-folks Kate Rainey. In her telling, Danäe (Snowdie MacLain) is impregnated by Zeus (King), who immediately disappears. On the other hand, Kate Rainey's exuberance makes her a fitting bard for an ancient myth. "I believe he's been to California. Don't ask me why.

But I picture him there. I see King in the West, out where it's gold and all that. Everybody to their own visioning" (p. 11).

This emphasis on the myth-making process is underscored by the final story, "The Wanderers." The occasion is Kate Rainey's funeral. Thus the work itself, the lyric song, is coextensive with the life of its bard. That life is a narrative frame, enclosing the story and allowing Miss Welty sufficient distance from the material to give it the golden aura of myth.

Thus we may view the slight story, "Sir Rabbit," as a reprise, reminding us of King's sexual force, the force that through the green fuse drives the flower. Mattie Will Sojourner, the narrator, connects the twins with their father. When they were fifteen, Ran and Eugene took her in the woods. Now, married to Junior Holifield, she is taken by King himself. Both halves of the story are united in her consciousness. Mattie Will reenacts the role of Danäe, not once but thrice, just as the twins repeat the action of their father. Like King and like the wandering Aengus before him, they seek "the glimmering girl/With apple blossom in her hair."

The sexual pursuit then is an ancient form of celebration. As archetypal action it occurs in each of the first five stories. (Certainly the rescue of Easter from the mud bottom of Moon Lake and her resuscitation have sexual overtones.) Sex in *The Golden Apples* celebrates the fertility of nature and of man:

> *In the night time,*
> *At the right time,*
> *So I've understood*
> *'Tis the habit of Sir Rabbit*
> *To dance in the wood—.* (pp. 110–111)

The final celebration in the book is the funeral. Like the ceremony in *Delta Wedding*, the funeral serves to unite the community for a moment. All the wanderers recognize in Kate Rainey's death the end of the journey. The impact is especially strong on Virgie, who sees in her mother's death the isolation which Miss Eckhart's life had prefigured. That life had been an oblation of music, which Virgie rejected in rejecting Miss Eckhart. Now music once again echoes isolation and the victory of art: "In Virgie's reach of memory a melody softly lifted, lifted of itself. Every time

Perseus struck off the Medusa's head, there was the beat of time, and the melody. Endless the Medusa, and Perseus endless" (p. 276).

The insight is of the doubleness of things, "love close to hate, living to dying; but of them all, hope and despair were the closest blood." Like Lorenzo Dow in "A Still Moment," like Rosamond's father, and in the manner of Hopkins's "Pied Beauty," Virgie sees all things counter, original, spare, and strange. Man is a sojourner on the earth, searching for the dream he once knew. (The story recalls in title, tone, and theme Carson McCullers' poignant "The Sojourner.")

But the experience is double. The imagination converts isolated suffering into group experience, celebrates loss in myth and music. At the end of the book, Virgie steps into the role which her mother had at the beginning, bard and intermediary betwen time and art:

> She smiled once, seeing before her, screenlike, the hideous and delectable face Mr. King MacLain had made at the funeral, and when they all knew he was next—even he. Then she and the old beggar woman, the old black thief, were there alone and together in the shelter of the big public tree, listening to the magical percussion, the world beating in their ears. They heard through fallen rain the running of the horse and bear, the stroke of the leopard, the dragon's crusty slither, and the glimmer and the trumpet of the swan. (p. 277)

If I read her correctly, Endora Welty is saying that art alone transforms the stuff of experience into coherent shape. In this she echoes the practice of Elizabeth Bowen, to whom Alfred Appel compares her at the end of his study: [5] "Illusions are art, for the feeling person, and it is by art that we live, if we do." [6]

The Ponder Heart (1954) differs from *The Golden Apples* in being an individual rather than a corporate celebration. In its own way it deals with the duality of experience. Uncle Daniel's innocence and Ran MacLain's pathetic isolation are the same; at the end the comic surface gives way to isolation. [7]

The three celebrations in *The Ponder Heart* are marriage, a funeral, and a courtroom trial. In each case the social responses run counter to form and produce the tragicomic quality that is most characteristic of Miss Welty's work. The marriage, for instance, is an instantaneous act. Uncle Daniel walks into the dime store, sees Bonny Dee behind the counter, and proposes: "I've got a great big house standing empty, and my father's Studebaker. Come on— marry me" (*The Ponder Heart*, p. 26). The wedding is a private ceremony, almost a secret.

The funeral, on the other hand, has comic elements, both in itself and in its consequences. Grief is forestalled by Edna Earle's criticism of the white trash Peacocks. The flowers are set out in pie pans; there is no grass in the yard; Mrs. Peacock wears tennis shoes to the funeral. Most significant here is the technique. The narrator holds a tight rein on Uncle Daniel. His experience becomes her story. Note the comic tension between her commentary and his responses in a passage like the following: "It was there at the graveside that Uncle Daniel had his turn. There might have been high foolishness or even trouble—both big red-headed Baptist preachers took hold of him. It was putting her in the ground *he* didn't like" (*The Ponder Heart*, p. 66).

If the wedding is entirely uncelebrated, and the funeral is described in clucking disapproval, the murder trial is conducted in an uproar. For the first time Uncle Daniel is unleashed, by Miss Welty and by his legal counsel, with catastrophic results. The Ponder heart turns justice into a festival. Hitherto no social form has contained Uncle Daniel. But the murder trial at last turns attention to himself; the defendant becomes the celebrant.

Like Honora in *The Wapshot Scandal*, he runs into the crowd, giving away his money on the eve of his conviction. Both incidents are festive protests against the dehumanization of man. And ironically in each case the festive spirit of the celebrant is completely lost on the avaricious group. The action is a self-release which at the same time imprisons the giver in his charity:

> The Baptist preacher—Brother Barfield, always on hand—rose up and made his voice heard over the storm. (Our preacher was home praying for us, where he belonged.) He said he thought all the money here unclaimed by Mr. Daniel Ponder (*that* was a funny way to put it) should be turned over to the Baptist Church, which needed it. But old lady Peacock—and such a Baptist, you remember *two* preachers at the funeral—hollers back gay as a lark, "Finders keepers!" and showed him her hands full. (pp. 123–124)

Uncle Daniel's acquittal for the murder of Bonny Dee is anticlimatic. The judge can barely shout the verdict over the commotion. No matter; the trial has beecome a liturgical celebration by now, anyhow. "He brings out more money than you could shake a stick at. He made every row, like he was taking up collection in church, but doing the very opposite" (p. 119). Uncle Daniel's boundless heart has found an adequate expression of his love, a virtual emptying of himself for others. Of course, Edna Earle does not fail to point out the ironies involved.

In each case, then, Uncle Daniel's private celebration runs counter to the prevailing motion of his society. Yet the wider society of readers restores the balance in their comic response to the situation. One is reminded, again, of the epigraph for this chapter: *only the merry heart hath a continual feast.*[8]

While an analysis of all Miss Welty's stories is beyond my scope here, I would like to consider some forms of celebration that appear in her short stories. Ruth Vande Kieft has done us a service in editing *Thirteen Stories* with a perceptive introduction.[9] I should like to consider three of her selections, "The Wide Net," "A Still Moment," and "Powerhouse"—certainly three of the best stories by any standard.

"The Wide Net" celebrates a timeless place and its rural ways. The particular feast involved is a ritual hunt for a presumably drowned wife. The action is a full, obvious feast with several components thereof: a celebrant, Old Doc; two deacons, the husband, William Wallace, and his friend, Virgil Thomas; two little Negro acolytes, Sam and Robbie Bell; a liturgical action, dragging the net up the Pearl River; a river deity, the King of the Snakes; and a ritual combat between Virgil and William. Moreover, the path of the hunt is always the Old Natchez Trace, suggesting a traditional action; and the whole society participates in a secular feast and procession which even nature imitates: "Once they went through a forest of cucumber trees and came up on a high ridge. Grady and Brucie who were running aread all the way stopped in their tracks; a whistle had blown and far down and far away a long freight train was passing. It seemed like a little festival procession, moving with the slowness of ignorance or a dream, from distance

to distance, the tiny pink and gray cars like secret boxes. . . ."
(*Thirteen Stories*, p. 23).

Since the characteristic attitude in the story is a reverent performance of ritual duties, the characteristic tone is a subdued but
joyful affirmation of existence. As Doc says, "the excursion is the
same when you go looking for your sorrow as when you go looking for your joy." Thus individual identity is sublimated in corporate action. The group emerges empty-handed from the hunt for
Hazel, but it ends with a triumphant procession of fecund nature.

> William Wallace walked through the town as though he did not
> see anybody or hear anything. Yet he carried his great string of fish
> held high where it could be seen by all. Virgil came next, imitating
> William Wallace exactly, then the modest Doyles crowded by the
> Malones, who were holding up their alligator, tossing it into the
> air, even, like a father tossing his child. Following behind and
> pointing authoritatively at the ones in front strolled Doc, with Sam
> and Robbie Bell still chanting in his wake. . . . (p. 35)

"The Wide Net" is a romance, cut from the same cloth as *The
Robber Bridegroom*. Like all romances, it shows the reunion of
lovers at the end. Hazel has hidden from William all day. The hunt
then has been meaningless on the rational level. But as celebrative
action, it has revealed the context of communal love within which
the marriage will find meaning and foison.

Like *The Ponder Heart*, "The Wide Net" is a trial of love. The
difference is the context. The early short story springs from a
world of love. The novel reveals a fallen world full of buffoonery
and avarice—redeemed only for a moment by Uncle Daniel's love.
The difference may indicate a failure of faith on Miss Welty's
part that society can any longer maintain a corporate celebration.

Since public celebrations are unavailing, the artist must take refuge in private ones, if for no other reason than to assure the continuity of communication between artist and audience. "A Still
Moment" reveals that continuity better than anything else Eudora
Welty has written. Love and separateness are resolved in a celebration of reality through art. "A Still Moment" demonstrates the
analogous unity of three distinct experiences.

The first is a minister's. Lorenzo rides furiously in the night, always towards death: "On the back of one horse after another, winding them all, he was always riding toward it or away from it, and the Lord sent him directions with protection in his mind" (*Thirteen Stories*, p. 86). His vision of an interior wilderness, a darkness of souls that he must dispel, goads him into his apostolate. Religious conversion is his way to the light.

The second experience is the outlaw Murrell's. Himself a dark evangelist, Murrell is accustomed to revealing his identity to his victim before murdering him. "Destroy the present!—that must have been the first thing that was whispered in Murrell's heart—the living moment and the man that lives in it must die before you can go on. It was his habit to bring his journey—which might even take days—to a close with a kind of ceremony" (p. 89). The revelation of himself as outlaw vindicates his belief in the intrinsic evil of experience. Like Flannery O'Connor's Misfit, he holds for nihilism: "No pleasure but meanness."

Each position is abstract. It takes a third, Audubon's, to put human experience into a real context. That context is natural abundance. "All life used this Trace, and he liked to see the animals move along it in direct, oblivious journeys, for they had begun it and made it, the buffalo and deer and the small running creatures before man ever knew where he wanted to go, and birds flew a great mirrored course above" (p. 91). Audubon has taught himself to be humble before the mystery of existence.

The occasion for the illumination of these three men who meet by chance in the falling dusk is the appearance of a snowy heron. Lorenzo sees the bird as a sign of God's immanence: "Praise God, His love has come visible." Murrell "looked at the bird with the whole plan of the Mystic Rebellion darting from him as if in rays of the bright reflected light," seeing himself as a Natchez Satan in a kingdom of slaves and brigands. Audubon, on the other hand, "felt again the old stab of wonder—what structure of life bridged the reptile's scale and the heron's feather? That knowledge too had been lost."

The narrator comments on the shared experience, the silent celebration of the heart's need: "What each of them had wanted was simply *all*. To save all souls, to destroy all men, to see and record all life that filled this world—all, all—but now a single frail yearning seemed to go out of the three of them for a moment and to stretch toward this one snowy, shy bird in the marshes. It was as if three whirlwinds had drawn together at some center, to find there feeding in peace a snowy heron. Its own slow spiral of flight could take it away in its own time, but for a little it held them still, it laid quiet over them, and they stood for a moment unburdened . . ." (p. 95). The experience is an esthetic moment, a unity of disparate experiences.

Yet the resolution quite clearly balances separateness against love. Audubon shoots the heron, destroying life for art. He could remember the heron's beauty, "but it was not from memory that he could paint." The paradox is a cruel one.[10] Murrell feels vindicated by the act. "Each must go away alone, each send the others away alone." The moment of community has been an illusion for him; isolation is the only reality. Lorenzo is powerfully moved by the heron's beauty, but like Murrell, he rejects this world for the camp meeting ahead up the Trace—"and then he shouted into the marshes. 'Tempter!' "

Clearly, the moment is past. By the logic of their value schemes, Murrell and Dow are forced to discount the apparition as one more enigma in an enigmatic world. Audubon, as naturalist and painter, is forced to murder the beautiful bird. But he alone is human, living in a world of objects. For him the bird is not enigma but mystery. His painting will be a tribute and an addition to the mystery of existence; ultimately, his shot celebrates and affirms the real. "A Still Moment" gives us Eudora Welty's central celebration: the celebration of art itself.

"Powerhouse" is a third kind of celebration, this time musical. The title figure (who looks and acts like Fats Waller) is a pianist who manages to express his total experience in his music. Suffering, deprivation, and death are significant elements of that experience. Powerhouse's wife Gypsy may be dead. At any rate, Powerhouse recognizes and muses about Uranus Knockwood, a mythic double-figure who "come in when we go out" and "go out when we comes in." Uranus is the anti-self, the denial of love, hope, and celebration in one's own experience.

Powerhouse is the celebrant who exorcises this demon from the assembly. At first, at the white folks' dance, the exorcism is muted. But even here the narrator distinguishes three musicians from the rest of the band: "Only those playing around Powerhouse are the real ones." Later, in the Negro bar during intermission, these three are the nucleus for the congregation.

Like Audubon, Powerhouse is the artist whose art celebrates life. As the scene shifts from the dance hall to the bar, the drive shifts from the musical to the verbal. But the action is one: celebration of the will to live and to affirm experience. This affirmation radiates from Powerhouse at the center to include his sidemen, the Negro waitress, and all the patrons of the cafe.

In the central section of the story, Powerhouse assumes the fears and threats incumbent on the Negro and expresses them boldly. His wife has jumped from the window, spilling her brains and insides on the sidewalk, where she has been discovered by Uranus Knockwood: " 'Ya! Ha! You talking about her brains and insides— old Uranus Knockwood,' says Powerhouse, 'look down and say Jesus! He say, Look here what I'm walking round in!' " (p. 137). Then a litany follows, in which all the patrons express their own experience of Uranus—be he Chance, Fate, Suffering, or Death. But Powerhouse has assumed that experience on himself and contained it.

After the litany, "Everybody in the room moans with pleasure. The little boy in the fine silver hat opens a paper and divides out a jelly roll among his followers." This offering expresses the shared experience in a sharing of food. Others step forward and introduce themselves to Powerhouse. Then the celebrant finishes the exorcism with a telegram to Uranus Knockwood: "Here's the answer. I got it right here. 'What in the hell you talking about? Don't make any difference: I gotcha.' Name signed: Powerhouse" (p. 139). This defiance of Knockwood expresses the pianist's affirmation of life, his celebration of experience.

Back at the dance hall, the celebration takes on musical form once more. The song is another defiant gesture—"Somebody Loves Me." Chorus after chorus tumbles from his fingers, until we realize that Powerhouse's struggle with Uranus Knockwood never ceases. As Virgie Rainey says at her mother's funeral, "Endless the Medusa, and Perseus endless."

" 'Maybe . . .' He pulls back his spread fingers, and looks out upon the place where he is. A vast, impersonal and yet furious grimace transfigures his wet face. '. . . Maybe it's you!' " (p. 140).

The final refutation of Uranus Knockwood is neither musical nor verbal, but volitional. Love is the last celebration, and ultimately the only one.

The essential celebration in Eudora Welty's work therefore is a private act. Her feast is a deliberate choice between the open heart and the closed fist. In this sense Uncle Daniel Ponder is the composite Welty hero—romantic, larger than life, essentially childlike, eager to open himself to experience. Sometimes her narrators work against that composite, generating a comic tension between point of view and the author's values, for instance Edna Earle in *The Ponder Heart*, Leota in "Petrified Man," and Sister in "Why I Live at the P.O." But more often the narrator reveals a poetic approval of experience, a desire for "what we all want—a story of Beauty and Passion and Truth."

Given the nature of her subject and of her approach, Miss Welty's achievement is clearly in the short story. Her lyric style, her reliance on the moment of vision, her sense of the uniqueness of the individual and of his experience, her almost religious sense of wonder at being, and her sensitive response to physical setting are all characteristic of the poem, not the novel. And the celebration of these things is a paramount achievement in contemporary fiction.

5 ❧ Flannery O'Connor: A Hidden Celebration

UNLIKE Eudora Welty, Flannery O'Connor is not a lyric writer. Her sense of the South is prophetic. She tried to combine the prophet's role and the novelist's craft. Her work reveals that religious sense of life in striking and unusual fashion. The typical O'Connor short story is built on sacramental action: baptism, confirmation, the eucharist. At their best, these stories reveal the priesthood of the laity, sacred celebration in the secular world.

Flannery O'Connor's work consists of two collections of short stories, *A Good Man Is Hard to Find* (1955) and *Everything That Rises Must Converge* (1965), and two novels, *Wise Blood* (1952) and *The Violent Bear It Away* (1960). Probably her best work is in the short story; no finer collection than *Everything That Rises* has appeared in recent years. Somehow the novels don't quite measure up—she had little interest in sustained plotting or in the slow evolution of character. Hers was a nervous talent, one for lightning strokes and quick illuminations of human darkness.

As Pieper notes in the conclusion of his book, darkness can mask celebration. "But what is hidden is nonetheless real. . . . Two extreme historical potentialities have equal chances: the latent everlasting festival may be made manifest, or the 'antifestival' may develop in its most radical form" (Pieper, p. 65). In Flannery O'Connor's work, celebration is hidden beneath banality, grotesquerie, and deformity—"But what is hidden is nonetheless real."

In Miss O'Connor's mind, the novelist's vision enables him to celebrate the hidden reality: "The fiction writer should be characterized by his kind of vision, not by his function. His kind of vision is prophetic vision. Prophecy, which is dependent on the imagination and not the moral faculty, need not be a matter of predicting the future. In the novelist's case, it is a matter of seeing near things with their extensions of meaning and thus of seeing far things close up. The prophet is the realist of distances, and it is this kind of realism that goes into great novels. It is the realism which does not hesitate to distort appearances in order to show a hidden truth." [1]

The Catholic novelist, furthermore, has the special burden of using his talent to shape tradition. His celebrations of prophetic vision must reveal the hidden Christ in the welter of contemporary experience: "For the Catholic novelist, the prophetic vision is not simply a matter of his personal imaginative gift; it is also a matter of the Church's gift, which, unlike his own, is safeguarded and deals with greater matters. It is one of the functions of the Church to transmit the prophetic vision that is good for all the time; and when the novelist has this as part of his vision, he has a powerful extension of sight." [2]

Vision is Flannery O'Connor's central concern. Sacrificial action is hidden under the barren surface of her stories. Her purpose is not to separate feast from famine, but to reveal their inseparability. Her first collection of stories shows Christ amidst one-armed con men, homicidal maniacs, hermaphrodites, and a virgin existentialist with a Ph.D. and a wooden leg. Once she has established the reality of her rural eccentrics as everyday people, she can push her artistic vision toward mystical illumination—roughly the difference between *A Good Man Is Hard to Find* and *Everything That Rises Must Converge*.

The polarities of her work, of hidden feast and public famine, she describes as "mystery and fact." "When I write a novel in which the central action is baptism [*The Violent Bear It Away*], I know that for the larger percentage of my readers, baptism is a meaningless rite; therefore I have to imbue this action with an awe and terror which will suggest its awful mystery. I have to distort the look of the thing in order to represent as I see them both the mystery and the fact." [3] Flannery O'Connor is quite sensitive to the antifestive tendency that drives celebration underground. Her feasts, like Ellison's, Malamud's, and Baldwin's, are guerilla raids on the unfestive society overhead—a society that refuses to acknowledge the divine mystery of existence.

In Miss O'Connor's first volume of stories, vision and sacrifice are disguised by ugliness and deformity. Sometimes the hidden feast is an ironic comment, the testimony of physical nature against the example of humankind. In stories such as "A Temple of the Holy Ghost," "The Artificial Nigger," and "A Circle in the Fire," only the narrator sees the gulf between the human and his world. Miss O'Connor concludes the first of these stories, for example, with an allusion to the continual crucifixion of Christ: "Her mother let the conversation drop and the child's round face was lost in thought. She turned it toward the window and looked out over a stretch of pasture land that rose and fell with a gathering greenness until it touched the dark woods. The sun was a huge red ball like an elevated Host drenched in blood and when it sank out of sight, it left a line in the sky like a red clay road hanging over the trees." [4]

Some of the stories, like "A Stroke of Good Fortune," "The Life You Save May Be Your Own," "A Late Encounter With the Enemy," and "Good Country People," are ironic throughout. No setting, vision, or narrative commentary relieves the grimness of the story. In such stories Miss O'Connor is most concerned with the fact of life, with its prevalent public famine. Such celebration as there may be in these stories is hidden too deeply to see. Each one is reductive, destroying the communal bond which celebration presupposes. But each gives testimony to the reality and to the power of the devil in modern life—especially to the devil of self-delusion.

In three of her best stories, however, Flannery O'Connor turns mystery against the prevailing fact and in a moment of vision illuminates the human condition. "A Good Man Is Hard to Find" suggests a double illumination—a vision of evil and a vision of sonship. The impact of the story depends upon our seeing them together as the vision of one man under different aspects.

Throughout "A Good Man" the characters react to one another with unsuppressed hostility. On a Sunday drive through Georgia the children quarrel with each other and insult the grandmother. Bailey, her son, scarcely tolerates her, and his wife ignores her completely. They are stopped by three men on a deserted country road. Significantly, it is the grandmother who first recognizes the Misfit and his fellow escaped convicts. "The Grandmother shrieked. She scrambled to her feet and stood staring. 'You're the Misfit!' she said. 'I recognized you at once!' "

The recognition has fatal consequences for Bailey, his wife, and their children. It also anticipates the recognition at the moment of her own death. After hearing the Misfit's tale of lost faith—a grotesque account under the circumstances—she sees him as her own son: "She saw the man's face twisted close to her own as if he were going to cry and she murmured, 'Why you're one of my babies. You're one of my own children!' She reached out and touched him on the shoulder. The Misfit sprang back as if a snake had bitten him and shot her three times through the chest" (*Three by Flannery O'Connor*, p. 143). The Misfit *is* one of her own children, toward whom the grandmother reaches out with love. The resurrection, which the Misfit cannot accept, becomes personal for the grandmother, affording her the grace of salvation.

The hidden celebration in "The River" is baptismal. A little boy is baptized by a zealous river preacher while his parents sleep off a hangover. The river, the preacher tells us, is the river of pain itself, "moving toward the Kingdom of Christ, to be washed away, slow, you people, slow as this here old red water river round my feet."

When Harry returns from his baptism his parents mock him and refuse to admit that now "he counts." So the little boy leaves the next morning—"He hadn't taken a suitcase because there was nothing from there he wanted to keep." He returns to the river seeking the preacher, now gone. Mr. Paradise is there, though, and follows him to the bank with a big piece of peppermint candy and lust in his heart. Drawn by the kingdom of Christ upriver, Harry jumps in, hotly pursued by Mr. Paradise. "He plunged under once and this time, the waiting current caught him like a long gentle hand and pulled him swiftly forward and down. For an instant he was overcome with surprise; then since he was moving quickly and knew that he was getting somewhere, all his fury and fear left him" (p. 159). In his innocence Harry finds the Kingdom of Christ, literally though unconsciously putting the devil behind him. Mr. Paradise, the pederast, rises from the river like some ancient water monster, defeated in his pursuit of flesh.

Celebration is hidden here under the shock of the boy's drowning. But Miss O'Connor challenges us to see the act with the eyes of mystery and not with those of fact. In order to make the baptismal action count, she must make it violent. In this sense, "The River" anticipates the action and the resolution of *The Violent Bear It Away*.

"The Displaced Person" is at once the finest story in the first collection and the most significant manifestation of hidden celebration. The title refers about equally to Mr. Guizac, a Polish refugee, and to Christ. Mr. Guizac comes to Mrs. McIntyre's farm through the offices of Father Flynn. In contrast to the Pole and his family are the Shortleys, hired hands who feel threatened by the industry of the displaced persons. The farm Negroes, Mrs. McIntyre, and Mr. Shortley must share the guilt for inaction when a tractor rolls over Mr. Guizac and snaps his spine.

If the vision of personal guilt is the final one in this story, it is foreshadowed by abundant alternative visions. The peacock who preens around Mrs. McIntyre's house, the last of his kind, is the occasion for the priest's vision of Christ, for a celebration of eternal glory in barnyard beauty: "The priest let his eyes wander toward the birds. They had reached the middle of the lawn. The cock stopped suddenly and curving his neck backwards, he raised his tail and spread it with a shimmering timbrous noise. Tiers of small pregnant suns floated in a green-gold haze over his head. The priest stood transfixed, his jaw slack. Mrs. McIntyre wondered where she had ever seen such an idiotic old man. 'Christ will come like that!' he said in a loud gay voice and wiped his hand over his mouth and stood there, gaping . . . His attention was fixed on the cock who was taking minute steps backward, his head against the spread tail. 'The Transfiguration! he murmured" (pp. 290–291).

Mrs. Shortley's vision is appropriately narrow. As narrator in the first section, she sees the Guizacs in a black light: "Mrs. Shortley had the sudden intuition that the Gobblehooks, like rats with typhoid fleas, could have carried all those murderous ways over the water with them directly to this place" (p. 264). Later, her visions multiply. "She was seeing the ten million billion of them pushing their way into new places over here and herself, a giant angel with wings as wide as a house, telling the Negroes that they would have to find another place. She turned herself in the direction of the barn, musing on this, her expression lofty and satisfied" (p. 267). As her imagination becomes apocalyptic ("She saw plainly that the meaning of the world was a mystery that had been planned and she was not surprised to suspect that she had a special part in the plan because she was strong"), she begins to prophesy: " 'The children of wicked nations will be butchered,' she said in a loud voice. 'Legs where arms should be, foot to face, ear in the palm of the hand. Who will remain whole? Who will remain whole? Who?' " (p. 277). Mrs. Shortley sees the struggle to survive as a contest between herself and the priest—and we see it as a contest between true celebration and false. On the day that they leave the farm (before Mrs. McIntyre can give them notice), Mrs. Shortley has a final, terrible vision during a massive stroke: "They were frightened by the gray slick road before them and they kept repeating in higher and higher voices, 'Where we goin, Ma? Where we goin?'" while their mother, her huge body rolled back against the seat and her eyes like blue-painted glass, seemed to contemplate for the first time the tremendous frontiers of her true country" (p. 280).

The second half of the story is told from Mrs. McIntyre's point of view. It balances comedy and realism against the visionary perspective in the first part of the story. But as Mrs. McIntyre replaces Mrs. Shortley as "giant wife of the countryside," she endures a vision of her own part in the passion and death of Christ, the original displaced person.[5] Badgered by the now-returned Mr. Shortley, she plans to fire Guizac. Her vision narrows. The transfiguration of her peacock is lost on her. She rationalizes her moral obligation to fire Guizac and turns against Father Flynn.

This rejection of grace ("That man is my salvation") leads literally to paralysis. On the morning that Shortley manages to have the tractor roll over the Displaced Person, Mrs. McIntyre goes out to give him notice with "the cold climbing like a paralysis up her feet and legs." And "she . . . felt her eyes and Mr. Shortley's eyes and the Negro's eyes come together in one look that froze them in collusion forever, and she . . . heard the little noise the Pole made as the tractor wheel broke his backbone" (p. 298).

In their shame, Shortley and Sulk desert her. Thereafter, abandoned and impoverished, Mrs. McIntyre lies bedridden and helpless before the relentless catechizing of Father Flynn. Miss O'Connor implies that the death of Guizac is a bloody oblation for the conversion of the woman. In due time the hidden feast will be made manifest.

The purifying fire of vision is a central motif in the three prophetic novels. They are concerned not so much with the prophet's mission as with his formation. In learning how to see, her prophets learn to celebrate the death of the Lord. Miss O'Connor says of such people: "I'm not interested in sects as sects; I'm concerned with the religious individual, the backwoods prophet. Old Tarwater is the hero of 'The Violent Bear It Away,' and I'm right behind him 100 per cent. . . . He lacks the visible Church, but Christ is the center of his life." [6] The two novels and the novella reveal the shift in her concern from purgatorial vision to mystical vision. But in every instance, visionary celebration is anchored in reality.

Wise Blood is the story of a prophet's education. The novel describes the conversion of a backwoods St. Paul. Haze Moats returns from the army to found the Church Without Christ. His atheism is simply an inverted piety, however; at least no one fails to recognize him for a preacher. Haze develops faith through protest, humiliation, and blindness.

Vision is a central motif in *Wise Blood*. Haze looks out at the world through a fog, yet everyone notices his eyes: "his eyes were what held her attention longest. Their settings were so deep that they seemed, to her, almost like passages leading somewhere and she leaned halfway across the space that separated the two seats, trying to see into them" (p. 10). Perversion of vision is marked by perversion of language. Asa Hawks, blind evangelist, preaches Jesus. But Hawks is neither blind nor religious, as Haze discovers one night while holding a match under his eyes. The one man whose secret he had to discover, the one witness for Christ, is a fraud. At this point Haze begins to make that fraudulent identity a real one in his own life.

Hoover Shoats, alias Onnie Jay Holy, is another religious con man. Haze's "new jesus" strikes him as a good fast-buck idea.

"Listen!" Haze shouted. "It don't cost you any money to know the truth! You can't know it for money!"

"You hear what the Prophet says, friends," Onnie Jay Holy said, "a dollar is not too much to pay. No amount of money is too much to learn the truth!" (p. 85)

Hoover Shoats sweet-talks the people and flaunts his lavender handkerchief (the color frequently signifies sexual perversion in Miss O'Connor's work). His Church of Christ Without Christ parodies Haze's genuine difficulties with belief, even to the point of substituting another prophet dressed exactly like Haze and driving another "rat-colored car." The man's name is Solace Layfield. He gets three dollars a night. Perversion of identity is marked by counterfeit form. When Haze runs over Layfield in his Essex, he is reclaiming an identity stolen from him. But he is also reclaiming a delinquent prophet for the Lord; Haze hears the man confess his sins to Jesus just before his death.

Haze is a catalyst for religious indifference. As comic as the novel is, Christ is at its center. The real subject is freedom, as Flannery O'Connor notes in her foreword to the 1962 paperback edition: Freedom is "a mystery and one which a novel, even a comic novel, can only be asked to deepen." Asa Hawks responds to Haze with flight, his daughter with curses, Enoch Emery by choosing gorillahood, Solace Layfield by choosing Christ. None of them can retain indifference.

The final choice is Haze's. Robert Fitzgerald tells us that Miss O'Connor discovered the Oedipus plays while trying to resolve the book. Thus she has Haze blind himself with quicklime, completing the action that Hawks, the spoiled priest, did not have nerve enough to perform. After his blinding Haze escapes the world into the darkness of the self, where "If there's no bottom in your eyes, they hold more."

His landlady is the narrator of the final chapter; we see the blind Haze through her eyes only. Her conniving for him becomes awe at his spiritual struggle. When the policemen club him to death and bring him back to her, the narration glows with metaphors of vision. Not yet knowing that he is dead, she searches into his ruined eyes for the secret he has hidden there. He recedes with that secret into eternity, until the blind man becomes for her "the pin point of light."

Miss O'Connor's comic irony inverts celebration in *Wise Blood*.

Yet the elements of celebration are present in the ritual blinding. But the communal context of that act is ethereal, like the direction of the novel itself. The sacrifice has the elements, if not the form, of sacrament.

In *The Violent Bear It Away* Miss O'Connor projects the prophet's calling with greater violence, a smaller cast of principals, and greater control. The issue is more than the education of a prophet now; it is his vocation to baptize. The action turns on the baptism of an idiot boy, Bishop Rayber. The prophet, like Haze, is a reluctant dragon. From the outset his vocation afflicts him. Young Tarwater is the victim of God's grace. He goes to Memphis to live with his agnostic uncle "with a certainty sunk in despair, that he was expected to baptize the child he saw and begin the life his great-uncle had prepared him for. He knew he was called to be a prophet and that the ways of his prophecy would not be remarkable" (p. 357).

Miss O'Connor tightens the second novel by polarizing belief and infidelity in the same family. Old Tarwater (Old Testament) had once stolen his nephew Rayber, baptized him, and fired him with zeal for the word of the Lord. But Rayber ran away. Now he is a school teacher. When the old man dies, Young Tarwater comes to his uncle's house to resolve his vocation.

Rayber tries to destroy it, of course. "The boy would go either his way or old Tarwater's and he was determined to save him for the better course." With no particular love for either course, Tarwater tries to escape his dilemma by drowning Bishop. But at the crucial moment the words of baptism escape his lips; Tarwater unwillingly unites Bishop's death with the death of the Lord. The implication is that Bishop will share in the Lord's Resurrection.

The mystery which Flannery O'Connor celebrates in this novel is precisely that: the identity of baptism and death. Drawing on Pauline theology, she shows that the essential violence in every life is the death of the self that accompanies baptism. The antecedent action prepares us to accept this paradox. Rayber was baptized in the woods, Tarwater in the nursery. Both baptisms were covert and hostile actions. In Bishop's case, Rayber anticipates the boy's death by trying himself to drown him one day at the beach. At the last moment his nerve fails and Bishop survives. A second foreshadowing of the essential action occurs later, at a fountain. Bishop is playing happily under the spray when Tarwater is seized with his mission. He hesitates on the rim of the basin just long enough for Rayber to come and snatch the boy away. The final act combines the theological with the dramatic paradox: baptism into death.

Two motifs help to unify the novel and to direct it toward its sacramental resolution. Both of them are visionary. The first one, fire, indicates a burning clean of impure ways of seeing. Tarwater's development consists of various painful illuminations: he sees his role as prophet in the burning of the shack where his great-uncle died; he sees it in the burning lights of Memphis, and he sees it in the burning trees at the end of the novel. Each fire reinforces his vocation, whether he accepts it or not: "The Lord is preparing a prophet with fire in his hand and eye and the prophet is moving toward the city with his warning. The prophet is coming with the Lord's message. 'Go warn the children of God,' saith the Lord, 'of the terrible speed of justice' " (p. 339).

At the end of the novel Tarwater has a revelation of his great-uncle seated on the hillside eating the loaves and fishes and of his own vocation:

> He whirled toward the treeline. There, rising and spreading in the night, a red-gold tree of fire ascended as if it would consume the darkness in one tremendous burst of flame. The boy's breath went out to meet it. He knew that this was the fire that had encircled Daniel, that had raised Elijah from the earth, that had spoken to Moses and would in the instant speak to him. He threw himself to the ground and with his face against the dirt of the grave, he heard the command. GO WARN THE CHILDREN OF GOD OF THE TERRIBLE SPEED OF MERCY. The words were as silent as seeds opening one at a time in his blood. (p. 447)

The sacramental significance of the fire is pentecostal. At the end of the novel Tarwater has been confirmed by the fire of the Spirit and advances on the city to bear witness to God's mercy.

The second motif is that of fish-water-bread. Old Tarwater's eyes are "fish-colored"; at one point in his struggle with Rayber, on the fishing trip, Tarwater's eyes are fish-colored. Fish keep reappearing in the novel, suggesting the ichthus, the early Christian symbol for Christ. The pervasive water imagery throughout the book signifies baptism and man's thirst for it. The bread element, for instance, suggests the corresponding spiritual hunger. Tarwater begins with "the certain, undeniable knowledge that he was not hungry for the bread of life," and proceeds to develop "the heart of his great-uncle's madness, this hunger . . . so that nothing would heal or fill [him] but the bread of life."

Tarwater's struggle for faith reaches a climax in the fishing boat. He defies Rayber and his vocation. But the rejection nauseates him; he vomits into the lake. Afterwards he is always hungry and thirsty. He cannot eat a sandwich offered to him by a truck driver, though he hungers for it. He tries to slake his thirst with drugged bourbon in another car, but he is violently disappointed by the result: the driver (the devil) rapes him in the woods. Earthly food cannot satisfy spiritual thirst and spiritual hunger.

At the end of the novel Tarwater hungers and thirsts for the loaves and the fishes, for the body of Christ: "The boy too leaned forward, aware at last of the object of his hunger, aware that it was the same as the old man's and that nothing on earth would fill him. His hunger was so great that he could have eaten all the loaves and fishes after they were multiplied" (p. 446).

With cleansed vision and an insatiable appetite for God, Tarwater leaves the burning woods behind him to encounter the world anew, confirmed in his sacred mission. Once again Flannery O'Connor suggests that celebration is a part of the visible world, and that the world is rooted in God.

In his introduction to *Everything That Rises Must Converge* Robert Fitzgerald suggests that Flannery O'Connor's dissatisfaction with Rayber led her to a neater working of the same material in "The Lame Shall Enter First." But the novella achieves compression at the cost of the rich symbolic and thematic overtones of the novel. It gives us a better Rayber in Sheppard, but it sacrifices the drama of the Tarwater figure. Sheppard is now the central character, whereas Rayber never occupied the central position in *Violent*.

The novella concerns Sheppard's attempt to adopt and to reform Johnson, an orphaned delinquent with an IQ of 140. Like Tarwater, Johnson was reared by his grandfather in a shack. Like Old Tarwater, he has a profound sense of evil: " 'Satan,' he said. 'He has me in his power.' " The difference is that Johnson is a perverse prophet, giving witness through his own evil. As in *Vio-*

lent, a young child is the middle term in the struggle between an adolescent prophet and an unbelieving father. Norton does not seek baptism, though, as Bishop seems to. He wants to see his dead mother in heaven, beyond the stars. He spends his nights in the attic with a telescope, searching the heavens in vain. Johnson seizes on his need to instruct him in the ways of the Lord, but Norton's conversion is not of primary importance: Sheppard's is.

Johnson approaches Sheppard and Norton in different ways. Norton, the innocent, seeks love: thus Johnson preaches Christ to him. Sheppard clings to naïve assumptions of invincible natural goodness: thus Johnson preaches sin to him. By making Johnson an instrument for very different purposes, Flannery O'Connor throws the essential problem of parental love into a stronger light. Furthermore, Johnson's instrumental role reduces his dramatic possibilities as a person.

In his struggle with Sheppard, Johnson tries to force an admission of personal evil. He begins by burglarizing the neighborhood. When the police bring him back to Sheppard, Sheppard refuses to believe the charges, exhibiting his faith in Johnson to disguise his refusal to accept personal evil. Later, however, Johnson is caught red-handed, and Sheppard is forced to face the truth. Thus Johnson destroys Sheppard's humanistic self-deceptions by insisting on his own evil and on redemption through Christ alone. "Johnson hurled himself forward. 'Listen at him!' he screamed. 'I lie and steal because I'm good at it! My foot don't have a thing to do with it! The lame shall enter first! The halt'll be gathered together. When I get ready to be saved, Jesus'll save me, not that lying stinking atheist, not that. . . ." [7]

This brutal rejection awakens Sheppard. Like Rayber, he has failed to educate the prophet in the ways of the world. The failure shocks him into an awareness of a deeper failure: "He had stuffed his own emptiness with good works like a glutton. He had ignored his own child to feed his vision of himself. He saw the clear-eyed Devil, the sounder of hearts, leering at him from the eyes of Johnson. His image of himself shrivelled until everything was black before him. He sat there paralyzed, aghast" (p. 190).

For the first time Sheppard realizes the enormity of his pride. The devil he derided in Johnson's raving becomes hideously real in himself. He rushes upstairs, filled with repentance and love for his neglected son, only to find him hanging from an attic beam, the telescope at his feet. Norton is at last with his mother. Self-knowledge desolates Sheppard and reduces him to belief—or at least to the numbed condition of personal awareness that precedes belief. His son is destroyed so that he might live.

We can see a shift in emphasis in this third novel from the role of the prophet to the effect of prophecy on human choice. Though the resolution reminds us of that in "The Displaced Person," the tone is less comic, less ironic. Flannery O'Connor has sacrificed some of the richness of her story for the sake of its tragic illumination.

The novella polarizes hope and despair in the dead son and the living father. Sheppard's vision of himself is like Mrs. Shortley's. It anticipates similar epiphanies in Flannery O'Connor's last collection. Norton, like Mrs. May in "Greenleaf" and the little boy in "The River," plunges into the mystery of death in an act of wonder, an act of faith. Never before has Miss O'Connor so juxtaposed the finite and the infinite. Though this story is probably the weakest of her three long works, its conclusion suggests the increasingly mystical illuminations of her last stories.

That mystical quality indicates a shift in the nature of celebration in her work. Hidden celebration becomes a matter of personal illumination. The festive company is more likely to be the communion of saints than fellow Georgians. Here and elsewhere in *Everything That Rises Must Converge*, the principal characters move beyond human community into dim anticipations of the heavenly feast. Yet the will is still free to reject human community and its celestial corollary. Some of these final stories dramatize that rejection and its demonic consequences. In any event, Miss O'Connor continues to celebrate the mystery of human freedom: heaven and hell begin on earth.

Everthing That Rises Must Converge is a collection of stories about the enlargement of vision. The characters share in the rising action of the title, toward a convergence with Christ at the summit of time. Of course, Miss O'Connor protrays degrees of illumination, and uses a variety of genres: tragic, comic, tragicomic, satiric. When the enlargement of personal vision overflows into social consequences, ceremony becomes liturgy.

Though similar to *The Violent Bear It Away*, "The Lame Shall Enter First" emphasizes love instead of violence. Norton joins his dead mother in the stars; Bishop simply endures his drowning. More important, Sheppard feels the searing knowledge of his own evil, while Rayber feels nothing. Love for his son underlines Sheppard's sense of guilt and shocks him back to life.

Miss O'Connor tends to pair the remaining eight stories, often as variations on a similar subject. The first two stories, the title story and "Greenleaf," present death as the illumination of the self. The enlargement of vision is individual, but total. As ironic counterstatements, she includes "A View of the Woods" and "The Comforts of Home," in which death functions as the demonic refusal to believe and to celebrate reality. Here the enlargement of vision reveals the damned self.

Flannery O'Connor broadens the vision from individual to social in another pair of stories. "The Enduring Chill" and "Revelation." Her concern here is life, not death; the vision connects the individual with the communion of saints. The last two stories, "Parkers Back" and "Judgement Day," dramatize belief as martyrdom, in life and in death. All these stories rise toward belief.

"Everything That Rises Must Converge" is in a sense the paradigm of all the rest. The central situation reveals a conflict between mother and child in which the mother expresses condescending, complacent love towards her bright but contemptuous offspring. Flannery O'Connor balances fondness against intellectual pride; generally the son or daughter experiences the illumination that the mother either does not need or cannot undergo.

As the story opens, Julian is riding the bus with his mother. He is a self-conscious liberal who sits next to Negroes; she, a sentimental lady who gives nickles to colored children. As in "Good Country People," the motif of the generations matches the head (the child) against the heart (the mother). The would-be artists in such situations are sitting ducks for Miss O'Connor. Julian wishes to shock his mother out of her fantasies of southern glory, but of course he succeeds only in miring himself further in his own.

The story reveals not one but two illuminations. The first is bogus. A Negro lady gets on the bus wearing the same hat his mother wears—a green and purple job. "His eyes widened. The vision of the two hats, identical, broke upon him with the radiance of a brilliant sunrise. His face was suddenly lit with joy. He could not believe that Fate had thrust upon his mother such a lesson" (p. 17). The bogus illumination is vindictive and triumphant. But his mother rejects the lesson in her affection for the woman's little boy; she wants to give him money.

The real illumination soon follows. The four of them leave the bus, whereupon Julian's mother tries to give the child a penny; the Negro mother flattens her with her pocketbook: "He don't take nobody's pennies," she says. The shock of having her charity spurned completely upsets Julian's mother. She starts out in the wrong direction, going home to Grandpa and Caroline. She does not know her own son.

The illumination is dual, however. The mother dies on the sidewalk, leaving Julian to face the world from which she had always protected him: " 'Help, help!' he shouted, but his voice was thin, scarcely a thread of sound. The lights drifted farther away the faster he ran and his feet moved numbly as if they carried him nowhere. The tide of darkness seemed to sweep him back to her, postponing from moment to moment his entry into the world of guilt and sorrow" (p. 23).

Only at the end of the story is Julian born; his mother's death has been the birth pangs of the self. Even here the fact of death is part of the ritual rebirth; this in turn is framed by a vision which at its furthest reach is Christian hope. "Everything That Rises Must Converge" is not yet celebrative, however. Julian still looks backward towards his mother; he has not yet accepted reality.

"Greenleaf," on the other hand, is a celebration. Mrs. May, a farm widow like Mrs. McIntyre in "The Displaced Person," wishes to assert her power over her hired man, Greenleaf. The issue is a bull among her milk cows. The bull belongs to either O.T. or E.T., Mr. Greenleaf's tenant-farming sons. These sons in turn balance against her own children, loafers and intellectuals. The metaphor for the experience here is sexual. Mrs. May has already emasculated her sons and wants to do likewise for Greenleaf. She will have him shoot the bull.

But the sexual overtones are fruitful rather than violent. Mrs. "May" would rather have had the "Greenleaf" boys than her own. Her will to power is more than Freudian; it is vernal. She grows toward the illumination of life in the rising action of her death.

That death, finally, is a lovely marriage ritual.

At first Mrs. May fears the bull: "That's the awfullest looking bull I ever saw." But later, as she realizes that she can force Greenleaf to shoot him, she brightens: "The exhilaration of carrying her point had sharpened her senses. Birds were screaming everywhere, the grass was almost too bright to look at, the sky was an even piercing blue. 'Spring is here!' she said gaily" (p. 48). She can manipulate the man with the gun. What she really wants, of course, is to be subdued. Miss O'Connor makes sex the metaphor of the encounter with God.

Prior to her death, she has been an unbeliever. She tells Mr. Greenleaf that religion has warped his wife. Even now, at the moment of death, she remains perfectly still, "in frozen unbelief," as the bull charges.

> She stared at the violent black streak bounding toward her as if she had no sense of distance, as if she could not decide at once what his intention was, and the bull had buried his head in her lap, like a wild tormented lover, before her expression changed. One of his horns sank until it pierced her heart and the other curved around her side and held her in an unbreakable grip. She continued to stare straight ahead but the entire scene in front of her had changed— the tree line was a dark wound in a world that was nothing but sky—and she had the look of a person whose sight had been suddenly restored but who finds the light unbearable.
> . . . She did not hear the shots but she felt the quake in the huge body as it sank, pulling her forward on its head, so that she seemed, when Mr. Greenleaf reached her, to be bent over whispering some last discovery in the animal's ear. (pp. 52–53)

Thus Mrs. May's expanding vision is both sexual and spiritual. The violence of her death reveals the dark beauty of the story, the beauty of a rising action that resolves harsh opposites into a converging unity.

"A View of the Woods" also dramatizes violent death in the country, but the ironic context is harshly restrictive. Rather than enlarging vision, this "View" narrows it. Mr. Fortune owns the woods and takes perverse pride in holding them over his son-in-law, Pitts. The woods are his, but the view is Mary's. They can never be reconciled on this count.

The tragedy of the story lies in the corruption of love by pride.

Fortune uses his power over the land to tempt Mary Fortune away from Pitts, who blocks his access to her. The struggle has sexual overtones. Fortune violently objects to Pitts' punishing her; Fortune himself wants that right. Mary loves her grandpa, but she respects her father. Hence, quite rightly, she refuses to accept Fortune's version of the punishment he has seen her take. " 'He nor nobody else has ever touched me,' she said, measuring off each word in a deadly flat tone. 'Nobody's ever put a hand on me and if anybody did, I'd kill him' " (p. 64). Her statement is prophetic.

The woods hide the darkness of his own heart. Toward the end of the story Fortune is caught up "in the midst of an uncomfortable mystery that he had not apprehended before. He saw it, in his hallucination, as if someone were wounded behind the woods and the trees were bathed in blood" (p. 71). The crucifixion of Christ goes on for all time. And yet the woods are himself as well—his legacy to the girl he kills and his deathbed.

When Fortune tries to usurp Pitt's position he brings on the death of love. He turns his mulberry Cadillac down a lovers' lane into the woods. There he will have it out with her. But Mary is the stronger. As they wrestle on the ground she pins him and crows her victory: she is "pure PITTS." The attack has destroyed her love for him.

Furious at being rejected as lover, father, and benefactor, Fortune forgets the rules of the game, overthrows his granddaughter, and smashes her head against a stone. Her eyes glaze, disregarding him. His own heart literally expands and he collapses. Miss O'Connor uses physical enlargement in ironic counterpoint to spiritual vision. His heart bursting, Fortune "felt as if he were being pulled after it through the woods, felt as if he were running as fast as he could with the ugly pines toward the lake" (p. 80). The camera eye supplants him here, pans the lake, and returns for the final shot of the two corpses beside the yellow bulldozer.

The last image is most apt: "The place was deserted except for one huge yellow monster which sat to the side, as stationary as he was, gorging itself on clay." The heart enlarges all right, to the dimensions of the yellow machine. The demonic vision of the ending is the darkest among these stories. Fortune's fate is death without resurrection.

One can scarcely call "A View of the Woods" a celebration;

indeed, the yellow machine symbolizes the impossibility of human enlargement here. Only the trees bear mute witness to the presence of Christ, as they do in most of these stories. Much the same action occurs in "The Comforts of Home." The impersonal and melodramatic discovery is made by an outsider. The only enlargement will be a front-page headline.

"The Comforts of Home" is the weakest story in the collection. Miss O'Connor allows her flair for the macabre to run amok here, destroying her sense of mystery. Thomas is an overprotected intellectual who cuts himself off from the world around him. His dead father is the demonic voice we have heard in *The Violent Bear It Away*; his mother is a complacent do-gooder who wants to renovate Sarah Ham, an alcoholic "nimpermaniac." Once again Miss O'Connor balances protective love against arrogant innocence. And once again, that innocence is homicidal.

When his mother takes Sarah Ham into her home, Thomas thinks he can escape her. But gradually she invades his dining room, his study, and his bedroom. His hatred for her corrupts his love for his mother. Like Julian in the title story, Thomas wishes to destroy his mother's illusions; his efforts succeed only in destroying her life.

Miss O'Connor places the action in a larger context. Pride destroys charity; excessive innocence sunders the communal bond. The climax reveals the anti-celebration appropriate for Thomas's life. He fights with Sarah over the revolver he has planted in her purse. His mother intervenes to protect Sarah and takes the bullet meant for her. Thus Thomas destroys whatever love remained in him.

The discovery, though, is incomplete. Thomas never realizes his own guilt, as do Julian and Sheppard. Farebrother, the legal equivalent of the yellow machine, surprises the trio at this moment and puts the whole action in a sardonic framework:

> The sheriff's brain worked instantly like a calculating machine. He saw the facts as if they were already in print: the fellow all along had intended to kill his mother and pin it on the girl. . . . Over her body, the killer and the slut were about to collapse into each other's arms. The sheriff knew a nasty bit when he saw it. He was accustomed to enter upon scenes that were not as bad as he had hoped to find them, but this one met his expectations. (pp. 141–142)

Farebrother is the only sardonic narrator in the collection. The irony is neat, but too easy. On the other hand, one sees in these two stories the power of Flannery O'Connor's devil.

As if to counteract that force, Flannery O'Connor now shifts from scenes of death and isolation to those of life and the communion of saints. Significantly, the enlarging vision is both sacred and communal in "The Enduring Chill" and "Revelation."

"The Enduring Chill" is comic. Asbury Fox, would-be writer and intellectual, returns to the South from New York. He is convinced that he will die. We see the typical family situation once more: education is a principle of estrangement between mother and child. The comic quality of the story lies in the private rituals of death with which Asbury surrounds himself.

Myth critics, beware! Miss O'Connor parodies the fashionable archetypes of contemporary criticism here. Asbury sees himself in the myth of the unknown god, the myth of the suffering artist, the myth of the dying god ("He looked like one of those dying children who must have Christmas early")—even Mailer's myth of the white Negro: ("Suddenly he thought of that experience of communion that he had had in the dairy with the Negroes"). The point, of course, is that these are phony rituals, false ceremonies, illusions.

Miss O'Connor arrays a whole gallery of rural realists against these illusions. Asbury's mother wants him to write plays in the morning and help with the dairy in the afternoon; his spinster sister wears Girl Scout shoes; the Negroes pocket his communal cigarettes; the subtle Jesuit says he's a good boy at heart but very ignorant; and Block, the country doctor, discovers that his angst is really undulant fever.

In "The Enduring Chill" the South does rise again. This is the biblical, rural, real South, scoring victories against these New Yankees at Agnostic Station, Joyce Junction, and Vedanta Hollow. Beneath this comic riposte at false gods, however, lies a deeper mystery. Despite himself, Asbury is drawn into the real community of the South, the family, and the faith. Miss O'Connor reveals the incorporation in her conclusion:

> The old life in him was exhausted. He awaited the coming of the new. . . . He saw that for the rest of his days, frail, racked, but enduring, he would live in the face of a purifying terror. A feeble

cry, a last impossible protest escaped him. But the Holy Ghost, emblazoned in ice instead of fire, continued, implacable, to descend. (p. 114)

"Revelation" is the purest example of the expanding vision of the communion of saints. Tragicomic now, the story reveals the rebirth of a woman of the Pharisees. Mrs. Turpin sits in a doctor's office, waiting. Around her sit the publicans she and Claud can afford to ignore: white trash, a runny-nosed child, a common couple, and a Wellesley girl with acne. The waiting room symbolizes both the womb and society. Mrs. Turpin must be reborn into both.

The agent of her rebirth is the Wellesley girl. Like Hulga in "Good Country People," she cannot listen to pious bromides. Finally, enraged at Mrs. Turpin's, she hits her over the eye from across the room with her physiology textbook. Before they can subdue her, the girl has given Mrs. Turpin her first revelation: "The girl raised her head. Her gaze locked with Mrs. Turpin's. 'Go back to hell where you came from, you old wart hog,' she whispered" (p. 207).

Completely off-balance, Mrs. Turpin plunges from euphoria to dejection. She cannot sleep; she snaps at Claud. Suspicious of her Negroes now, and shaken in faith, she seeks the answer to her doubts among the pigs. There she challenges God Himself, as she struggles with pigs, field, and crimson sky.

But she cannot see again until her vision has been purified. When she does see, the sight is the communion of saints. In that vision of the swinging bridge to heaven, the lame enter first—the Negroes, the white trash, the battalions of freaks and lunatics. Last of all come the people like herself; "even the virtues are burned away."

The final two paragraphs of "Revelation" enlarge Miss O'Connor's vision and our own into a full celebration, a total and eternal hymn to God. ". . . At length she got down and turned off the faucet and made her slow way on the darkening path to the house. In the woods around her the invisible cricket choruses had struck up, but what she heard were the voices of the souls climbing upward into the starry field and shouting hallelujah" (p. 218).

"Parker's Back," though less dramatic than the other stories, reveals the slow growth of self-awareness. O. E. Parker is a tenant farmer who prides himself on his tattoos. One day he smashes his employer's tractor into a tree and runs to the city, leaving wife and job. Like Young Tarwater, he flies from his vocation only to be caught by it—in this instance, by a picture of "the haloed head of a flat stern Byzantine Christ with all-demanding eyes." He has the picture tattooed on his back (it takes two days) and begins to make his way home.

But he is no longer what he was. His buddies in the pool hall tease him and throw him out. He drives home then, "as if he were himself but a stranger to himself," and tries to get in. Sarah Ruth has locked the door: the old O. E. Parker is dead.

He first becomes aware of his reconstruction when Sarah Ruth forces him to speak his name. It is biblical, Obadiah Elihue. Next he takes off his shirt; she scorns the idolatrous image of Christ. She beats him with a broom and drives him out of doors, where he sits under a pecan tree and weeps like a baby.

Parker is a comic Tarwater; he never realizes his role as prophet. The pool hall casts up its Jonah to the sidewalk; his wife dishonors him in his own country. But as she does in so many of her other stories, Miss O'Connor makes nature itself comment on man's transformation. The sun seems to shine on him from all sides in the field. It pours through his spider web soul when he admits his names. Finally, his own flesh bears witness to Christ. As Sarah Ruth beats him, "large welts [form] on the face of the tattooed Christ."

Thematically, Miss O'Connor has shown the rebirth of a dead soul. As she does in her best stories, she shows the soul burned clean, shocked back into life. The theme is from the Psalms : "By the waters of Babylon I sat down and wept." But from the pun on the title right through to the end, the treatment is controlled, detached comedy. "Parker's Back" reveals Flannery O'Connor at her best.

"Judgement Day" is a weaker variation on this same theme of martyrdom. Technically the most complex of her stories, it makes greater use of the countryside she knew so well. Tanner, an old man who is forced to live with his daughter in New York, wants his body shipped back to Georgia when he dies. New York is "no kind of place." Georgia is closer to heaven.

The story unfolds through a series of flashbacks, showing Tanner's shrewdness in outwitting backcountry Negroes. He assumes that northern Negroes are no different. Several times he encounters a Negro actor on the landing and each time tries to establish a country footing with him. But the Negro is agnostic and short-tempered. Tanner persists in calling him Preacher; infuriated, the actor throws him down the stairs. At this point flashback and fantasy are confused. But Tanner's last statement reveals the truth beneath the confusion: "Hep me up, Preacher, I'm on my way home!"

Tanner comes off nicely, but the Negro does not. One is convinced that Miss O'Connor never knew any northern Negroes. She is not at home in that New York apartment, either; for her as for Tanner, Georgia is closer to heaven.

Flannery O'Connor's Catholic celebration is unique in contemporary literature. Her literal, banal style disguises a sense of participation in the sacred action of the universe: the salvation of man. She remains firmly grounded in the physical scene, the rural, biblical South, but she shows us the mystery on which that scene is built. At times communal, more often personal, the hidden celebration in her work is perhaps the finest testament of her ability to connect fact and mystery.

Although Flannery O'Connor and Eudora Welty are both southern ladies (Miss O'Connor would be amused at the term) whose literary imagination is thoroughly grounded in the rural South, they are not really comparable. Eudora Welty's countryside is rich, historical, and mythical; her lyric style has its closest affinities with poetry; her essential subject is the incommunicable uniqueness of life. Flannery O'Connor's South is all red clay and pinewoods—often aflame in one way or another; she used ugliness, grotesquerie, suffering, and Old Testament violence to point up the need for a salvation greater than ourselves. To this end she was anti-humanist and conservative, fearing the false comforts of liberal compassion and urban civilization. Her closest affinities are not with southern literature at all, but with French literature. One hears in her work the tragic echoes of Pascal, the prophetic thunder of Leon Bloy, and the dying words of Bernanos's country priest—"Does it matter? Grace is everywhere."

6 ⁊ James Agee:
The Elegies of Innocence

LIKE Eudora Welty, James Agee makes extensive use of the rural South in his two novels. And like Flannery O'Connor, he has a strong biblical sense and works within a Catholic framework: nature and grace, sin and redemption are ultimately at stake in his work. Among all these writers, however, he is best seen in juxtaposition with J. D. Salinger. Both men find childhood the repository of ultimate goodness; Manichee-fashion, both tend to equate sexual experience with evil; both are writing fables of identity. A crucial distinction remains, nonetheless: for Salinger, ultimate identity, the supreme realization of the self, lies in Seymour Glass, his alter ego. For Agee, ultimate identity lies in his own boyhood. Put simply, Salinger reaches out into fantasy and hagiography for his hero; Agee reaches back into his past.

Agee began as a poet, developed as a journalist for the Luce organization, and ended as a fine film critic and screenwriter. Yet he felt guilty about his commercial success, and turned to fiction only at the end of his life. The truly extraordinary point about his fiction is the subject matter. He was eminently qualified to write novels about the writer's life, as George Gissing did; or about the sharecropper, as John Steinbeck did; or about Hollywood, as Scott Fitzgerald and Nathaniel West did. That he chose to ignore all his adult experience and to turn back to his childhood amounts to a rejection of his adult experience. The central fact of his childhood was the death of his father when he was six; both novels turn on such an event.

For both personal and temperamental reasons, then, James Agee is an elegist. All his work suggests a time when life was finer, simpler, and more natural. Probably his father's death helped to limit that time in his memory. As we know from his letters to Father Flye, his childhood was deeply affected by that death. For whatever reason, his work attempts to reconstruct his childhood and to make that individual past the only locus of values. By implication it denies the goodness of life in the here-and-now.

This equation of innocence and goodness may also result from Agee's frequent guilt feelings at being a successful journalist. He began as a poet and always considered himself one. *Permit Me Voyage* (1934: now most readily available in *The Collected Poems of James Agee*, edited by Robert Fitzgerald, 1968) takes its title from a line in Hart Crane's "Voyages III," and looks at reality with elegiac compassion. Probably Agee's concept of the artist's life was unduly influenced by the tragic example of Crane; in any event, in his later work Agee deprecated his profession and his professionalism, despite the fact that his scripts and his film criticism are fine achievements.

In reviewing *Letters to Father Flye*, John Updike put the point well:

> If Agee is to be remembered, it should be for his few, uneven, hard-won successes. The author of the best pages of *Let Us Now Praise Famous Men* and *A Death in the Family* owes no apology to posterity. As to "the quarter of a million unsigned words," surely a culture is enhanced, rather than disgraced, when men of talent and passion undertake anonymous and secondary tasks. Excellence in the great things is built upon excellence in the small; Agee's undoing was not his professionalism but his blind, despairing belief in an ideal amateurism.[1]

The comment reveals as much of Updike as it does of Agee: the complete professional versus the ideal amateur. Both men have celebrated styles and a quick poetic imagination, though Updike probably has more sheer talent than any writer of our time; both write in several genres; both are novelists who find their regional origins important to their fiction; both stress the theme of identity as innocence. The difference is simply one of attitude. Agee's innocence is completely separate, prior in every way to present living. Whatever Updike's difficulties in connecting past and present, he insists on the necessity of doing so; professionalism requires it.

A related point, also from Updike's review of the *Letters to Father Flye*: "He simply preferred conversation to composition. The private game of translating life into language, of fitting words to things, did not sufficiently fascinate him. His eloquence naturally disposed itself in spurts of interest and jets of opinion" (p. 206).

Let Us Now Praise Famous Men is largely talk, but talk in the grand manner. It fuses poetry and journalism, praise and diatribe, household inventories and personal meditations. Agee wishes to make it a record of experience, as formless and chaotic as life itself: "It is simply an effort to use words in such a way that they will tell as much as I want to and can make them tell of a thing which happened and which, of course, you have no other way of knowing. It is in some degree worth your knowing what you can of not because you have any interest in me but simply as the small part of it is of human experience in general." [2]

This hybrid book is of vital importance despite Agee's disclaimer. Lionel Trilling calls it our best portrait of the Thirties. But the book has a personal importance to Agee as well. It is his bridge between the nonliterary world where he made his living, the world of photography, journalism, and memoir, and a secret, inner world, where he could write "a sort of amphibious style—prose that would run into poetry when the occasion demanded poetic expression" (*Letters*, p. 48).

The book is a case study of the two months in 1936 that Agee and Walker Evans spent among three Alabama sharecropping families. Evans's photographs comprise Book One. The first section of Book Two is a lengthy preamble in which Agee explains the genesis of the book (it began as an article on tenant farmers for *Fortune* and kept growing) and his first encounter with his subjects. Part One, "A Country Letter," is an impassioned lyric, elegy, and night song. Next is a reprise, "Colon." Agee organizes Part Two by topic: money, shelter, clothing, education, and work. After a brief attack on professional litterateurs, "Intermission," Agee launches into Part Three, a chronicle of his first few days with the sharecroppers. The book closes with two short descriptions, one of Shady Grove, Alabama, the other of sleeping children. In the

Notes and Appendices, Agee gives us a gallery of his heroes: Beethoven, Margaret Bourke-White, Anglo-Saxon words, William Blake, and the nightsong of two unseen birds.

There remains the title. "Let us now praise famous men and our fathers that begat us . . . (Ecclesasticus 44: 1–14). The context of the passage is a catalogue of patriarchs; Enoch, Noah, Abraham, Isaac, and Jacob. On one level the title is ironic, suggesting that these sharecroppers are among those "which have no memorial; who perished, as though they had never been born; and their children after them" (verse 9). But on balance, the book is in praise of famous men, and that praise is liturgical.

Whether Agee's style be invocatory or journalistic, his intention is always the same: a celebration of the poverty, the joy, and the suffering of the human condition. His heightened style, his allusions, and certain organizing elements in the book are biblical. Most of the time the celebration is elegiac, but sometimes Agee celebrates reality with joy: "the memory of the piccolo notes which rise and transfix Beethoven's pastoral storm: the odor of a freshly printed newspaper; the stench of ferns trapped in the hot sunlight of a bay window; the taste of a mountain summer night: the swaying and shuffling beneath the body of a benighted train; the mulled and branny earth beneath the feet in fall; a memory of plainsong or of the first half hour after receiving a childhood absolution. . . ." (pp. 227–228). The catalogue goes on, in the manner of Thomas Wolfe.

In sum, *Let Us Now Praise Famous Men* celebrates fatherhood, family life, courage, and anti-institutional humanism. Although its achievement is extremely uneven, the book contains passages of lyric beauty as good as anything James Agee ever wrote. But that achievement disguises a major deficiency. In order to celebrate these tenant farmers and to share in the sacrifice of their lives, Agee must isolate both himself and them from the mainstream of American life. As is the case in so many contemporary novels, celebration is possible only under seige.

The book masks self deception and self-pity, too. For all his attacks on *Fortune*, journalism generally, and the literatti, Agee is inescapably a commercial writer. *Let Us Now Praise Famous Men* is thus an excursion for him, a polemical pastoral in which he can flay the demon of commercial values in himself and in his world.

But when he tries to lose himself in his subject, as he often does in the book, he is denying the professional competence with which it is written. Agee wants to have it both ways.

The essential difficulty with Agee's fiction is the split between religious faith and literary effort. He felt that he had outlived belief, at least the institutional belief on his childhood. But he could not eradicate the religious sense from his vision of life; it is simply the basis of it. As he says in a letter to Father Flye in 1950:

> At times or moments I feel virtually sure that nothing short of coming back into a formal religion (probably the one I was brought up in) will be nearly enough for me: at others, just as sure I never will. But at all times I feel sure that my own shapeless, personal religious sense, whatever that may be, is deepening and increasing; even the swings away are less far away from it: keep some kind of relation with it. (*Letters,* p. 184)

Agee's elegies of innocence then result from pious memories of his childhood. Amateurism, faith, and innocence are a composite past for him, one that later experience could not sustain. Probably his drinking, his incessant fears of death, and his constant self-accusation are the result of a need to punish himself for forsaking church and poetry. We do not know; David McDowell's forthcoming biography should help us to find out.

We do know that the two novels, and to a lesser extent the film scripts, present celebration as a courageous secular act. Agee attempts to convert his religious impulses into purely secular form, and to make that form a substitute for ecclesiastical form. In each novel the death of a father, clearly autobiographical, represents a deeper death for Agee—the death of God. Yet his feelings and his talent refuse to accept that death as a permanent reality. The visible world must present a substitute. Like Joyce, whom he much admired, Agee uses the novel as the assertion of identity and a weapon against the inhuman counter-identity offered by institutional religion.

Much of the lyricism in the two novels attempts to extract the religious core of secular experience. *The Morning Watch* (1951) is quite clearly split between the school chapel and the world outside. Agee uses liturgical patterns to assert the religious supremacy of that world. He attempts to reconcile belief and experience in a secular resurrection from sin to life. Agee wrote of *The Morning Watch*: "Not a good winter and spring, for me. I got a lot done last fall. Spent most of the winter and spring on a *Life* piece, turned it in not long ago, worked a week and finished a first draft, anyhow, of the story about Maundy Thursday" (*Letters*, p. 181).

Agee's title comes from the penitential Psalm 130, expressing David's trust in the mercy of God. On the allegorical level, the Watch is the Garden of Gethsemane, in which Richard, the twelve-year-old protagonist, is Peter. The literal level recounts his arising at 3:45 on Good Friday morning for an hour's adoration in the school chapel, followed by a trip to the mountain pond for a dawn swim with two other boys.

The Morning Watch is a scenic novel; most of the action takes place in Richard's mind. Public events check his private attempts to make the world conform to his convictions. He never succeeds, but the attempt sharpens his self-awareness and leads to his physical and spiritual rebirth at the end of the novel.

The novel begins in the school chapel as Richard tries to evoke pious feelings while meditating before the crucifix. Naturally enough, his efforts are distracted by the boys around him and by his own fantasies of crucifixion and self-deification. Slowly the minutes pass. Richard's meditation becomes a struggle with himself in which he relies more and more on the formulas of hymns, remembered prayers, and pious phrases. What afflicts him most of all as his hour ends is a feeling of defeat, a sense of alienation from the penitential spirit of Maundy Thursday.

He leaves the chapel in the third chapter to join his friends Hobe and Jimmy outside. Here his courage is put to the test: going out into the dawn and into the natural world, Richard leaves behind him night, the chapel, and the rules of the school. The conflict is between man and the church, or more precisely, between Richard's personal religious sense and ecclesiastical forms. Symbolically, the three boys echo the action of the Apostles on Gethsemane when Christ is captured.

Hobe and Jimmy discuss their tardiness as the cock crows. At first Richard wants to go back to the dormitory, but he remains silent because he is afraid to speak. As the cock crows a second time, Richard suggests that they get their tennis rackets. A third time the cock crows, and he leads them to the Sand Cut, an off limits gravel pit.

The triple denial is Peter's; Agee underscores the saint's weakness here, not his strength. At least Richard is no Pharisee, and acts with a clear knowledge of his own sin. He feels remorse immediately; he sees himself in the hog that they pass on the way. But a counterforce is at work; against his sense of personal guilt the listening, joyful spring asserts itself. The spring catches the boy up with the shell of a locust: ". . . at the far side of the clearing Richard stopped short and the others passed him; for here, abject against sharp bark, he found a locust shell, transparent silver breathed with gold, the whole back split, the hard claws, its only remaining strength, so clenched into the bark that it was only with great care and gentleness that he was able to detach the shell without destroying it" (p. 129).

The locust shell is a figure of the Resurrection, the shell of a reality that lives reborn. Agee uses the locust to chide Richard's pride in believing himself to be the sole cause of his salvation or damnation. In the liturgical allegory, the locust shell stands for the central Christian paradox, the crucified Redeemer. Symbolically the locust shell dominates what we might call the Good Friday section of the novel, replacing the gold monstrance of Maundy Thursday.

Stylistically the sense of exuberance over the physical scene echoes the film scripts—specifically the river journeys in *The African Queen* and *The Night of the Hunter*. In both, the journey motif has suggested a spiritual awakening, a journey into the self. Living in the physical world demands a courageous response. Richard makes it with a feeling of joy.

His plunge into the gravel pit is a complex action. At its simplest, the plunge demonstrates his physical courage: he stays under water the longest. Furthermore the plunge demonstrates his union with the physical world, a world in which Richard must live. Given manhood by nature, he exercises it by going all the way to the bottom. At its deepest level, then, his dive recalls the spiritual conflict in the chapel between his desire for martyrdom and his remorse at having that desire. He emerges, lungs bursting, his enchanted body singing "*Here I am.*"

But as this new Adam rises from the pool, Agee reminds us once

again of the struggle between good and evil. Hobe and Jimmy
see a snake, an undulant ambiguity of the Risen Christ, their own
discovered sex, and the serpent in Eden. (For Agee, any experience contains the elements of good and evil.) Constrained by their
fallen natures, Jimmy and Hobe pounce on the snake and torture
it. And Richard, once again hesitant, takes the lead. He lunges past
them at their victim, rock in hand, and beats the skull to splinters.
His motives are mixed: simultaneously he desires their applause, is
ashamed of that desire, and wishes to put the snake out of its suffering.

The snake represents most clearly original sin, which man assumes all over again as he asserts his manhood, since all experience
is inevitably tainted with corruption. Significantly, Richard does
not wash the slime from his hands, but only dips them into the
pool. Man is not baptized into angelism, but into the weakness and
the glory of the flesh.

As Hobe and Jimmy fling the battered body of the snake to the
hogs, Richard is again crushed with remorse. His cruelty makes
Christ's passion real for him for the first time, and he asks, in the
words of the penitential psalm, *"Forgive! Forgive! O God forgive!"* As if to emphasize his guilt, he picks the locust shell off the
tree and carries it back to school. Here at the end of the story,
Richard's reliving of the Passion hints at the Resurrection. The
priests will not understand, of course. But Richard has assimilated
his experience. He has integrated his personal resurrection from
the pool with Christ's: "When the boys turned from the sty he
followed them towards the Main Building carrying, step by step
with less difficulty, the diminishing weight in his soul and body,
his right hand hanging with a feeling of subtle enlargement at his
thigh, his left hand sustaining, in exquisite protectiveness, the bodi-
less shell which rested against his heart" (p. 156).

The Morning Watch, Agee's "Maundy Thursday novel," develops both elements of the liturgical feast: the love of Christ for
his disciples in giving them his own body (the locust, the snake),
and the suffering in Gethsemane at the prospect of his own Passion. But the novel is more than a pious exercise in Christian allegory. It retains the integrity of felt human experience, principally
in its lyric realism, its attempt to render the physical world afresh.
Nature here is more than it was: it is the instrument of God's com-

munication with man, an answer to David's psalm. The Watch itself is a waiting for personal resurrection, a personal experience that must be undergone alone.

Opposed to this personal religious experience is formal religion. The priests of *The Morning Watch*, like those in *Noa Noa* and *The Night of the Hunter*, are menacing. Richard's is a Christianity without Christendom, a church in diaspora. The harsh formalism of chapel worship gives way to the freedom and beauty of outdoor life. Like Huckleberry Finn, Richard will break the law and *go* to hell, but he will do so on his own terms.

If *The Morning Watch* shows the growth of a personal religious sense in one boy, *A Death in the Family* (1957) shows it in one family. The restoration of the family to itself is the real subject of Agee's posthumous novel. Just as Richard had to rebuild himself in a knowledge of his own weakness and God's love, so Mary, Rufus, and Catherine must rebuild their family through an acceptance of suffering. The father dies, but the family continues, each member in a search for courage.

Agee was reluctant to talk about his novel. He alludes to it only once in his letters to Father Flye: "I think I'd better not talk much about the piece of writing. A novel, short but longer than I had foreseen or thought best for it, about my first 6 years, ending the day of my father's burial. I read you the little I had done of it. On the whole, I feel hopeful about it, and I certainly need to feel hopeful. Underlying the hopefulness is utter lack of confidence, apathy, panic and despair. And I'd better not dwell on that just now, either, for I could much too easily slip into it" (*Letters*, pp. 170–171).

The plot consists of an action and two reactions. In Part One Jay Follett, father of Rufus and Catherine (as a boy Agee was called Rufus), drives to the supposed deathbed of his own father. On the way home he runs off the road and is killed. The fatherhood search is the dominant motif of the rest of the novel.

In Part Two, his wife Mary must come to terms with death by rejecting, among other things, the bitter cynicism of her own father. Part Two is the story of her growth in courage. Part Three belongs to the children: Rufus and Catherine must discover courage and maturity in their grief for the dead Jay. Their problem unifies the novel. In each part, the protagonist must overcome his isolation to find himself in family obligations. That act of finding becomes a religious experience; as a corporate action it celebrates the reality of the family.

Part One is Jay's story. Like the other parts, it shows a test of faith. Called to his father's bedside in the middle of the night, Jay finds that his alcoholic brother Ralph has exaggerated their father's illness. While at home, Jay must redefine his obligations as father and as son. After berating the weak-kneed Ralph, he starts back to Mary and the children. Enroute in the early dawn, he falls asleep at the wheel and slides off the road and down an embankment. In his death he succeeds, however. His life has been spent in generous love, and his death is a challenge to Mary, Rufus, and Catherine to respond with love for each other.

Although Part One is largely Jay's story, one incident in the life of Rufus is significant there. In chapter seven, before he knows of his father's death, he goes out with his Aunt Hannah to buy a cap. The cap he wants is much too large, "a thunderous fleecy check in jade green, canary yellow, black and white, which stuck out inches to either side above his ears and had a great scoop of visor beneath which his face was all but lost" (p. 65). He cannot *wear* a man's cap, but he much prefers it to the boys' caps before him. Hannah honors his choice; the cap is a badge of manhood, a foreshadowing of Rufus's role in Part Three.

Part Two returns us to the adult world and Mary's attempts to cope with death, "the prevailing word." Through a series of evasions she tries to deny it. Her family offers her comfort in the attempt, but she cannot, finally, accept either comfort or her family.

At the end of chapter eight, Mary's sister Hannah is tempted to deny God, until she sees Mary at the family prayer. "And as they continued, and Hannah heard more and more clearly than her own the young, warm, earnest, faithful, heartsick voice, her moment of terrifying unbelief became a remembrance, a temptation successfully resisted through God's grace" (p. 105).

Brother Andrew's reaction, however, is angry blasphemy. Having brought them the news of Jay's death (like Richard's father, Jay dies with a small bruise on the point of his chin), Andrew blurts out, "He wasn't a *Christian*, you know. . . . He didn't have to make his peace with God. He was a man, with a wife and two children, and I'd say that sparing him *that* horrible knowledge was the one thing we can thank God for" (p. 116).

Mary's father poses a greater difficulty. His cynicism, a "blind animal sympathy," strains her faith. He had never accepted her choice of Catholicism, anyway; her piety is too soft a response to man's monstrous existence—rage is more appropriate. Agee isolates Mary from her father, the further to test her faith. It survives, not so much Catholic as personal.

Mary responds to death with the words of Psalm 130. A voice speaks the words within her; she joins it, making the words of David her own: "Out of the deep have I called unto Thee, O Lord: Lord hear my voice. . . ." With this act of faith, Part Two ends.

Mary's faith has survived its test. Her test, like Jay's, is familial. Both make the same choice—to return to the living. Agee balances her family's denial of faith against her own love for her children. Mary's acceptance of faith reinforces that love. And only when she has fully experienced the loss of Jay can faith become meaningful. Like Richard, she comes from pious abstractions to a personal commitment—through the medium of the same psalm.

In Part Three the focus shifts to Rufus. He is the principal narrator of the action. Rufus sees his father's death as an opportunity for self-dramatization; he rushes into the street to seek sympathy from strangers. Like Richard, his first tendency in a spiritual crisis is to attitudinize. But the stranger he meets rebukes him for seeking public sympathy at his father's death and sends him back indoors, where he finds the family waiting for the priest.

Now the climax: united by understanding and by shared grief, the family asserts itself against the Church. First Father Jackson tries to intimidate them. Then he usurps Jay by sitting in his chair. Once again the fatherhood motif enters the story, in multiple ways. The family unites behind the dead father. The new father strikes a false note; he is no more representative of the Heavenly Father than he is of the earthly one.

Agee's distrust of formal religion, apparent earlier in the film scripts for *Noa Noa, The Night of the Hunter*, and in *The Morning Watch,* is founded on a deeply personal, private sense of God. Those who presume to represent Him and to interpret Him for others only insult him. In all probability the struggle reflects Agee's own problems with the Episcopal church of his childhood.

In any event, the difference between personal and formal religion is that between Walter Starr and Father Jackson. The layman, with his knowledge of Jay the man, is the natural priest. He tells the children: "He wanted a good life, and good understanding, for himself, for everybody. There never was a braver man than your father, or a man that was kinder, or more generous. They don't make them. All I wanted to tell you is, your father was one of the finest men that ever lived" (pp. 227–228).

In the final chapter, Andrew becomes the spokesman for Jay, insofar as he protects Rufus from the full impact of his father's death. Andrew is a father figure, but he is also Andrew. He can offer substitute fatherhood, but not faith; bitterness, but not love. The problem is, finally, religious and personal.

On his walk with Andrew, Rufus makes his first mature choice. Like his mother, Rufus refuses to accept Andrew's bitterness. Father Jackson may be "a priggish, mealy-mouthed son of a bitch," but Rufus will not think so. For Rufus, life expands in love and affirmation; it does not contract into vindictiveness. Like his mother, he rejects the temptation of rejection. Instead, he begins the slow, quiet process of picking up the pieces. "He wished he could ask his uncle, 'Why do you hate Mama?' but he was afraid to. While he thought he looked now across the devastated Fort, and again into his uncle's face, and wished that he could ask. But he did not ask, and his uncle did not speak except to say, after a few minutes, 'It's time to go home,' and all the way home they walked in silence" (pp. 254–255).

In the two novels we see the essential quality of Agee's art. The novels are lyric—like the camera he understood so well, they focus on static scenes to portray universal reactions to human sorrow: guilt, courage, awakening, love. Such scenes work well. But the saddest thing about them, and about Agee's fiction in general, is his inability to believe in the present reality of his celebrations. They are of a certain time and place, protected, nurtured, and embalmed by memory. Agee's ideal world is a lost world, out of touch with present living. Even stylistically, none of Agee's abundant personal charm and vitality enters these books. In large measure, Agee's penchant for innocence is a death wish.

But his lyric style, his technique of isolating characters from their environment so that they can unfold, and the slow development of a moral courage that is finally religious—these are the achievements for which he will be remembered. He sees ordinary life in religious, noninstitutional terms. The novels and the hybrid documentary are the record of talent grappling with faith. Like Jacob, Agee wrestles with an angel, in order to know his name.

7 &ᵃ J. D. Salinger: A Solitary Liturgy

So MUCH has been written about Salinger in the last fifteen years that one scarcely knows where to begin—with the books themselves or with their latest critic. George Steiner called this phenomenon the Salinger Industry, an operation rolling along on its own momentum, under no man's control. We have to begin with the books and not the critics, however. Salinger has one brilliant novel, several fine stories, and a problem: Seymour Glass. Unlike Agee, who restricts his point of view to childhood innocence and sensibilities, Salinger expands the age of innocence and reinforces it with wisdom, winsomeness, and karma. And this combination is the problem: the more Salinger develops the legend of Seymour, the more incredible that legend becomes. Seymour is a dead end, but Salinger cannot accept that fact.

Let us begin with the fateful day in March, 1948, when Seymour shot himself in a Miami Beach hotel room. Seymour's suicide in "A Perfect Day for Bananafish" is the irrevocable central action around which all the Glass stories revolve. It is the ultimate negation of living in the present. Salinger tries to compensate for that act by showing Seymour on progressively higher levels and earlier ages. His spiritual power radiates to his brothers and sisters. It was and is their ultimate spiritual resource. Seymour's suffering and death are meant to be sacrificial and redemptive for those who love him—in short, they are liturgical acts. But the liturgy is vitiated by a gradual stagnation of action, by a lapse from liturgical into purely contemplative form. Seymour, like Humpty-Dumpty, cannot be put back together again.

The central conflict in Salinger's world then is that between the sensitive self and reality. The attempt to reshape the conflict in liturgical terms involves a rejection of real conditions for a more elevated state of human existence. But one of the principal truths about liturgy is its fundamental grounding in reality. As the eminent liturgist Louis Bouyer puts it: "First of all, let us repeat again: the world of the sacraments, the world into which the liturgy introduces us, is not a world in its own right, standing aloof from the world of ordinary living. It is rather the meetingpoint of the world of the resurrection with this very world of ours in which we must live, suffer and die. And this very fact implies that liturgical life, far from taking us out of real life, far from making us indifferent to or uninterested in real life, on the contrary positively sends us back into it in order to carry out fully in it the Mystery which has come to us through the sacraments." [1]

Liturgy, then, must recognize and assert the realities of life: time, death, pain, and evil. Sacramental action works in and through human realities. The problem with Salinger's liturgy is that he extrapolates the sacramental action out of time altogether; he appears to mitigate the disintegration of the self by lifting Seymour out of the human situation, thereby divinizing him. Through some fiat of the author the distinction between finite and infinite vanishes; Seymour's suicide becomes meritorious action, bootstrap salvation. This, I venture, is unacceptable on liturgical, humanistic, or artistic grounds.

Yet Salinger's liturgy is not suddenly thrust upon us midway in the Glass cycle. We can see it developing in Holden Caulfield, assuming various forms in the *Nine Stories*, and finally asserting itself in *Franny and Zooey*.

The Catcher in the Rye vests its liturgical action in Holden, the natural priest. The sacrifice that makes the liturgy meaningful is that of his position at Pencey Prep. Holden's expulsion is a scapegoat ritual and a purging of the temple of learning. When he leaves Pencey, Holden takes the sins of the community on his shoulders; his expulsion is all-inclusive and charismatic.

To his history teacher Mr. Spencer, for instance, he offers identity and forgiveness, consoling the man for having to fail him. Mr. Spencer badly needs his identity restored. Ackley, the pimply, awkward outcast, is an earlier version of Seymour's Fat Lady. Holden restores Ackley by listening to him and by asking him about his religion. Even Stradlater, whom Holden suspects of seducing Jane Gallagher, gets Holden to write his English theme for him. In each relationship Holden makes himself vulnerable: the priest immolates himself for his congregation. Holden attempts to sanctify Mr. Spencer by confessing his sins, to sanctify Ackley by listening to him, and to sanctify Stradlater by wrestling with him.

The liturgical action continues as Holden plays out his sacrificial role on the train with Mrs. Morrow, mother of an insensitive classmate. He protects her from that knowledge with elaborate lies about the boy. Later he dances with three girls from Seattle who are looking for movie stars in a second-rate cocktail lounge; Holden pays the bill. Still later he protects a prostitute named Sunny (a sly allusion to Salinger's own nickname) by paying but refusing to take her. In each relationship Holden is indeed a catcher in the rye, extending his life for others and protecting them: Mrs. Morrow from the knowledge that her son is a rat, the girls' illusions about glamorous New York, Sunny from meretricious sex.

As befits his sacerdotal role, Holden is a virgin. When Maurice intimidates Holden after Sunny's visit, he must suffer humiliation as a penance for Sunny and for his own sexual desires. His relations with girls always balance desire against pity—he feels sorry for them. Desire always succumbs to pity, his manhood to his priesthood. Thus Holden victimizes himself, sharing in the suffering that he endures for others.

Two extensive incidents in the novel reveal his ministry, and both culminate in a significant illumination. The first is Holden's relationship with Sally Hayes. Sally is a phony, but a good-looking phony. When Holden takes her to see the Lunts in a Sunday matinee, he sees the whole experience in a context of falsity. Broadway, the movies, the Lunts, and Sally Hayes are the unredeemed world for which he sacrifices his innocence.

After the play Sally suggests that they go ice-skating at Radio City. She wants to see herself on the ice in a skating skirt. Like all phonies, Sally is a narcissist. She lives before the mirror; Holden is a window man. Sally's style cannot carry her on the ice, however; they are the worst skaters on the rink. When they sit down for a drink, Holden tries to shake her out of her illusions; the drinks become a metaphor for real communion between them. First he indulges her (and himself) with a fantasy of escape to New England.

But Sally insists on keeping in line—first college, then marriage. She will not indulge his fancy, so Holden tries to shatter the mirror by denouncing the banalities of marriage. Sally is frightened: she cannot accept his honesty. Finally, in despair at reaching her, Holden tells the truth: she gives him a royal pain in the ass. The illumination is harsh; the liturgy fails to renew Sally.

In counterpoint to his failed ministry with Sally is his success with Phoebe. Hints of the dual relationship appear throughout the Sally Hayes section, chapters 16 and 17. While waiting for Sally, Holden walks toward Broadway to get a scarce record for Phoebe, "Little Shirley Beans." Among the massy mobs on Broadway he sees a poor family with a little boy about six. The boy is walking along in the gutter, singing and humming "Coming Through the Rye." Innocence counterpoints sham.

Another time, as he is buying the theatre tickets, he thinks of Olivier's *Hamlet* and of the one genuine note in the movie, Laertes' horseplay with Ophelia before leaving for France. Genuine love is nonsexual, fraternal.

A fourth counterpointed incident is the little girl at the museum. Unlike the Broadway theatre, the museum is innocent and genuine. Unlike Sally Hayes, the little girl whose skate he tightens is a good skater (we presume). Holden's memories of museums and roller skates move him to reject Sally for Phoebe, his sister.

In contrast to Sally, Phoebe is genuine. She and Holden exchange meaningful experiences: her role in the Christmas pageant, his expulsion from Pencey, his future. To Phoebe Holden propounds the central, redemptive myth of the book, the catcher in the rye. When he leaves she insists that he take her $8.65, which was to have gone for Christmas presents. The money is a sacrifice analagous to his own.

Their relationship is interrupted by the return of the Caulfields from a party. Holden escapes into the night to the Antolinis', where he is or is not accosted toward morning by the English teacher. The point here, I suppose, is not Antolini's sexual interest in Holden, but his dubious position as a sympathetic member of the established order. In fictional terms his position in the novel comes too close to Holden's own; theirs is an identical ministry. In effect Salinger creates him and cancels him out.

But there is thematic significance to the head-stroking incident as well. Throughout the novel Holden never sleeps in his own bed. At Pencey Prep he chooses to sleep in Ackley's room rather than in his own, with Stradlater. When he goes to the hotel in New York on Saturday night and to the Antolinis' on Sunday night he demonstrates his alienation from the establishment. Holden remains the outcast, while Antolini does not, as his marriage plainly indicates. If Antolini has confused or ambivalent sexual drives, he only shares the mortality of his fellow humans, becoming one more burden for Holden to carry.

The Antolini episode only interrupts the Holden-Phoebe relationship. Phoebe too wishes to opt out, and comes to meet Holden on Monday afternoon dragging her suitcase behind her. For once Holden is not the only scapegoat. Phoebe is real; instead of commuting her guilt to him (she has none, of course) she attempts to join him—and we are prepared for the major epiphany of the novel, Phoebe on the carrousel.

The ride integrates Holden into the community, reversing the estrangement he had felt at Radio City with Sally Hayes. The atmosphere for this act is genuinely festive: children riding a carrousel in a zoo during the Christmas holidays. The atmosphere of Radio City, on the other hand, is entirely unfestive; the simple ritual of ice-skating becomes a contest of egos and illusions.

Holden's first reaction to Phoebe's riding the carrousel is akin to his earlier realization that you couldn't wipe out all the "Fuck You's" scrawled on the walls of the world if you had a million years. Now he realizes that children must fall from innocence in their own way, and that one can never be a catcher in the rye. The gold ring represents the chances one must take in life.

But the gold ring is also a symbol of community. It immediately enlarges into a ring of people, driven by a sudden shower under the shelter of the carrousel. Holden, as observer and celebrant, stays seated on his bench. But his sudden happiness is a response to a genuine celebration. The cohesiveness of all the parents and mothers around the turning carrousel is a beautiful action, an epiphany of love in a musical dance. This wordless group is Holden's final congregation, restoring him at last to faith in the victory of the good, however much surrounded by "Fuck You's."

On the final page of the novel, Holden is still underground, like Ellison's Invisible Man. But he is no longer in flight. He looks forward to his return from California. He accepts his experience and admits that he misses Stradlater, Ackley, Maurice, and the rest. The admission indicates, as Richard Wilbur puts it, that love calls him to the things of this world.

The Catcher in the Rye is a beautiful lyric novel. Holden's experience, from innocence through alienation to accommodation, ends in a meditation. Somehow he realizes that he is the center of a world that is nourished by his memories. Pity and nostalgia are strong emotions. They filter Holden's awareness of the world, distancing otherwise unacceptable experience. The celebration at the carrousel charges his experience with liturgical significance, offering Holden a community that he can affirm and accept. The sacrifice of his innocence has brought him round once again to society.

Yet a few objections remain. First, a minor one: the events of Saturday night in the novel seem to exceed the time available for them. Holden goes to bed at Pencey, gets up and leaves, catches a train from eastern Pennsylvania to New York, checks into a hotel, drinks and dances with the girls from Seattle, goes to the Village for another drink and walks forty-one blocks back, meets Sunny, quarrels with Maurice and Sunny—and then goes to bed!

More substantial objections arise regarding the resolution of the novel. Granted Holden's restoration to society, how substantial is it? Holden is no longer a child; he can neither ride nor contemplate carrousels at length. Furthermore, his scapegoat role is itself a passive action, forced upon him by circumstances. He is a priest in spite of himself. Again, as outsider and as victim, he never gets very far outside or very hurt. Like the little boy who runs away from home, he always stops at the corner.

Finally, the sacrificial action is sentimental. The cheerful, innocent, colloquial style completely contains evil and suffering, so that Holden and Salinger have it both ways—a comfortable alienation from school and society, and a return in time to take the College Boards. Freedom and reality are at stake in Salinger's work, but even in *Catcher* he hedges his bet. Despite these objections, the novel is a fine and moving work.

The *Nine Stories* confront experience more openly and withdraw from it more painfully. The first of them, "A Perfect Day for Bananafish," introduces us to the Glasses with the story of

Seymour's suicide at Miami Beach in the spring of 1948. His death is a liturgical action from which the rest of the Glass family will draw sanctification.

Section one of "Bananafish" describes the context of the suicide. Muriel is talking long-distance to her mother in New York. The subject is Seymour. We sense the hostility and snobbery of the two women as an indication of the unseen man's desperate situation. His alienation is much greater than Holden's, as we discover in the second section.

There Seymour is lying on the beach, talking to Sybil. They go into the water for a swim, and Seymour tells her the story of the bananafish who swam into a hole and ate so much that he could not get out. As a means of giving the narrative and the relationship heightened importance, Salinger isolates them from the first and third sections of the story, which take place in the hostile environment of the hotel. In section two, life is free, sunny, and childlike. The bananafish myth is an explanation of himself, of the artist's sacrifice. The only congregation for the act is three-year-old Sybil. The suicide has meaning, then, only for her (though she does not witness it) and for all the spiritual Sybils who follow her.

The emphasis is on seeing (Seymour, Sybil), even while the action is sacrificial. The test is to see the subsequent suicide as a fruitful sacrifice, and to believe in its efficacy. Yet what form can such a belief take? The answer is in the ceremonies of family living, specifically of Glass family living. For the Glasses are the spiritual heirs of Seymour. Salinger's dramatic problem is to find liturgical actions which appropriately reenact Seymour's sacrifice, and to find them within the family circle. His difficulty is having to redraw Seymour in the later stories to fit the demands of his theme. The Seymour of "Bananafish" and that of the later stories are two different persons. This one is vague, weak, humorless, and utterly lacking in the charism that oozes from Seymour's every pore in the later stories.

"Uncle Wiggily in Connecticut" develops the family liturgy by indirection. Seymour's salvific function is transferred to his dead brother Walt. Marriage in suburban Connecticut is a hell without love. This truth develops "in vino" as Eloise and her college roommate, Mary Jane, drink themselves under one bleak winter afternoon. Love is possible only in a state of innocence—in Eloise's case, only with the dead Walt Glass. She works out her unhappiness in endless martinis and aggressive behavior toward her husband and child.

Uncle Wiggily is the symbolic extension of Walt and ultimately of Seymour. As the limping rabbit who solves riddles, Walt reenacts his brother's role with Sybil. But as dead lover, he reenacts Seymour's courtship of Miriam. Eloise tells Mary Jane about it; but Mary Jane is too drunk, too callous, and too indifferent to listen. Eloise cannot accept a world without Walt. His death in the explosion of a souvenir Japanese stove is simply meaningless.

The finest of these nine stories by virtue of its sheer emotional power and its relentless development of a heart starved for love but damned by its inability to extend it, "Uncle Wiggily" is a demonic feast. The martinis that Eloise and Mary Jane consume anesthetize but do not liberate them. Similarly, conversation degenerates into monologue. Mary Jane is hopeless, the maid is sullen, Ramona is unreachable, Lew is insensitive. Eloise is imprisoned in herself, in memories of an identity she has long since surrendered. She cannot accept life in the present—love, especially, is only a memory. Through Walt Glass Salinger polarizes heaven and hell in Glass and non-Glass. Ironically the split between liturgy and community, between sanctity and reality, begins here with Salinger's finest story.

"Just Before the War with the Eskimos" is a slighter work, suggesting the world of Holden Caulfied rather than that of suburban Connecticut. Though their language is interchangeable, the principal difference between Eric Graff and Holden is Salinger's irony. Eric has no epiphany and does not understand his role as priest. But Ginnie Mannox, the fifteen-year-old narrator, does. Disappointed in love with Ginnie's older sister, bleeding from a cut finger, and about to go out with a homosexual, Eric is an appropriate victim. Ginnie's half-conscious sympathy moves Eric to a liturgical gesture: he offers her half a chicken sandwich. She accepts it, finally, giving him some slim significance as celebrant. Though the chicken sandwich is unavailing for himself, it moves Ginnie to a reconciliation with Selena. They will not bicker over cab fare and tennis balls now.

The pain in "The Laughing Man" is dual—a child's terror at the death of a hero, and the hero's anguish at the loss of love. The story of the Laughing Man is a fantasy impromptu on a character in Victor Hugo as told by John Gedsudski, law student, to the Comanche Club, one of whose nine-year-old members tells the story to us. The three frames generate meaning as they spark against each other. The chief liturgical action, however, is suffering without redemption: The Comanche Club is a congregation whose gospel is defeat. When Mary Hudson breaks off with John Gedsudski, life loses its meaning. Reality destroys love, represented by the Laughing Man, but it also sunders the communal bond between priest and congregation. Thus the child's terror. Life is too stark to be contained by the celebrations of childhood.

Such is the point also of "Down at the Dinghy." True, childhood terror is averted by the presence of an understanding adult, Seymour's sister Boo Boo. But the reality of anti-Semitism can not be hidden from her son Lionel. The maid has called his father a kike; he escapes to the dinghy at the end of the dock. Boo Boo reassures him by defusing the bomb. But there is more communion between the two maids in the kitchen than there is between mother and son. Protection from reality and not celebration of it is the point of the story.

"For Esmé—With Love and Squalor" is Salinger's most famous short story. It contains numerous liturgical elements: Sergeant X and Esmé meet in church; they eat together in the tearoom; the gift of the watch with the shattered crystal restores X after his breakdown, as does Charles' HELLO HELLO HELLO. But the restoration is only a small part of Sergeant X's total experience of squalor. Significantly, Salinger's narrator cannot allow the story to end without commentary. Although the sergeant comes out of his trauma in his letter to Esmé, the burden of the evidence indicates that the liturgical communion between X and Esmé is too fragmentary to shore against his ruin.

A further problem with the story is its repetition of the pity-nostalgia syndrome. Pity is the only emotion and nostalgia the only context for a rapprochement with reality. Life in the present is at best tolerable for Sergeant X. Though the story begins in 1950 with Esmé's wedding announcement, the clue to X's problem is his condescending description of his wife. At the same time he romanticizes his communion with Esmé. X is no more able to cope than Seymour: all goodness is innocent, all maturity evil. And, curiously enough, the anagram of the title "For Esme with Love and Squalor," is somber: "Few Last." In any event, the renewal of Sergeant X is special, remote, romantic, and fleeting. "For Esmé" demonstrates no evidence of a livable present.

"Pretty Mouth and Green My Eyes" is a better story than "For Esmé." The anguish is not filtered through nostalgic cheesecloth. Lee and Arthur are real; the need for communication is desperate. Though Lee is a false priest, he is for Arthur a Thou and not an It. The telephone takes on the sacramental significance that it carries in the Glass stories to follow. Salinger matches cruelty against need in the story and succeeds. A sign of its enduring value, I think, is the substitution of an ambivalent sympathy for the characteristic pity. Arthur's suffering damns Lee much more completely than it does Arthur, despite his lie at the end and his futile attempt to preserve appearances.

"De Daumier-Smith's Blue Period" is a transitional story in the Salinger canon. It marks the point at which Salinger begins to discard the language and conventions of realism for the mysticism of his later work. Probably his funniest story, it tells of an adolescent painter's elaborately unsuccessful attempt to escape reality. The liturgical element is his joyful return to the real through the painting of Sister Irma, who teaches cooking and drawing. The celebration is both religious and artistic; Sister Irma's best painting is of Christ's burial. De Daumier-Smith cannot abide the work of his other correspondence students at *Les Amis Des Vieux Maitres,* however. But Sister Irma's restorative innocence is enough to sustain him and to move him to write her a long, impassioned letter.

Salinger balances communion against confusion in the story. Only the boy is interested in the students; the inscrutable Japanese couple who run the school are not. Only Sister Irma can feel; the other students cannot. The resolution balances falsity against genuiness. The experience clears his mind of pretense and gives him a sense of his own identity. It involves a woman in the show window of an orthopedic appliance shop.

The trusses and dummies in the window are hideous; but when the woman slips and falls flat, humanity illuminates the scene. The fall reminds Smith of Sister Irma. He feels a mystical bond with both women; he alone has witnessed their humanity in an inhuman context. He confirms the mystical union with a diary entry that night; with a grand, adolescent gesture, he renounces his claims on Sister Irma. Everyone is a nun, he says. Such indeed, is the refrain in the Glass stories which move toward mystical moments and sublime liturgies.

"Teddy" marks the next stage in the decay of sacrificial action. Though the boy is murdered by his sister, nothing really happens in the story. If "Pretty Mouth" is a real advance in Salinger's grappling with pain and evil, "Teddy" suggests a radical evasion of those realities. Teddy himself clearly foreshadows Seymour—or Seymour the second. The story is a failure, and one with pernicious consequences for Salinger's art. It posits a nondiscriminating acceptance of pain, including Teddy's death; it suggests a dim resurrection effected by foreknowledge of that death. To know the moment of death is to deny one's mortality. Indeed, Teddy is immortal, enjoying one of his many incarnations enroute to final illumination. "Teddy" simply doesn't come off.

On the whole the *Nine Stories* are a fine achievement. They confirm Salinger's ability to wring great significance from very slight material. They manifest his ear for the cadences of colloquial speech. The dialogue of his adolescents and young adults celebrates the irresisible vitality of youth and innocence. But the tragic confrontation of reality in "Bananafish," "Uncle Wiggily," and "Pretty Mouth," the best of these stories, leads to a faltering confrontation in "For Esmé" and "The Laughing Man" and to outright denial in "Teddy." From this point on, Salinger's characters do not so much redeem the time as they refuse to admit its existence. The world becomes other than our own, an illusion and an escape, "a world in its own right, standing aloof from the world of ordinary living," as Bouyer puts it.

With "Franny" Salinger separates the liturgical life from its realistic context. There are two worlds in the story—the outer, collegiate world of Franny and Lane, professors and football weekends, and the private, inner world of the Jesus prayer. "Franny" begins with those meticulous stage directions for which Salinger is famous, but it steadily descends into Franny's soul. One might almost call the plot platonic, for the photographic realism of the luncheon with Lane Coutell only shadows a higher reality. That reality is Franny's preoccupation with a Russian pilgrim and his search for God. The surface story echoes this pilgrim's progress in the restaurant, but sacred and profane love counterpoint the two levels of action throughout the story.

The heart of the pilgrim's story is an agape. In his search for God the pilgrim wanders onto a family who invite him in for dinner. Husband, wife, family, and servants all eat together in a Christian love-feast. Franny's preoccupation with the meal indicates her desire to love on such ideal terms with the world, and to have Lane do so as well.

But Lane's egotistical and brutal assault on his lunch parodies that agape, just as his lust for Franny parodies sacred love. Franny sees herself as an apostle, offering him a higher way, *The Way of a Pilgrim*.[3] Her liturgical action, her version of the pilgrim's command to pray always, is the Jesus prayer: "Lord Jesus Christ, have mercy on me." When both pilgrim and prayer fail to move Lane, she faints.

The story parallels "Bananafish" with a sexual reversal of roles. Lane here plays the oafish and insensitive Muriel to Franny's Seymour. Instead of Sybil, she has her pilgrim for an audience. In each case the listener is isolated from the oppressive real world. Once again the Glass figure offers himself for his fellows and once again they reject him. In such fashion Salinger gets distance from the surface realism of his story. Franny's subsequent retreat to the Manhattan apartment of the family is analogous to Seymour's permanent withdrawal from society. In the "real" world, Lane not only rejects the spiritual element of love; he even profanes the temple by offering himself as a carnal substitute.

The Glass liturgy is not a dead end, however. It is simply inoperative in the unredeemed present. When the scene shifts to the inner world of the Glass family circle, the liturgy becomes restorative and redemptive. But Salinger pays a high price for Franny's redemption: the rejection of the real world.

"Zooey" develops that rejection at length. True, the rejection is partly a necessary withdrawal for Franny's recuperation. Yet a more radical dissent is involved. Franny's Jesus prayer, which functions as a kind of antiphon in her story, rejects human sin and weakness.

In conversation with his mother, Zooey says that although the Jesus prayer in its complete form acknowledges personal sin, neith-

er Pilgrim book emphasizes guilt. Zooey clings to a perverse innocence here. Glass sanctity demands a rejection of personal guilt, a
rejection ordinarily expressed in truculent honesty. Sanctity is individual and exclusive, a denial of personal guilt and of the social
bond on which liturgy is based.

Even the epiphanies in "Zooey" are isolationist. At one point
Zooey is standing at the window, staring down five floors at an
eight-year-old girl hiding from her dachshund. When the little dog
finds her and rejoices, Zooey is moved to respond with the always
sacred profanity of Salinger's characters: egoism prohibits a poetic
response to the world.

Yet Zooey only observes the little girl and the dog; he cannot
share their joy. The physical distance between his apartment window and the scene below is too great for communion between it
and him. The festive act occurs outside the family, unlike Hold-
en's celebration at the carrousel. The liturgical pattern set up by
Seymour's suicide imprisons as it sanctifies. Perhaps the greatest
cruelty under these circumstances is the illusion of freedom which
Franny and Zooey derive from the myth of the Fat Lady.

Paradoxically, the myth absolves the Glasses from social responsibilities even as it seems to call for them. The Glasses have only
to be their beautiful selves on the radio program and a charismatic
relationship with the audience of Fat Ladies will follow. For all
of the Glasses the Fat Lady is "out there," conspicuously remote.
Seymour loves her precisely because she is remote and does not
exist in any prudential way for him. This is to say that the Glasses
think of themselves not as people but as works of art.

At the end of the story Salinger has Zooey tell Franny to love
the cup of consecrated chicken soup, to love Lane Coutell, to love
her audience in summer stock. But Salinger is contradicting the
implications of Glass spirituality; he is asserting a social bond that
does not exist. The irony is that Zooey's telling Franny to love is
itself a mere performance, a purely rhetorical resolution of problems that none of the Glasses, not even Seymour, can live with.
Salinger makes love a matter of aesthetic feeling for one's own
beauty.

The apparatus of the telling is a kind of liturgy. The old unlisted
phone number, the handkerchief over the mouthpiece, the imitation of Buddy (and the consequent evocation of Seymour him-

self) all suggest a ritualistic activity that expresses and deepens a shared belief in Seymour's spiritual power. Interestingly enough, Franny rejects the false minister (only Buddy can be the ordained intermediary between Seymour and his siblings), but she accepts the relevance of the message.

In liturgical terms "Zooey" is a dialogue, first between Zooey and Bessie, then between Zooey and Franny. Common household objects (the cup of consecrated chicken soup) assume sacramental significance. But this liturgy is truncated. It ends with the liturgy of the word; once the gospel message of the Fat Lady has been proclaimed, the sacramental action ceases. "Zooey" is a liturgy without sacrifice, a Mass that ends at the Creed. No action follows from hearing the word. Indeed, no action *can* follow. Only "world-hating saints" achieve satori. Zooey's apartment window separates him not only from the girl and her dachshund, but from the Fat Lady as well.

As for Franny, the message of the Fat Lady is only an affirmation. To put it in dramatic terms, she retreats from an engaged position with Lane Coutell into disengaged myth. Liturgical action slows to a halt. Indeed, as the cycle develops, withdrawal and inaction become ideals.

The whole of "Raise High the Roofbeam, Carpenters" reveals Seymour's refusal to act. Like "Franny," "Carpenters" counterpoints public and private liturgies. Buddy serves as the link between the two. In the public marriage ritual he substitutes for his brother as victim. By eloping, Seymour undercuts the empty public gesture; Buddy must suffer the consequences with the in-laws. But it is through Buddy also that we enact the private ritual on the toilet seat.

The core of that ritual is introduced by Boo Boo's soaped message (the title of the story) on the bathroom mirror. The text is a marriage hymn or entrance rite, built on a Sappho lyric. Next follows a scripture reading from the book of Seymour, written in exile at Fort Monmouth during the early months of the war. All the tensions of misunderstanding so obvious in the first part of "Bananafish" are here revealed in the diary entries.

The diary records Seymour's response to things rather than to people. He loves all things with an undiscriminating love. The reading concludes in an outburst of love. Seymour suspects people of trying to make him happy.

"Carpenters" resolves in comic anticlimax. After the guests have left, Buddy explains Charlotte's nine stitches to the deaf-mute great-uncle. The grinning, agreeable little man is beyond the reach of the secular society to which he nominally belongs—so naturally he is an appropriate audience for Buddy's story. He has the proper spirit of celebration. The noncommunication between the Glass world and the outside world does not matter for the moment.

Here as in *Franny and Zooey* Seymour is the absent good. Though not yet mythologized, he is abstracted. The note of happiness that runs through his diary entries is a curiously static one, however. Seymour *offers* his all-inclusive love to mothers-in-law, psychiatrists, and fiancées who cannot understand Rilke, but we do not see that love in operation. Indeed, the elopement is the only act that Seymour performs in "Carpenters."

Seymour's failure to act otherwise makes his avowed happiness highly questionable. For the elopement is only a reaction. Essentially it denies the social context of love and marriage. "Carpenters," like "Franny," ends in disengagement from the real world.

The greatest failing of "Carpenters," however, is the awkward attempt to reconstruct the Seymour of "Bananafish" into a joyful lover. Anticipating the difficulties of marriage to Muriel, Seymour marries her anyway. He offers himself to her as a private sacrifice. Yet his rejection of her and of the world six years later contradicts the sacrificial action. The suicide in "Bananafish" repudiates the marriage in "Carpenters." In "Bananafish" we see the lover as Indian-giver.

"Seymour: An Introduction" (1959) completes the transformation of its subject from person to myth. Once again Buddy mediates between the reader and Seymour. The technical virtuosity with which Salinger distances Seymour is a tour de force in point of view, but technique alone is insufficient to bring the story off. Perhaps Salinger's uneasiness about presenting Seymour as a real saint causes him to push the dead man steadily backward in time and distance. The emphasis now falls on the child's spiritual maturity.

This emphasis establishes Seymour as a guide to spiritual elevation. As narrator, Buddy can place the action firmly, even cozily, in the family context. Seymour thus has an almost private meaning, as evidenced by Buddy's calling the piece he is writing "a prose home movie." Anecdotal, discursive, enthusiastic, and reverent, "Seymour" is out-and-out hagiography. For Salinger, Seymour must mean, not be—thus the progressive dissolution of Seymour as a man. As a wise child and a teacher of children Seymour tends to be little more than an allegorical Wise Innocence. His sanctity is directly proportionate to his unreality. Seymour stands outside being, an Omega Point toward which all rising action converges— or so Salinger would have us believe.

The sacrificial action of the Glass cycle, already sluggish, here ceases entirely. "Seymour" is simply a prolonged contemplation. The man has been arrested in flight: indeed, he is almost always standing still. His immobility indicates the story's failure as a story, whatever value we may give it as spiritual reading.

In liturgical terms the action of "Seymour" becomes silent meditation. Buddy has passed from family priest offering sacrifice to a monk kneeling quietly in his choir stall. But even as spiritual reading "Seymour" is unconvincing. Though Salinger's narrator calls the piece "a prose home movie" and deprecates the short story form, he cannot thereby resolve his formal problems. He wants us to take Seymour's sanctity for granted, which we cannot do. And he wants us to accept his charismatic function as an act of genuine liturgical value. But if Bouyer's definition of the liturgical life is correct, Seymour is neither fictional hero nor effective sacrifice.

Salinger's difficulties with Seymour become even greater in the most recent Glass story, "Hapworth 16, 1924" (1965). For one thing, he gives up the task of narration and presents a long letter from Seymour to Bessie and Les without further comment. For another, the work is clearly didactic. Salinger is talking over the heads of his presumptive audience to the reader, in a way calculated to intimidate him. Even James E. Miller must demur on "Hapworth," though he is generally laudatory in his pamphlet on Salinger: " 'Hapworth 16, 1924,' ends with a long list of books that Seymour requests be sent to him at summer camp. The list ranges from the complete works of Dickens and Tolstoi to *The Goyatri Prayer* and Porter Smith's *Chinese Materia Medica*. Few men could get through this interminable reading in a lifetime, let alone in a summer." [4] In "Hapworth" Seymour comes perilously close to being the mystic as prig.

The letter tells us of Seymour and Buddy, ages seven and five, who are spending a summer at Camp Simon Hapworth, Hapworth Lake, Hapworth, Maine. Buddy's four-paragraph headnote tells us that he has just received the long-buried letter from Bessie on May 26, 1965, and will pass it along verbatim.

In liturgical terms, "Hapworth" is an epistle and a homily. For the first time, Seymour reveals directly what he thinks of God, life, adults, and his future. The letter shows how the Glasses ought to respond to a world which Seymour will erect for them. Again the element of sacrifice, so essential to corporate worship or liturgy, is entirely missing.

Structurally "Hapworth" consists of three parts. The first part (pp. 32–77) demonstrates Seymour's and Buddy's victories over the stupid adults who nominally direct them at the camp. Part two (pp. 77–88) is a list of admonitions to the Glasses back in New York. Part three (pp. 88–113) is the book list.

Salinger's tactic in "Hapworth" is to transcend the limitations of reality by refusing to accept them as real. Time, death, pain, and evil simply have no place in Seymour's world. Like Teddy, Seymour predicts his future with cheery equanamity. He writes while lying in bed with the clock stopped "at yesterday or the day before." We learn that he can enter and leave time voluntarily. Death itself is only the cessation of the body, leaving the soul free to reincarnate itself at will. After fulfilling their obligations in the present, Seymour and Buddy will die cheerfully, something which they have not always done in the past.

Although Seymour cannot see a way to eliminate painful experiences, he is quite capable of suppressing any suffering in himself. When he is wounded in the thigh by an axle, he simply suspends communication between his nervous system and his leg.

The problem of pain is closely related to the problem of evil. And this perhaps is the most significant denial in Salinger's happy world: the denial of evil. People may be comical, stupid, or insensitive, but no one is evil. Seymour attacks the problem indirectly by describing and dismissing his sexual urges. Mrs. Happy arouses his precocious sex impulses. He hopes to see her standing in the raw after swimming some day. Yet he says immediately that he does not relish the charming distractions of lust; his life is too short for them. Passions are transient but sweet. In any event, lust is not evil.

Merely by recognizing sensuality, Seymour deprives it of its power. By a further extension of amused sympathy to the older campers, Seymour and Buddy can dispassionately accept their widespread homosexuality. To see evil from an innocent perspective is to contain it, to deny its existence. Thus even the sodomites at Camp Hapworth are absolved by Seymour's charismatic understanding.

The list of books in part three is a substitute world, complete with its book-villains, for the real world. Having rejected human society with its multiple ills, Seymour projects a wholly illusory world of fictive creatures, almost as if, and here I am being quite tentative, almost as if Salinger were recreating his own childhood. He posits an ideal childhood with an ideal family. He superimposes a wisdom gained from a wide and mature reading in literature and religion on his seven-year-old hero, and suffuses the whole with condescending charm and warm-hearted wisdom.

"Hapworth" even lacks the Fat Lady, Salinger's acknowledgement of human ills. There is no Fat Lady in Seymour's world. Indeed, there never was—only an avowed love for man in the abstract, a love much like Gulliver's lover of rationality. The love of abstractions (innocence, childhood, honesty, loving itself) carries with it a corresponding rejection of particular people (Lane Coutell, the woman in the elevator at Miami Beach, Mr. Happy). In the Glass world, Salinger has rejected the pain, vices, and absurdities of ordinary human life for the Land of the Houyhnhnms (neé Glass). Seymour returns to us from his spiritual voyages a jovial Gulliver, i.e., a monster.

To recapitulate, let us review Seymour's development. In the first Glass story, "Bananafish," Salinger begins with the central fact of the Glass family, Seymour's redemptive suicide. In "Uncle Wiggily in Connecticut," Salinger dramatizes the consequences of a world without love. In *Franny and Zooey* Seymour becomes the guru who will help his brother and sister transcend the world. In "Raise High the Roofbeam, Carpenters," Seymour gives himself to Muriel, a gift he will take back in "Bananafish." In "Seymour" and "Hapworth" he ceases to be real altogether.

In order to dramatize the religious significance of Seymour's life and death, Salinger has used liturgical parallels. But his liturgy is a Glass liturgy, private and solitary—a contradiction in terms. The Glasses respond by a progressive withdrawal from reality; thus liturgical action degenerates into mere exhortation. A liturgy without sacrifice, a liturgy without the fruit of social commitment, is a self-destructive liturgy.

Though *The Catcher in the Rye* is a fine and unique achievement, as are the best three or four stories, Salinger seems unable to resolve the spirit and the flesh. His celebration is a mendacious affirmation, proclaimed by etherealizing the human. Salinger recognizes our need for feasts, but his religious myths are narcissistic, denying the goodness of reality upon which all great art and all liturgical worship are based.

Lest we take the whole thing too solemnly, however, we should remember Salinger's reputation as a leg-puller. Perhaps the Glasses, the Fat Lady, and Seymour himself are only elaborations on an elaborate private joke. Perhaps Salinger is wrapping one of those Japanese stoves that will one day explode in our faces.

If Agee cannot face the implications of living in the present, Salinger refuses to allow that present to exist. One might distinguish passive and active dissent from reality here. Both men overvalue youth and innocence—both use ritualized forms to protect a private reality. But at least Agee plays fair; *A Death in the Family*, especially, is a moving elegy for a real loss. Salinger on the other hand plays us false. Although *The Catcher in the Rye* is a fine novel, the Glass stories are increasingly slack, tedious, and mendacious affirmations of an illusory reality. Ultimately his liturgy denies life and love by denying the earth on which they occur. Frost puts the matter well at the end of "Birches":

> ... Earth's the right place for love:
> I don't know where it's likely to go better.

On Salinger's planet, love doesn't go at all.

8 ⮑ James Baldwin:
The Search for Celebration

> It is the responsibility of free men to trust and to
> celebrate what is constant—birth, struggle, and death
> are constant, and so is love though we may not think
> so—and to apprehend the nature of change, to be
> able and willing to change. I speak of change not on
> the surface but in the depths—changes in the sense of
> renewal.[1]

JAMES BALDWIN and Ralph Ellison present an interesting study in
constrasts. Doubtless the best of our Negro writers, they demonstrate that "the Negro writer" is a myth. They differ in almost
every significant respect: Baldwin is anguished, solemn, sublimely
idealistic, and a little prissy. Ellison is Rabelaisian, funny, tough-
minded, and awkward. Clearly Baldwin is a Paleface and Ellison is
a Redskin, to use Philip Rahv's distinction. (Le Roi Jones, who
qualifies as a real revolutionary, does not qualify as a serious writer.) But the most telling difference between Baldwin and Ellison is
their attitude toward celebration. Festivity, present in Baldwin's
early work, declines into hopelessness as his fiction develops,
whereas Ellison, using a variety of tricks, styles, and modes, embraces the world with jokes and riotous laughter.

Baldwin's sense of isolation is magnified by the split between
the wish and the reality in his work—and this is the difference,
roughly, between his essays and his fiction. In the essays Baldwin
asserts his hopes for an ideal American society, transcending guilt,

race, and violence. Like Whitman before him, he asserts a celebration of the American experience. But Baldwin's fiction projects an increasingly violent and incoherent world, incapable of celebration. Baldwin's search cannot resolve his personal hopes with his artistic vision. The failure to do so results in the destruction of the self.

To begin with, Baldwin's celebrations are nostalgic, individual, static recollections of a life no longer available to him. Only the innocent can celebrate that reality; experience drives one relentlessly away from the community into the hermitage of the self. The only way out is empathy and endless pity. But the pity turns to self-pity. Perhaps, indeed, all Baldwin's rhetorical efforts only evade responsibility, as Marcus Klein maintains.

Apart from the first novel, *Go Tell It on the Mountain*, and a few moments of mystical union expressed in his essays, no real celebration exists for Baldwin. His thinly-disguised selves—for though many, the heroes and the stories are one hero, one story—never celebrate as members of a community, but only as isolated individuals. The speaker in his fine story "Sonny's Blues," for example, looks at his brother's celebration from the distance of middle-class Negro respectability. And Rufus Scott, a later version of Sonny, cannot live the celebration he finds at his drums in *Another Country*. The failure of celebration results in the obliteration of the self: Rufus leaps to his death from the George Washington Bridge.

Yet Baldwin insists upon the need "to trust and to celebrate what is constant." If any phrase summarizes his theme, it is this one. "To trust" is the personal response to one's real situation; "to celebrate" is the social response of like-minded persons. Baldwin learned it years ago in the songs and shouts of his church. Like Agee, he left the church, but it never left him. He hopes for a secular celebration to replace the one he left behind.

In *The Fire Next Time* Baldwin projects this vision of American life, a life in which blacks and whites must "like lovers, insist on, or create, the consciousness of others. . . ." He places primacy on the spirit of celebration, trusting that adequate forms will follow. This of course is the mystic's prerogative, and the Christian's. If the spirit is strong enough, the politicians will find the way.

But for all Baldwin's eloquence and moral power, his vision reveals the search more than the solution. Man must celebrate reality, and ultimately the God of creation, but need and fact are not one. The wish awaits fulfillment for Baldwin; the celebration awaits its guests. And the imperative is not only moral and spiritual, but vital: "God gave Noah the rainbow sign, No more water, the fire next time."

This gap between the wish and the reality summarizes Baldwin's inability to develop further celebrations after *Go Tell It on the Mountain.* Celebration requires corporate existence; but since personal identity is such a pervasive concern for Baldwin, he has no room left for a corporate identity. His fiction reveals an increasingly desperate attempt to recapture the spirit of growing identity within a corporate structure, the spirit of celebration. The problem is the widening chasm between the dynamic experience of living in the world and the static, innocent idyll of corporate life as Baldwin knew it when young.

Baldwin's hero typically begins as a young boy in a tension-ridden family. He develops in religion, but his development is checked by his sexual awakening. The awareness of sex is an automatic loss of innocence, the prerequisite for incorporation and celebration. Concomitant with the loss of innocence is the awareness of isolation, which in turn produces guilt for the inability to love. (As Klein points out, love is a ceremony of innocence.) The lack of love spurs the hero to establish social connections once again, but he must do so through sex, jazz, or violence. (Rufus Scott, the quintessential Baldwin hero, tries all three.) For various reasons, each attempt fails, and the hero has only two responses: to reject society as evil and to insist upon the integrity of his own wish to love.

Yet his essays are increasingly mystical in their affirmation of a transcendent social mission. Growth, love, and the need for involvement echo through his three collections, *Notes of a Native Son, Nobody Knows My Name,* and *The Fire Next Time.*[2] Such social concerns are exhortations to renew American life. Here we see a dramatic difference from what we might expect. A classification by theme reveals that only nine of these twenty-six essays express Baldwin's alienation; six deal with the search for a usable past, four with the Negro as American, four more with the need for love, and three with the search for identity.[3]

While some essays embody two or more themes, only two of the six essays on American life (apart from those dealing with Harlem) profess Baldwin's alienation. Surprising—but not so surprising if we see the essays as rhetorical attepts to establish social connections, connections which the fiction cannot sustain. Consider the conclusion to "Nobody Knows My Name":

> Human freedom is a complex, difficult—and private—thing. If we can liken life, for a moment, to a furnace, then freedom is the fire which burns away illusion. Any honest examination of the national life proves how far we are from the standard of human freedom with which we began. The recovery of this standard demands of everyone who loves this country a hard look at himself, for the greatest achievements must begin somewhere, and they always begin with the person. If we are not capable of this examination, we may yet become one of the most distinguished and monumental failures in the history of nations. (p. 116)

Now this passage very narrowly escapes pulpit oratory in its oracular tone and formal style. Yet the rhetorical tactics are immediately clear if we see the essays and the fiction as disjunctive halves of Baldwin's self, as the wish and the reality. The essays envision a community based on love, freedom, and an achieved individual and social identity. Yet in the light of his fiction, one is tempted to call such passages holy fantasy.

A clearer sign of this disjunction is evident in the treatment of autobiographical material in "Down at the Cross" and *Go Tell It on the Mountain.*

As we compare the late essay with the early novel, we see two quite different narrators. Baldwin the spokesman sounds like an unfrocked preacher. The voice, inflections, and diction are churchy. Here Baldwin is the priest in spite of himself. On the other hand, the stance is not entirely voluntary; he has been pushed into a public pulpit by the politics of the 1960s.

But when Baldwin the young novelist is dealing with the same experience, the rejection of formal religion, the tone is nostalgic. Furthermore, it is free, unself-conscious, and decidedly unspokesmanlike. Here is the passage from "Down at the Cross":

> It is not too much to say that whoever wishes to become a truly moral human being (and let us not ask whether or not this is pos-

sible; I think we must *believe* that it is possible) must first divorce himself from all the prohibitions, crimes, and hypocrisies of the Christian Church. If the concept of God has any validity or any use, it can only be to make us larger, freer, and more loving. If God cannot do this, then it is time we got rid of him. (*The Fire Next Time*, p. 67)

The rejection of the Church places all the burden on the individual. For Baldwin, the true Christian lives in diaspora, unable to relate to the hypocritical, loveless fraud of organized religion. Yet the rejection of the Church involves a rejection of the deepest joys in his own experience. Here is the passage from the novel: "There is no music like that music, no drama like the drama of the saints rejoicing, the sinners moaning, the tambourines racing, and all those voices coming together and crying holy unto the Lord" (*Go Tell It on the Mountain*, p. 49).

Here indeed was a full-throated celebration, total, visceral, ecstatic. Even in his relentless insistence on individual love, Baldwin could not reject its religious corollary, community worship. Indeed, the rest of Baldwin's work reveals the search for a secular equivalent of that religious celebration.

Once we see the spiritual context of Baldwin's desire for celebration, our major difficulties regarding his intention disappear. The measure of his achievement in the three novels is directly dependent on the spiritual energy of his characters. Among the three fictive societies, none is more close-knit or more drenched in religious passion than *Go Tell It on the Mountain*.

The novel describes a fourteen-year-old boy's coming of age. The tremendous forces that mark this rite of passage carry him out of a childhood inheritance of lust, violence, and death, into freedom and identity. Three deaths go into his making, including that of his own father. He is born in a context of rape and bloodshed. But when John Grimes emerges from the Temple of the Fire Baptized early one Sunday morning, he does so in the perilous grasp of love.

We may distinguish two contexts for John's resurrection, the spiritual and the familial. The connection between them is his foster-father, Gabriel. As sinner, deacon, tyrannical father, and husband, Gabriel molds the plastic stuff of John's life into a shape distinct from his own. The struggle for identity is dual—the father's need for a son balances against the son's need to free himself.

Baldwin divides the novel into three parts. The opening part reveals John's emotional entanglements with a mother who loves but cannot help him, a father who rejects him, and a brother who sneers at him. He goes to the temple and wrestles with Elisha, a seventeen-year-old preacher in the church and a benign alternative to the wrathful Gabriel.

The long second section gives us three points of view: Florence's, Gabriel's, and Elizabeth's. These are "the prayers of the saints," and each reveals a portion of John's identity. "Florence's Prayer" casts Gabriel in a cruel light as a youthful rakehell and a betrayer of his first wife Deborah, whose frigidity results from her rape at sixteen by a band of white men. Now sixty, Florence hears the call of death. Bitter at Gabriel, she can only question a heaven big enough for them both.

"Gabriel's Prayer" reveals the tremendous pull of lust and guilt that drives the man first to Deborah, then to Esther, and finally to Elizabeth. Like another preacher, Arthur Dimmesdale, he cannot acknowledge his child. Only after Royal's death in a Chicago bar does he confess to Deborah his child by Esther. The two women, Esther and Deborah, project the irreconcilable elements of his nature, passion and piety. If he is to retain his pride, he must reject his share in their deaths and in that of his son.

"Elizabeth's Prayer" describes John's proud, lost father—the victim of race hatred and social indifference. Humiliated by a false arrest on a burglary charge and unable to endure the memory of his degradation, Richard slits his wrists and leaves Elizabeth to bear John. Clearly, John is another Royal, Gabriel's second chance to admit his lust and sin. But Gabriel rejects the chance again, fastening all his hopes on the legitimate son. Roy is the bad seed, however, and is destined to follow Royal to a violent death. These two half-brothers, John and Roy, reveal the ambiguity of paternity and of grace.

A short third section brings us to the present, where John must thresh out his own identity amidst the prayers of the saints. Here is Baldwin's most remarkable feat in the novel, the union of familial context and religious context. His Temple of the Fire Baptized is a viable community, bound together by blood and sin, prayer and baptism. The religious context envelops the familial, offering John an opportunity to escape the family and enter the church. The two contexts, secular and sacred, merge in the communion of saints.

John's own experience prepares him for conversion. His sins recapitulate that family guilt which he is powerless to reject. By his masturbation he shares in that guilt; by their prayers they share in his conversion. John's rebirth, indeed, is won by the suffering of the saints. For Baldwin, suffering is the only prayer.

Songs and hymns echo that suffering throughout. The title relates the joy of the free Christian at his task, climbing the steep mountain. Elisha reminds John of this at the end of the book. Florence sings of the need for grace. Gabriel's song is one of desperate confidence in the Lord, while Elizabeth sings of acceptance:

"The consecrated cross I'll bear
Till death shall set me free
And then go home, a crown to wear,
For there's a crown for me." (Go Tell It on the Mountain, p. 132)

In his essay "The Harlem Ghetto" Baldwin describes the Negro hymns as a ritual triumph over social oppression. Harlem Christians identify almost wholly with the Jews in Egypt. Yet something sinister clings to their celebration; the triumph is a fantasy revenge on the new Egyptian, the white man. The novel is different, however. Indeed, a curious quality of Baldwin is his refusal to accept violence or hatred; he dissociates himself from these reactions by writing about violent, hateful conditions. Through writing, Baldwin exorcises his own devils.

Essentially, *Go Tell It on the Mountain* is a community celebration. John accepts the conversion that Baldwin himself rejected. Principally because this experience is rooted in his own past, Baldwin convinces us of its reality. His problem in the later fiction is to find a social context that will give form and meaning to celebration. In *Giovanni's Room* this becomes impossible; the social context narrows to the point of strangulation. It widens again in *Another Country,* but the fissure between the self and society destroys the ability of the characters to relate to each other. By the same token, the chief artistic value of *Go Tell It on the Mountain* is the simultaneous development and social absorption of the self. The novel shows the passage from family to religion to identity as an integrated, communal action performed in love.

Baldwin posed special problems for himself in *Giovanni's Room*, and his efforts to resolve them impose an unbearable strain on the structure. None of the characters has spiritual roots in the community. All are pale shadows of living people; none has an achieved reality. Thematically the novel reveals the search for identity, the International Theme, and alienation from the self. But the Theme crushes the vehicle. *Giovanni's Room* lacks the felt life of the first novel, and as a result reaches for melodramatic effects and slips into sentimentality.

The trouble may arise from the setting. Paris is a place of exile. It is no place for an American, as Baldwin reveals in "Equal in Paris," "Encounter on the Seine," "Princes and Powers," and "The Discovery of What It Means to be an American." As he says of the American writer in this last essay,

> This is a personal day, a terrible day, the day to which his entire sojourn has been tending. It is the day he realizes that there are no untroubled countries in this fearfully troubled world; that if he has been preparing himself for anything in Europe, he has been preparing himself—for America. In short, the freedom that the American writer finds in Europe brings him, full circle, back to himself, with the responsibility for his development where it always was: in his own hands. (*Nobody Knows My Name*, pp. 9–10)

Paris is the antithesis of America. It is old, hostile, infinitely crafty. It abounds in professional homosexuals, hideous caricatures of lovers and of men. Indeed, for Baldwin the professional queer is a living contradiction of his idealized love. But if Paris is hostile to the American, the American is a positive menace to the European. Giovanni accuses David of the most unspeakable corruption in wanting to cling to his own purity like diamonds. In this sense, David is another Milly Theale. Nothing is so terrible as the effect of innocence upon experience.

Since Paris is a threat to the American identity, including his own, Baldwin must work very hard to surmount his aversions in the story. The complex fate of being an American is compounded by the racial role-reversal; here David is the archetypal American: tall, blond, Anglo-Saxon. And Giovanni, the dark Italian, fills the hole in existence that David has vacated—the passionate self. As an expatriate, and finally as a confirmed homosexual who seeks out sailors, David debases Giovanni and destroys him.

But Baldwin cannot handle David; he neither understands nor likes him. His comment in "Down at the Cross" reveals the situation aptly: *"Whoever debases other is debasing himself"* (emphasis his). Baldwin cannot accept debasement as a key to identity. As a result David becomes an abstraction: white oppression of the Negro.

As the dark man menaced by the white man, Giovanni obviously symbolizes the American Negro. His execution for the murder of his faggot persecutor Guillaume is the black man's martyrdom for the white man's iniquity. Extending the symbolism further toward allegory, one finds that Paris is really America, and the home which David seeks to return to across the seas is his illusion of American innocence. David himself therefore is only a younger and more vicious Guillaume. In rejecting Giovanni's love, David, white America, dooms himself. Giovanni, though dead, retains his dignity. David the corrupter must live with a taint he cannot cleanse. Neither he nor America can ever go home again. Both must remain in perpetual exile from themselves.

While the allegorical pattern is neat, I do not think it is essentially correct. For one thing, this novel is atypical of Baldwin in character, background, and theme. He is not at home among these strange white men in a strange land: consider "Stranger in the Village," for instance. Secondly, *Giovanni's Room* lacks the living society of suffering Negroes that gives meaning to his other fiction.

A more promising approach is to see these characters as versions of the self. So much of the novel consists of arguments about large questions—the weight of freedom, innocence and experience, the New World and the Old World, love and responsibility, the longing for a home—so much that the novel approaches the philosophic essay. The author is working out answers to his own questions. Finally Baldwin is neither David nor Giovanni, neither alienated forever nor a helpless sufferer. The book is an exorcism of these options, leaving the way open, if not for his characters, at least for himself. Baldwin *can* go home again, but there is no telling what he will find there. (*Another Country* does that.)

The action of *Giovanni's Room* alternates between the open world and the closed world. Insofar as Paris, the land of exile, is an open world, it is the arena of the encounter with others. Les Halles, Guillaume's bar, the streets, taxis, restaurants, and the Seine are an irrelevant reality for David. The Paris community is the antithesis of the Harlem community in *Go Tell It on the Mountain*. David can relate only to other foreigners: the Italian, Giovanni; Hella, the American homebody; and Sue, the lonely socialite from Philadelphia. Nothing corroborates David's experience in the open world; it has the texture of a nightmare from which he would gladly wake.

David seeks his home then in the closed world, where he can develop an illusion of dominance. Three rooms serve as fixed points of reference for him, and as arenas for his conquests.

The novel opens with the room in the south of France. It is raining, and David is looking out the window. It is the night of Giovanni's execution. The room reflects the consequent emptiness of David's life; the mirror mocks his domination over others.

> I am too various to be trusted. If this were not so I would not be alone in this house tonight. Hella would not be on the high seas. And Giovanni would not be about to perish, sometime between this night and this morning, on the guillotine. (*Giovanni's Room*, p. 7)

The novel ends in the same room, after the lengthy flashback that constitutes the action. David sees Giovanni's face everywhere; indeed, the flashback that follows is virtual evidence of the fact. The mirror suggests the motif of the double: Giovanni is the guilt David will not accept. Desperately David turns from the mirror to face the future. "I must believe, I must believe, that the heavy grace of God, which has brought me to this place, is all that can carry me out of it" (p. 248). This nameless room has brought him to the awareness that his flight from love has led only to the prison of the self.

Giovanni's room, of course, is the antithesis of this one. It is crowded with the confusion and squalor of Giovanni's life. Airless, fetid, with the odor of rotting potatoes and spilled red wine, crowded with boxes, a violin case, clothes, paints, and dirty laundry, the room reflects the vital chaos of that life. "I understood why Giovanni had wanted me and had brought me to his last retreat. I was to destroy this room and give to Giovanni a new and better life. This life could only be my own, which, in order to transform Giovanni's, must first become a part of Giovanni's room" (p. 127).

In other words, the New World must redeem the Old with its love. This is the challenge of Giovanni's room, but it requires a commitment that David will not make. Just as he destroys Hella's love for him in the south of France, so he destroys Giovanni's here in Paris. In the process David isolates himself from love altogether.

A third room, midway between the other two, is Sue's. Playing the role of expatriate has brought her to the final scene: the end of her youth and her hopes. She needs the love and illusion of America that David seems to offer. Her apartment reflects her inner squalor. It is "dark and full of furniture." After he has made love to her on the couch, "the dark, tiny room rushed back again." Sue's play has become a grim game of self-deception; their playing at love is only a variation. When she kissed him "It was a gesture of great despair and I knew that she was giving herself, not to me, but to that lover who would never come" (p. 145). David's experience in each room is essentially the same. The seduction of Sue reflects the main action in a small figure: to betray the love of others is to betray the self.

As a result the novel reveals self-betrayal at some length. The characters cannot connect with each other or with society at large. The social framework affords no context for celebration. These characters have no common experience except David on which to build a community. He is the American Dream, their vision of a society better than they know. And his failure to live up to the dream is less an indictment of the dream itself than of those who run from its responsibilities. By implication, *Giovanni's Room* holds out for a better country than we know, better than we deserve.

But the plane of action, like the title, is severely restricted. Baldwin's insistence upon the private struggle for identity in effect denies corporate existence or corporate responsibility. There is no social community in *Giovanni's Room*, only others, hostile persons conspiring against love, identity, and the self. Finally the self incarnates hostility and commits spiritual suicide. Thus we find no ritual, no music, no food, no laughter—only brandy and sex. These last represent a regressive attempt to regain lost innocence. And, as Elizabeth Bowen has said, once one has lost innocence it is futile to attempt a picnic in Eden. The novel raises this question: Given the quality of modern love, can a person ever relate to a meaningful group? Is celebration possible?

In *Another Country* we get the answer. It depends on the kind of people and the kind of person. For brief moments, through love and music, yes. But by and large, no. In *Another Country* Baldwin attempts to present the search for celebration in a realistic, intensely felt native setting. This is Baldwin's big novel. Like most big novels, it is seriously flawed. It does not tell the whole story, not even a very large part of it, as *Invisible Man* does, for instance. But it does suggest the terms of the search for celebration as Baldwin now sees it, removed from the uneasy grounds of racial allegory. Character rather than symbol predominates. By comparison *Giovanni's Room* is pallid. But at least it retains that sense of structure one finds in the first novel, a sense that seems entirely gone in the third one.

Rage is the emotional core of *Another Country*. These people are robbed of their inheritance by a society that refuses to allow love. Love indeed is another country, perpetually at war with this one. Those who love are exiles from life. As Cass puts it in the final section, "This isn't a country at all, it's a collection of football players and Eagle Scouts. Cowards. We think we're happy. We're not. We're doomed" (*Another Country*, p. 342).

Power or love: This is the choice Baldwin gives his characters in *Another Country*. They attempt to escape the claims of the power world on their lives through confused and ever-changing sexual relationships: Vivaldo, the would-be novelist, loves Ida, the sister of his friend Rufus, a Negro drummer who jumped from the George Washington Bridge. Richard Silenski is a white liberal novelist and a counterpart of Ellis, a crass television producer. Richard prostitutes his talent and produces a commercial success. In the process he alienates his wife, Cass, who turns for comfort to Eric, a homosexual actor who is waiting for his boyfriend Yves to arrive from France. Yves' arrival ends the novel on an ambiguous note. Homosexual love has no better chance than heterosexual love in the power world.

Artistically, *Another Country* fails to resolve its structural problems and leaves a sense of confused purpose behind it. The death of Rufus occurs at the end of Book One, "Easy Rider." With him go most of the vitality and the best dialogue in the novel. Baldwin sacrifices Rufus as a person in order to make him a victim, like Giovanni. His isolation and self-martyrdom produce the guilt among those who love him through the rest of the novel. The hero's role once abdicated now splits into seven fractured selves. Like Humpty-Dumpty they cannot put Rufus together again, no matter how they try.

Only the memory of Rufus holds these characters together, or purports to do so. Without this center, love becomes corrupt, hope fails, and lives disintegrate. Baldwin tries to impose a community on disparate people, all of whom share the guilt for Rufus' death but none of whom can turn personal suffering into redemptive living. This pattern works well as a demonstration of Baldwin's thesis, but it does not in fact work dramatically. At the end we have forgotten Rufus. He is not enough to create a community. Rufus is Baldwin's martyr, but these secular celebrations of his martyrdom are ungrounded in a social reality. As a matter of fact the novel seems to indict society for the failure of love; in *Another Country* Baldwin seems to be moving toward old-fashioned naturalism.

The personal disasters of the novel are so prevalent as to seem almost mechanical. We sense something schematic about the exploitation of sexual confusion and the consequent misery. Whatever a man's "thing" may be, the result is uniform, the death of love. Yet Baldwin sometimes rises above this schematic exploitation of misery to give us compelling individual scenes. The finest of these is the scene at the end between Vivaldo and Ida; others include Rufus at the restaurant window and Cass's rejection of Richard. But the novel vacillates between such moments and long stretches of character manipulation.

In this sordid imitation of the country of love, all affection corrupts itself. The ironic title of Book Three brings this home clearly. "Toward Bethlehem" refers not to the birth of Christ, but to Yeats' vision of the millenium in "The Second Coming": "And what rough beast, its hour come round at last, slouches toward Bethlehem to be born?" One version of the beast is Ellis, the producer who buys Ida's love in order to destroy Vivaldo's.

When Ida tells Vivaldo that she has betrayed him with Ellis, she suggests the terms of love in contemporary life. "I saw what he was doing, but I couldn't hate him. I wondered what it felt like, to be like that, not to have any real feelings at all, except to say, Well, now, let's do this and now let's do that and now let's eat and now let's fuck and now let's go. And do that all your life" (p. 356). Ellis is quite willing to live on terms of power alone, and to debase those with whom he deals. He symbolizes American's prostitution of love for power.

But *Another Country* is not all jeremiad, nor all structural chaos. Despite the undue length, the tiresome plotting, and the frenetic style, the novel attempts to celebrate reality. *Another Country* shows the encounter between the self and society in all its pain and tragic dignity, in the destruction of self-delusions and the evasions of truth. As Baldwin found the music of Negro spirituals to celebrate his world in *Go Tell It on the Mountain,* so here he finds the blues.

The essence of blues is the celebration of a spirit transcending its own misery. Whether the occasion be sad, joyful, or nostalgic, the blues and jazz reveal the human spirit fully participating in its own life.

"Sonny's Blues," a 1957 story in *Partisan Review,* demonstrates the thematic importance of jazz and blues for Baldwin. Sonny is a jazz pianist and ex-junkie. When his brother, the narrator, goes to hear him play, he experiences an almost sacred celebration in a secular context:

> Then they all gathered around Sonny and Sonny played. Every now and again one of them seemed to say, amen. Sonny's fingers filled the air with life, his life. But that life contained so many others. And Sonny went all the way back, he really began with the spare, flat statement of the opening phrase of the song. Then he began to make it his. It was very beautiful because it wasn't hurried and it was no longer a lament. I seemed to hear with what burning he had made it his, with what burning we had yet to make it ours, how we could cease lamenting. Freedom lurked around us and I

understood, at last, that he could help us to be free if we would listen, that he would never be free until we did. (*Going To Meet the Man*, pp. 121–122)

Rufus, like Sonny, is a musician, and a good one. When he comes to Vivaldo on the night of his death, trying to assuage his guilt for Leona, Vivaldo puts Bessie Smith's "Backwater Blues" on the phonograph.

> "*There's thousands of people*," Bessie now sang, "*ain't got no place to go*," and for the first time Rufus began to hear, in the severely understated monotony of this blues, something which spoke to his troubled mind. The piano bore the singer witness, stoic and ironic. Now that Rufus himself had no place to go—" '*Cause my house fell down and I can't live there no mo*'," sang Bessie—he heard the line and the tone of the singer, and he wondered how others had moved beyond the emptiness and horror which faced him now. (*Another Country*, pp. 46–47)

Jazz is part of Rufus's legacy to those who loved him. At his traps he celebrates the malignant complexities of life. As the book opens, he remembers his last job, a good job. The music united musicians and audience. A young saxophonist says it with him and for him: "*Do you* love *me? Do you love* me? This, anyway, was the question Rufus heard, the same phrase, unbearably, endlessly, and variously repeated, with all of the force the boy had. The silence of the listeners became strict with abruptly focused attention, cigarettes were unlit, and drinks stayed on the tables; and in all of the faces, even the most ruined and most dull, a curious, wary light appeared" (p. 13). For one brief moment the people in the club become a community and join the celebration.

Ida celebrates in similar fashion with Vivaldo. After their first night together, Vivaldo awakens to her singing at the sink:

> *If you can't give me a dollar,*
> *Give me a lousy dime—*

She had washed the dishes, cleaned up the kitchen, and hung up her clothes. Now she was making coffee.

> *Just want to feed*
> *This hungry man of mine.* (p. 153)

Most of the happy moments in the novel are closely identified with the blues; Bessie Smith echoes throughout like a musical fairy godmother.

Baldwin contrasts the authentic celebration of jazz and blues with bogus celebrations. The Silenskis' interracial cocktail party is a dreary desecration of the celebrative spirit and of the blues. More dramatically, Ellis's discovery of Ida as a singer is a profanation of Rufus' memory. The scene is set in a nightclub among Rufus' old sidemen, and plays in ironic contrast to his last, joyful gig. The group realizes that Ida is betraying herself and her brother for Ellis. She tells Vivaldo later, "Baby, if musicians don't want to work with you, they sure can make you know it. I sang *Sweet Georgia Brown,* and something else. I wanted to get off that stand in the worst way. When it was over, and the people were clapping, the bass player whispered to me, he said, 'You black white man's whore, don't you never let me catch you on Seventh Avenue, you hear? I'll tear your little black pussy *up!*' " (p. 357).

Ultimately the reality of personal relationships is betrayal: betrayal of love and the more basic betrayal of the self. Rufus Scott is Baldwin's most complete example of this double action, going the whole route from innocence to suicide. Unable to find authentic celebration, Rufus jumps from the bridge. The implications for Baldwin are grim.

On the other hand, the music of *Another Country* celebrates the need to know and to trust one's own experience. And yet the fatal, pathetic distance between the need and the reality cannot be bridged, it seems. In his subsequent writing Baldwin has shown even less indication of the ability to bridge the gap, and a distressing taste for sheer sensationalism, e.g., "The Outing," "The Man Child," and "Going to Meet the Man."

Nevertheless, Baldwin is searching for a spiritual connection between the self and society, between black and white. In a wider sense he wishes to force Americans to a confrontation of their own experience. Only when America faces herself, accepting and loving her distortions and weaknesses, can there be cause for real celebration. The conclusion of his "Notes for a Hypothetical Novel" restates his intention and his wish:

A country is only as good—I don't care now about the Constitu-
tion and the laws, at the moment let us leave these things aside—
a country is only as strong as the people who make it up and the
country turns into what the people want it to become. Now, this
country is going to be transformed. It will not be transformed by
an act of God, but by all of us, by you and me. I don't believe any
longer that we can afford to say that it is entirely out of our hands.
We made the world we're living in and we have to make it over.
(*Nobody Knows My Name*, p. 154)

But given the split between Baldwin's vision and his fictional
rendering of reality, how long can he continue to try?

9 ❧ Ralph Ellison:
A Riotous Feast of the Self

INVISIBLE MAN (1952) is probably the major festive novel in our period—curiously, since the mode and the celebration are ironic. But the irony protects the core of social commitment revealed at the end of the novel, when the Invisible Man promises to emerge from his coal hole. Commitment is the central question, not only for Ellison and Baldwin but also for Saul Bellow. But Baldwin's social perspective is chaotic and fragmented; Ellison's and Bellow's social perspective is organized around the central self. Unlike Baldwin, they insist that living in the present is a communal activity, and that identity is the sum of individual and social experience. Inevitably, their heroes expand to mythic dimensions in order to accommodate the social realities of our time. At the end of *Invisible Man, The Adventures of Augie March, Henderson the Rain King,* and to some degree *Herzog,* the hero is the gigantic generic I of "Song of Myself."

But the heroic pose is still a function of the individual in search of his identity, of his person-hood. As Ellison shows it, self-discovery involves a flight from family, homeland, native culture, and brotherly love, all occasions for celebration in his formerly innocent state. As the novel develops, innocent festivals are replaced by violent and ironic ones until the hero comes to accept himself and his past against a background of complete social dissolution. *Invisible Man* is thus a riotous feast of the self in which the hero flies from authentic celebrations only to come back to them full-circle at the end.

Three motifs recur in the narrator's search for identity: invisibility, his grandfather, and play. The action of the novel shows the hero grappling with his present (invisibility) in an attempt to relate a known but unassimilated past (his grandfather) to an unknown future. He attempts to forge the link through the various play elements at his disposal. Thus the book is a kind of game, but a deadly serious one.

Invisibility is Ellison's metaphor for the Negro. It is the perfect state for irresponsible action—both a temptation and a regrettable reality. But as a temptation, invisibility deprives a man of reality, of a real self. The hero must reject his invisibility and find a socially responsible role to play. But society will not allow him to escape his condition of permanent childhood. Only an abnormal, violent action can give the hero his manhood and awaken white America to his visible existence.

The boy's grandfather is both the origin and the object of his search. He has the identity that the boy must also reach. The boy ponders the deathbed advice throughout the novel: "Live with your head in the lion's mouth. I want you to overcome 'em with yeses, undermine 'em with grins, agree 'em to death and destruction, let 'em swoller you till they vomit or bust wide open." [1] The advice is ambiguous; under the yea-saying runs the sinister no. Finally, the hero must balance yea and nay in antiphonal chorus. "So I denounce and defend and I hate and I love." He goes beyond bitterness to the mystery of human community.

In the process, the hero lives by playing—music, first of all. Louis Armstrong's blues are a sardonic protest against segregation. The Negro did nothing to be so black and blue; his guilt is innate. His blackness makes him blue, as his bruises make him black-and-blue. Throughout the novel, the hero hears the blues, but he generally rejects them. They remind him too much of his past. The new man has no past, he feels.

Secondly, the hero must play the game of life. His grandfather tells him, the vet in the tavern, The Golden Day, tells him, and he tells us himself at the end: "humanity is won by continuing to play in the face of certain defeat" (p. 499). The game is crooked, of course. From the battle royal on, he is the loser.

Third, the hero plays many roles: valedictorian, chauffeur, assistant boiler-keeper, demagogue, lecturer, con man, rioter—the roles keep succeeding each other in an ironic series of rebirths.

Most of the roles involve words. But like Shakespeare's buffoons, instead of using words, he is used by them. This truth comes home to him when he sees Brother Tod Clifton spieling on the street corner, jiggling his little black Sambo dolls:

> *And only twenty-five cents, the brotherly two bits of a dollar be-cause he wants me to eat.*
> *It gives him pleasure to see me eat.*
> *You simply take him and shake him . . . and he does the rest.*
> (p. 374)

Clifton dangles on the strings manipulated by *Tod*—Death—whose creature he is in name and fact.

Invisibility, his grandfather, and the play element all prepare the hero for his encounter with experience. While he jiggles at the end of the string, he does so on four different sidewalks, each revealing a different failure: the failure of education (chapters 1–9); the failure of business and industry (chapters 10–12); the failure of politics, especially communism (chapters 13–22); and the failure of society (chapters 23–24). The climax comes when man revolts against the failure of his institutions and tears them down for a new start (chapter 25). The race riot presents the national pattern of death and rebirth, and it just may be enough to liberate the Invisible Man—but we don't know.

Throughout the novel Ellison reveals his awareness of the Negro past as a necessary foundation for living in the present. The real self in the novel is both the Invisible Man and his Negro institutions. Through the ironic mode and a fallible narrator, Ellison shows the fullness and richness of the Negro identity. The comedy lies in the hero's ignorance of that richness. The interplay between the communal identity and the hero's inability to accept it is the comic action of the novel. The story advances as the hero learns to become a man and a Negro. As a result, *Invisible Man* celebrates the Negro self in all its contradictions, defeats, and humanity.

This dialectical process begins with the battle royal. The hero is tricked into joining the fight with his young Negro friends. But he wants to get ahead, and he feels the fight will keep him from his moment of forensic victory. "I wanted to deliver my speech more than anything else in the world, because I felt that only these men could judge truly my ability, and now this stupid clown was ruining my chances" (p. 28). For the first time Ellison sets the ginger boy against other Negroes. Of course the comic irony cuts him down. Later in the evening, he does perform, but the white businessmen make him dance to their music—jiggle on the end of their string.

The ironic resolution of the ginger boy's first encounter with the whites is an illusory victory. He is an accomplished speaker (with all the hollowness that suggests). He receives a scholarship and a ginger-colored briefcase. He has raised himself over the "stupid clowns." But the last laugh is his grandfather's. In his dream that night the scholarship becomes a message from the dead: "To whom it may concern: keep this nigger-boy running." This is the truth behind the scholarship. This first piece of paper indicates that the ginger boy can never escape his past, but that he is condemned to try.

Celebration is thus bawdy and brutal at the town banquet. It becomes more formal at the next stage of his education. The ginger boy chauffeurs Mr. Norton, a wealthy trustee of the college. Again, language is irrelevant to reality. Behind Mr. Norton's pious inter-racial platitudes lie incest, madness, and monstrous self-deception. The dream is a rhetorical, utopian vision, but the reality is Jim Trueblood.

The college shuns Trueblood: the horror of incest is too real for it. Yet his tale fascinates Norton, completely destroying his version of his daughter's death. Incest undercuts Little Eva. Fur-thermore, Trueblood's earthy monologue, with its rich, idiomatic self-deprecation, contrasts effectively with Barbee's impassioned magnolia rhetoric. Incest and pulpit oratory are thus the social poles of Negro life. The appropriate place for celebrating such a dizzying set of contraries is The Golden Day, a brothel for shell-shocked soldiers, where a mad vet (veteran, veterinarian—Ellison puns on the word) tells Norton the truth about himself and about the hero: "I can tell you [Norton] *his* destiny. He'll do your bid-ding, and for that his blindness is his chief asset. He's your man, friend. Your man and your destiny" (pp. 87–88). Whores, drunks, and madmen appropriately celebrate the reality of southern life. And of course the ginger-colored boy loses this game, too. He is expelled.

Further undercutting the grandiloquence of blind Barbee's address is Bledsoe's power politics. When Bledsoe sends the hero north with letters of introduction to several white friends of the college, he completes the charade. This second piece of paper echoes the first, as the hero comes to see it: " 'My dear Mr. Emerson,' I said aloud. 'The Robin bearing this letter is a former student. Please hope him to death, and keep him running. Your most humble and obedient servant, A. H. Bledsoe.' " (p. 171). The initials mask a common insult; the full name indicates the indignity foisted on Bledsoe's Negro students.

Part of the failure is the complacency of white liberals. Mr. Norton reflects the unseen Mr. Emerson. Emersonian idealism, with its dogmas of self-reliance and the infinitude of the private man, is thus a sardonic joke. So the hero laughs. Ellison's comment on the delusory hopes and on the failure is the blues:

> *O well they picked poor Robin clean*
> *O well they picked poor Robin clean*
> *Well they tied poor Robin to a stump*
> *Lawd, they picked all the feathers round*
> *   from Robin's rump*
> *Well they picked poor Robin clean.* (p. 170)

The appropriate celebration for the hero's experience here is rueful self-mockery. But he fails to realize that his self-mockery is a ritualistic repetition of the group experience. A whole race of invisible robins has been picked clean. All you can do is laugh.

The second section, the hero's encounter with business, reveals Negro invisibility at the bottom of the economic ladder. Literally, the Liberty Paint Factory ("If It's Optic White, It's the Right White") is built upon the invisible black man who controls the boilers in the basement. Upstairs, of course, the factory is effectively segregated. The hero finds his proper place with Lucius Brockway, the suspicious Pluto who runs this underworld.

The following surreal sequence is built upon mutual distrust. Both Lucius and the hero think they have a position to protect; as a matter of fact, they do not. The basement is nowhere, an allegorical extension of invisibility among steam gauges. As the two fight on the floor for the prestige of being nobody, the boilers explode.

The explosion is an absurd comment on the human desires and delusions of the hero and Brockway. They fight blindly. Their insistence upon identity echoes the battle royal of the first section and anticipates the violence of the later sections. The hero's unconscious body is thrust under the white infirmary light where he is seen for the first time: "WHO ARE YOU? WHAT IS YOUR MOTHER'S NAME? WHO WAS BUCKEYE THE RABBIT? BOY, WHO WAS BRER RABBIT?"

The ensuing action is an ironic rebirth into the white world. But the ritual of death and rebirth is an enclosed action; once again the hero is forced to accept a dependent identity. They thrust another piece of paper under his face, this time a quitclaim for injuries suffered on the job. They buy him off again, just as the high school principal bought him off with the college scholarship.

As this second movement in the action ends, the reader realizes the total inability of business and industry to afford life to the Negro. Ellison's comments, scattered through chapter 11, counterpoint the action with Negro folklore and nonsense rhymes:

> *Did you ever see Miss Margaret boil water?*
> *Man she hisses a wonderful stream,*
> *Seventeen miles and a quarter,*
> *Man, and you can't see her pot for the steam*
> (p. 205)

> *Buckeye the Rabbit*
> *Shake it, shake it*
> *Buckeye the Rabbit*
> *Break it, break it ...* (p. 211)

All of this is the author's joke on the hero and a wider protest against his present lack of identity. The real celebration awaits the integration of origins and identity.

Part three of *Invisible Man*, the long Harlem section, presents the hero as more active in his self-delusion. The action is complex, involving two more pieces of paper, more violence, and death. The celebration is still external, still an ironic commentary on the hero's inability to see who he is.

For a brief moment the hero does see, though—that he is self-

deceived. Mary discovers him and takes him home to rest; indirectly she moves him to return to Men's House (all Negroes live in
the men's room) and to "baptize old Rev" with spittoon drippings.
He undermines the self-deception of his invisible peers who live
there. But immediately he relapses, becoming a tool of the Brotherhood.

The eviction scene is another opportunity for him. His protest
at the eviction of an aged Negro couple is a celebration. Together
he and his fellow Negroes have a chance to celebrate their poverty
and their victimization—to celebrate and to accept it with joyous
defiance. But he muffs the chance. He accepts another role, this
time as a public orator. Rejecting the eviction as a reality in his
own life is the first step in his newest self-deception. In playing
the role of public orator he plays the fool. Here as elsewhere
Ellison suggests that oratory itself is a form of deception. Like
Barbee, the hero is blind, and the blindness supports his fantasies.

The true identity is with him, nonetheless; he is simply unwill-
ing to accept it. Mary tells him at the opening of the section:

> *Here's my house right here, hep me git him up the steps and in-*
> *side, you needn't worry, son, I ain't never laid eyes on you before*
> *and it ain't my business and I don't care what you think about me*
> *but you weak and caint hardly walk and all and you look what's*
> *more like you hungry, so just come on and let me do something for*
> *you like I hope you'd do something for ole Mary in case she needed*
> *it, it ain't costing you a penny and I don't want to git in your busi-*
> *ness, I just want you to lay down till you rested and then you can*
> *go.* (p. 220)

And he stumbles onto it when he buys the hot yams from a street
peddler:

> "I can see you one of these old-fashioned yam eaters."
> "They're my birthmark," I said. "I yam what I yam!" (p. 231)

And he discovers the tragic meaning of his own past in the bureau
drawer of the old evicted couple. Among breastpumps, baby
shoes, and tarnished cuff links he finds the irrefutable legal link
with his past: "I read: *FREE PAPERS. Be it known to all men*
that my negro, Primus Provo, has been freed by me this sixth day
of August, 1859. Signed: John Samuels. Macon . . ." (pp. 236–237).

The hero recoils in disgust from the yellow parchment. He cannot accept his past, cannot be a victim with dignity. His speech abstracts from the real situation only to avoid it. Once more he begins to run, this time with the Brotherhood. Throughout the section, however, we always know that he runs from himself.

As he leaves Mary's house, for instance, he hears her singing "Back Water Blues." He feels the same nostalgia he felt with the yam-seller, the yearning for the simple celebration of his authentic, painful identity. But he doesn't act; he reacts. He takes the iron pickaninny bank (one thinks of Flannery O'Connor's Artificial Nigger) to destroy it, to obliterate this caricature of the Negro self. "For a second I stopped, feeling hate charging within me, then dashed over and grabbed it, suddenly as enraged by the tolerance or lack of discrimination, or whatever, that allowed Mary to keep such a self-mocking image around, as by the knocking" (p. 277).

But the figure reminds Mary of her enslaved past, a past she can live with and can see in her fellowmen. The preceding night he has had another such reminder from a joyful brother who insists on "the rights of the colored brother to sing." Brother Jack has him hustled out of the room. The hero, meanwhile, has betrayed himself again. For three hundred dollars he sells his dignity and receives a new identity—his fourth piece of paper. The ironic commentary throughout this action is musical: "Back Water Blues," "Go Down Moses," and "St. Louis Blues." And, for Ellison, music never lies. It is the authentic feast of Negro identity.

After his initial success at the rally, the hero rides a crest of self-adulation. All his projects succeed; he is another Frederick Douglass; he is what people tell him he is. Thus Ellison prepares us for the most profound identity crisis in the novel, the hero's choice of a personal or a political self.

The first step in the process is the fifth piece of paper: Brother Jack's anonymous warning not to go too fast. His pride is hurt; he turns to Brother Tarp for sympathy and receives only the sign of Jonah—a filed link from Brother Tarp's leg chain. That, of course, is the resolution of his problem. Real brotherhood is won by suffering, real identity by silent love. He sees his grandfather in Brother Tarp's eyes, but he still fails to understand his grandfather's meaning. The chain link becomes a rhetorical prop and so loses its meaning for him.

Celebration, as we have observed, is a corporate act revealing significant shared social and personal values, uniting separate individuals into a momentary but transcendent identity. Giving the hero the link from his leg chain is a private celebrative act for Brother Tarp; it is in fact a liturgical act, an offering of brotherly love. The hero does not share that understanding though; he lacks a sense of self that will enable him to celebrate and to love.

At this moment the personal self surrenders to the political self with disastrous consequences. Twice he is called up before the Committee of the Brotherhood and twice accused of deviant behavior. He is sent downtown to lecture on "the Woman Question" and ends up ignored, invisible even to the woman who seduces him. His attempt to reestablish connections later almost leads to a brawl in Barrelhouse's bar. In each case, the hero has pursued a false identity based upon political concepts he does not understand. The episode of Brother Jack's eye demonstrates his own personal invisibility for the Brotherhood. As a nobody he cannot assume personal responsibility.

Release from self-deception requires the death of Tod Clifton. That death would have been a rhetorical, political issue for the hero except for his inescapable personal involvement in it. He sees Tod selling little black Sambo dolls on a street corner: like the iron pickaninny, this is the ultimate burlesque of his high principles. Contemptuously, Clifton ignores him. As we have seen, the little paper dolls are his way out—and his meal ticket. They reflect Clifton's rueful self-knowledge. But they also symbolize the hero himself, dancing on Brother Jack's string. No matter what his role, the Negro reflects someone else's power; that is, he is invisible. When Clifton lashes out against the social strings that pull him, he becomes human, real, dangerous, and vulnerable. He is shot.

His death occasions the hero's funeral oration, whose bitterness suggests a new awareness in his public rhetoric. The address lacks the delusive vision of a new world, and the whole burial ceremony is as a result a sullen celebration. The hero fails to see that he as much as anyone has destroyed Clifton, however. By making him a Brother instead of a brother, he has condemned him to death.

Yet the discovery of the self is all the more urgent by reason of his blindness. It is the necessary act, and it will out at all costs. Indeed, Clifton's death simply foreshadows the massive will-to-be of the race riot in section four.

The hero is ready now for the social enlargement of his personal failure. The riot reveals the total lack of communication between people. It is the human response to inhuman rhetoric. The whole business has an insane gaiety about it, of course: Ras on his black horse charging policemen in his bear skins; the bonfire spirit of burning the tenement; the selective looting—"Git a side of bacon, Joe,—git Wilson's"—all contribute to the carnival atmosphere of the race riot. This is a bloody Mardi Gras in which all the invisibility and all the false identities are rejected in a Festival of Misrule.

The central character in this action is Rinehart. Like the hero, Rinehart has multiple roles: bag man, con artist, sport, and preacher. Unlike the hero, Rinehart revels in his roles. Rinehartism is the practical option for invisible men. "The world in which we lived was without boundaries. A vast seething, hot world of fluidity, and Rine the rascal was at home. Perhaps only Rine the rascal was at home in it. It was unbelievable, but perhaps only the unbelievable could be believed. Perhaps the truth was always a lie" (p. 430).

Significantly, Rinehart never appears in the novel. Why? Because he is an option, not a person. The hero is Rinehart, at least until he sees that the truth is not always a lie. People like Brother Jack, Sybil, and Rinehart's congregation are Rinehart, requiring illusions to live. One can still refuse to accept those illusions, but such an act requires an acceptance of the past, with all its failures and shortcomings, as a key to the present: "And now all past humiliations became precious parts of my experience, and for the first time, leaning against that stone wall in the sweltering night, I began to accept my past and, as I accepted it, I felt memories welling up within me. It was as though I'd learned suddenly to look around corners; images of past humiliations flickered through my head and I saw that they were more than separate experiences. They were me; they defined me" (p. 439).

Though the riot proper is the most dramatic single incident in

Invisible Man, it should not be isolated from the rest of the novel. The riot is a product of Rinehartism, of invisibility gone rotten. It is the popular refusal to accept a debased myth of origins. In this, the novel is part of a long tradition of American revolution: *The Rights of Man,* "The American Scholar," "Of Civil Disobedience," *The House of the Seven Gables, Leaves of Grass,* and *Huckleberry Finn* all reflect native belief in human possibilities greater than present circumstances. Unlike these works, however, *Invisible Man* looks backward to the enslaved self for its human dignity, not forward toward the New Eden. Real freedom lies in joyful acceptance of one's limitations.

The hero's awareness of this truth is not consciously shared by the other rioters; the action is an ironic celebration in which limited awareness is essential. But celebration finally is more important than irony. The festive element predominates, as does the emphasis on a shared activity and on conspicuous excess—all characteristic of a feast as Pieper defines it. Chapter 25 opens: "When I reached Morningside the shooting sounded like a distant celebration of the Fourth of July, and I hurried forward. At St. Nicholas [!] the street lights were out. A thunderous sound arose and I saw four men running toward me pushing something that jarred the walk. It was a safe" (p. 463).

Later in the chapter the hero recalls two other causes for celebration: today is Jack's birthday; the riot is thus his birthday party. More important, today commemorates Clifton, the racial martyr, with appropriate violence: "I laughed with the others, thinking: A holy holiday for Clifton."

The woman drinking beer on the milk truck demonstrates the spirit of festive excess in this celebration. And the one sustained action, the burning of the typhoid- and vermin-infested tenement, is an almost ritualistic sacrifice. In all this action, the play element reveals a ferocious human dignity. Ultimately, the riot celebrates death and rebirth; in a strange sense, Jack's birthday and Clifton's death are one and the same.

After he skewers Ras the Destroyer with his own spear, the hero overhears two Negroes describing that incredible man. Once again the festive spirit predominates. And once again the native idiom, rich in realistic humor and a sense of the absurd, undercuts the rhetoric of a public orator—Ras himself. By laughing at Ras' monstrous pretensions, these nameless observers elevate the high priest of hatred to the status of satiric butt. They represent both common sense and the communion between people that the riot unconsciously seeks to establish.

But killing Ras has another, more archetypal function. Just as Prince Hal deposes Falstaff, the Lord of Misrule, so the hero deposes Ras the Destroyer. His one bloody act then is an ironic peace offering, an attempt to introduce order and reality into riot and illusion: "And I knew that it was better to live out one's own absurdity than to die for that of others, whether for Ras' or Jack's" (p. 484).

The hero descends into his coal hole and destroys all those papers, the last shreds of illusory identity. This, too, is a small celebration, a flicker of the social bonfire overhead. The high school diploma, Clifton's doll, his Brotherhood name, and the letter from Jack all dissolve into ashes. Despite all the ironic qualifications, life is to be lived. He must act, he must love, he must denounce and defend, "since there's a possibility that even an invisible man has a socially responsible role to play." The aftermath of celebration is work. Without the context of work, leisure loses its form and becomes license.

The final state of the Invisible Man, then, is hope. The experience of life leads him to make connections. Part of the novel's paradox is his ability to connect with others through violence. The community emerging from his experience is one he has known all along but never really lived with—the spiritual community of those who have loved him and encountered him as a person. On the one hand, the sheep: his grandfather, the vet in The Golden Day, Mary, Tod Clifton, Brother Tarp. On the other, the goats: Norton, Barbee, Bledsoe, Brother Jack, Rinehart. The former compose a visionary company, a community whose celebration of life, hope, and shared suffering briefly echoes that consolidated world view of Chaucer's pilgrims.

We must not assume, nonetheless, that Ellison counts himself or his hero among the pilgrims. We are dealing with possibilities, for one thing, and not with achieved community. All the goats in the novel are rhetoricians, dealing in the fabricated illusions of public speech. All live as if by some shared communion with their audiences while simultaneously conning them. By talent and by temperament the hero (and the author?) is closer to the rhetoricians, not to the audiences. Thus the ending teases us ambiguously. The hero is about to emerge, but he has not done so. He rejects oratory for life, yet the book is a highly rhetorical structure. Is not the work itself of the devil's party? Ah yes, the narrator tells us, but he knows he may be boring us with his buggy jiving; he admits the failure of his own rhetoric. Is this not plain dealing? Perhaps. And one final twist: who knows, but on the lower frequencies, he speaks for you?

Who knows, indeed? Does the narrator finally escape isolation by sharing it with his readers? Does artistic illusion destroy insidious ones? If so, Ralph Ellison's feast of the self involves all of us in a corporate celebration of American experience. As he says in "The Seer and the Seen," "I think that art is a celebration of life even when life extends into death and that the sociological conditions which have made for so much misery in Negro life are not necessarily the only factors which make for the values which I feel should endure and shall endure." [2] In the face of chaos, one must assert order.

The singular achievement of *Invisible Man* is Ellison's ability to affirm our complex and varied American experience even as he shows us its ugliness and its brutality. No other novel of our time tells us so much and so completely what it means to be a Negro— and what it means to be an American.

The last phrase, of course, echoes Baldwin's celebrated essay and suggests the difference between the approach and the achievement of our best Negro writers. Baldwin's talent is split. He has a transcendental vision of America, expressed in his essays (essays in the Emersonian manner), and he has an apocalyptic sense of contemporary life that destroys the basis of his transcendental hopes. This split between his hopes and his sensibilities, between his essays and his fiction, has brought Baldwin to the impasse of disillusionment. He does not see the possibility of celebrating reality in contemporary America.

Ellison makes greater use of the blues than Baldwin does; he finds them vital and authentic celebrations of Negro experience. More important, though, is the range of his language. No one since Mark Twain is so rich, so varied, or so comic in his recreation of oral speech. Bracing peals of laughter echo on and under the surface of *Invisible Man*. The whole is an elaborate musical and verbal joke, celebrating love, sacrifice, and self-knowledge as our ultimate resources against the vicissitudes of life.

10 &~ *Bernard Malamud: A Party of One*

LIKE Saul Bellow, Bernard Malamud writes about the American Jew. But his approach and attitudes are quite different. To put it simply—too simply—Bellow finds ultimate reality in the many versions which the self can assume, in the endless possibilities of corporate American life, and in the future. Malamud, on the other hand, probes the past for the guilt that gives his Jews their primary identity. He cannot accept the pluralism of contemporary experience, as Bellow does. For Malamud, reality is an individual, retrospective view.

Suffering, humiliation, and ultimate defeat are the components of that reality. The encounter with the self involves inevitable loss: in *The Fixer* it is death itself. Ultimately Malamud's four novels fix the individual past in Jewish and Christian tradition. In so doing, they question the coherence of contemporary life without those traditions.

Malamud's central situation is the Jew's historical problem: escaping the ghetto. His novels stand on the boundaries of the pale, reluctant to abandon a coherent tradition, however painful, for the deracinated pluralism of contemporary American life. His characters adjust to that life with a wry self-mockery that preserves an inner core of private feeling.

As a result, Malamud's celebrations are brief and severely enclosed. I am what I can endure, his protagonists seem to say as they wrap their worlds tightly around them. Even the physical scene stresses encapsulation: a baseball diamond in a packed stadium; a dingy grocery in the slums; a furnished room in a small college town; most clearly, solitary confinement in a Tsarist cell.

The forms of celebration are similarly restricted. The basic form is the ritual lament; it may be a joint weeping over lost youth in a bakery, a confession of a misspent life after lovemaking, or a chant of the psalms of lamentation in prison. Whatever the particular form, any celebration that is not firmly anchored in one's identity as sufferer is a false feast, an attempt to dissipate the integrity of individual pain with joyless anodynes. Though strait the gate, all those who enter are redeemed.

Since such a celebration involves spiritual conversion, the feast is always a small one. Malamud is more concerned with the authentic renewal of the individual than with wholesale conversion. He hopes that private experience may become public, but the evidence proves contrary. The private feast is possible only in the ghetto. So the gap between private and public experience enlarges from novel to novel.

The problem of community is central to Bernard Malamud, as it is to most of the writers discussed in this book. In Malamud's case, we can distinguish the public novels, *The Natural* and *A New Life*, from the private ones, *The Assistant* and *The Fixer*. The difference between public and private is only relative, of course; by a public novel I mean one in which the protagonist seeks his identity largely in his social role. He believes in the standards of his society and tries to live by them. Such men are Roy Hobbs and S. Levin.

In the private novels, communal life is more narrow and more intense: celebration is authentic. In the public novels, where Malamud deals uneasily with a pluralistic society he does not trust, celebration is joyless and forced. In all likelihood the private novels are better, more realized works than the public ones, just as *Go Tell It on the Mountain* is a better work than *Another Country*. For one thing, the form and the context of celebration in *The Assistant* and in *The Fixer* are much closer than they are in the other two novels. In *The Natural* and *A New Life* Malamud must assert some context for significant feasting—and he does not trust his choice.

The Natural (1952) is the myth critic's delight. Critics have found parallels to the Fisher King, the Grail legend, and *The Waste Land* in the book. But the novel is also about baseball and sex: both are games which the hero loses. His losses define the man while they destroy the hero. *The Natural* celebrates mortality, the courage to err among the limited choices in a man's life, and to suffer the consequences thereof. The book celebrates man's immortal moment in the flux of time; but it does so badly.

The connection between baseball and sex is Roy Hobbs's identity. Malamud stresses the falsity of a public identity at the expense of a private one. Like Ellison's Invisible Man, Roy has many identities, each passing and insufficient. His final identity as loser offers a dim possibility of transcendence through Iris, who may be waiting outside the stadium with their unborn child, but the possibility is lost on this oafish hero. Roy never realizes that he has lived only in those rare, unselfish encounters with others, in fleeting celebrations of love.

Perhaps the greatest failing in *The Natural* is Malamud's sacrifice of the man for his scheme. Like *Another Country* and *Rabbit, Run*, this book offers a paradigm instead of an experience. Malamud tries to connect private and public experience by suppressing the individuality of his character. Yet whatever its excesses and weaknesses, the novel reveals his unvarying theme: man must die every day, over and over again, if he is ever to live. Iris Lemon, the good angel of *The Natural*, puts it this way: "Yet I was tied to time— not so much to the past—nor to the expectations of the future, which was really too far away—only to here and now, day after day, until suddenly the years unrolled and a change came—more a reward of standing it so long than any sudden magic. . . ." [1]

Since Roy is to be the victim of Malamud's scheme, he does not learn Iris' lesson. He crumbles the letter and throws it against the wall. With that action he destroys his possibilities of becoming a *Mensch* and remains only an actor, playing the rise and fall of the hero.

Each role, in both the baseball context and the sexual context, involves Roy as son and lover. Each stage in his development is marked by a particular kind of weakness. In the first section of the novel, "Pre-Game," Roy is the symbolic son of Sam Simpson, aging scout. On a train trip to his tryout in Chicago he challenges the current American League champion, Walter (The Whammer) Whambold to hit his pitches. Roy strikes him out, thereby hastening the end of The Whammer's career. But his third pitch hits Sam in the stomach and destroys him, too. Sam is the first to die that Roy might live.

If Roy is too strong a pitcher, he is too innocent a lover. Harriet Bird tests his motives for playing the game and finds them wanting. Roy desires only "the fun and satisfaction of playing the best way that you know how." Thus his athletic victory leads to his physical and moral defeat. In Chicago Harriet destroys his innocence in her negligee. His pride leads him to her hotel room, where she shoots him in the stomach with a silver bullet, and "making muted noises of triumph and despair, danced on her toes around the stricken hero."

When Roy finally makes the team at thirty-four, he is experienced but too disillusioned to love. Pop Fisher, manager of the New York Knights, assumes Sam's fatherly role. But Bump Bailey, the incumbent left fielder, now plays Roy's own role. Bump is simply The Whammer as practical joker. And Roy is Bump without a job or a girl; both belong to Bump. The girl is Memo Paris, Pop's niece and another Harriet. Only one of the men can be hero, son, and lover. Roy gets his chance when Bump slams into the left field wall chasing a fly ball for the love of Memo. Indirectly, of course, he dies for Roy. Roy steps in and leads the Knights into first place with Wonderboy, his marvelous bat.

His defeat by Memo is more serious than his previous one. Memo destroys both health and integrity. The silver bullet this time is a huge feast, a premature party to celebrate the pennant. Appropriately, the damage is internal. Roy's stomach rebels after the gastronomic orgy. He is taken to a maternity hospital, where Memo persuades him to throw the playoff game so that they can marry comfortably. In his role as young Percival he has destroyed The Whammer; now in his role as Lancelot, he is destroyed in turn by Memo.

If Sam and Pop are fathers, if The Whammer and Bump are alter egos, Herman Youngberry is Roy's mythical son. In the climactic game, the young knight slays the old one, robbing Roy of the heroic illusions on which he has built his identity. With the Knights trailing three to two in the ninth, Youngberry strikes him out.

The tragic element in his humiliation is his free choice of defeat. From time to time Malamud relieves the lyric naturalism of the book with moments of relative freedom; such a moment occurs in the seventh inning, when Roy comes to the plate with the bases loaded. Humiliated by his pact with the owner, Judge Banner Goodwill, Roy tells himself that the fix is off. Limping and twisted, he comes to the plate to hit. The sun breaks through. "Though it startled him to find it so, he had regained a sense of his own well-being. A thousand springlike thoughts crowded through his mind, blotting out the dark diagnosis of the white-mustached specialist. He felt almost happy, and that he could do anything he wanted, if he wanted" (p. 223).

His free choice is not to hit the ball and win the game, though. He fouls ball after ball at Otto Zipp (Double Zero), his tormentor in the stands. The efforts waste his strength. Worse, a ball hits Zipp and then Iris, who like Sam, Pop, and Bump, suffers for Roy. Love makes her vulnerable; if she had not stood up for him as she did that day in Chicago, she would not have been hit. Only after he has wasted his strength on Zipp and Iris does Roy take strike three.

In Iris Malamud unites the two contexts for celebration. Her belief in Roy allowed him to hit a homer for a sick boy and to redeem himself. There in Chicago the celebration was genuine, for it was based on Iris' faith in him: "Roy circled the bases like a Mississippi steamboat, lights lit, flags fluttering, whistle banging, coming round the bend. The Knights poured out of their dugout to pound his back, and hundreds of their rooters hopped about in the field. He stood on the home base, lifting his cap to the lady's empty seat" (pp. 147–148).

Later in the evening, the contexts of baseball and sex fuse. Roy and Iris are lying on the beach at midnight. Roy describes his life to Iris, who also submits him to a test. He says

> "I wanted everything." His voice boomed out in the silence.
> She waited.
> "I had a lot to give to this game."
> "Life?"
> "Baseball. If I had started out fifteen years ago like I tried to, I'da been the king of them all by now!" (p. 156)

Iris tells him that suffering "teaches us the right things"—in both love and baseball. Their sexual union is thus elevated into a personal giving, a promise of new life symbolized by a ritual cleansing and the kindling of fire on the bench.

The sick boy in Chicago also foreshadows Roy's second encounter with Iris, during the playoff game. This time, prone on the training table, she admits that she is pregnant; she tells him to "win for our boy." In each case, love is the context for suffering. Malamud's ending is thus ambiguous. Like all men, and not only fallen heroes, Roy must give place—to Herman Youngberry on the one hand, to his unborn son on the other. His final role in the death of the hero is father. His loss is ambiguous, not only because of the life-in-death suggested by his position at the end, but also because Malamud never tells us how much he now realizes about himself. Roy does not know what Malamud knows: that only in the context of loss can celebration be meaningful. His homer for the sick boy, his idyll with Iris on the shore of Lake Michigan, and his renewed love for her in the Knights' dressing room are meant to express his private involvement in the communal action of love and baseball.

The public celebrations in *The Natural* are false and orgiastic. Immediately following the beach idyll we read: "After a hilarious celebration in the dining car (which they roused to uproar by tossing baked potatoes and ketchup bottles around) and later in the Pullman, where a wild bunch led by Roy stripped the pajamas off players already sound asleep in their berths, peeled Red Blow out of his long underwear, and totally demolished the pants of a new summer suit of Pop's, who was anyway not sold on premature celebrations, Roy slept restlessly" (p. 164). The celebration rings hollow after his previous night with Iris.

Anti-celebration finds its apotheosis in Gus Sands, the Supreme Bookie. To Gus, games are mercenary feasts rather than celebrations. He bets on them and rigs them. Ultimately his view of baseball corrupts Roy's, for it is his money in all probability that rides on the play-off game and furnishes the $35,000 bribe.

Roy meets Gus Sands four times, always in the company of Memo. Each encounter pits knight against dragon, celebration against anti-celebration. Their first combat is at a nightclub, the Pot of Fire. Gus bets him that the next drink from the bar will be a pink lady, and he wins. The financial contest is a struggle between black magic and white. Roy counters by pulling silver dollars from Gus's ears and nose. The makeshift celebration gives him the first round and preserves his integrity.

On their second encounter, Roy disguises himself as a German waiter and dumps food all over Gus's lackey, Max Mercy. In such fashion Roy counters the anti-feast with a magic of his own, graceless as it is. In the third encounter, the level of combat sinks to a crap game. Roy beats Gus and Memo with a fantastic string of passes. Now the stakes are openly financial, but Roy's victories over Gus debase him just the same. Roy fails the fourth test, Memo's orgy. In this game Gus does not compete at all. He is simply there, turning Roy's sexual and physical appetites against him. Here Memo is Circe, making him forget his Penelope with food. And Gus, the one-eyed fixer, is Cyclops.[2]

Myth aside, these public celebrations do not work, simply because no communal solidarity can develop out of debased motives. Baseball and life cease to have meaning when Roy adopts Gus's anti-festive attitude and sells out. Malamud tells us why: when a man refuses to accept suffering as the only context for celebration, and love as the only reason for it, the human community—the team, the family—ceases to have any capacity to renew its members and falls apart. But in *The Natural* Roy Hobbs has no identity to begin with and simply blots up the social corruption around him. Malamud never gives his sucker an even break.

The Assistant (1957), by contrast, is surely Malamud's best novel. For one thing, he makes much better use of his context: Jewish and Christian traditions. *The Assistant* need not stretch for its sources in baseball and myth. All history is felt in the suffering of Morris Bober. The past reaches, encloses, and reinvigorates the present in the person of Frankie Alpine. Indeed, the central action of the book is the conversion of Christian to Jew, of holdupnik to son.

The novel describes this process of assimilation. Again, celebration is based on identity. And though Frankie does not know where he is going, he feels a responsibility to Morris that makes his choices more meaningful and his feasts, small as they are, more relevant. In *The Assistant* identity is communal, firmly grounded in a shared suffering that comes close to agape.

Unsurprisingly, identity is found in time and place. One lives only in the present and only in his day-to-day relations with others. The future is an illusion, especially when it prompts false hopes and desires to escape the present. Early in the novel the characters all make plans. Ida wants to sell the store; Helen dreams of a college education; Nat Pearl and Louis Karp want to marry Helen; Ward Minogue plans the perfect heist. Only Bober and Frankie make no firm plans; only they have no future. Bober lives in a past that is continually present, and Frankie keeps looking for a present that he finds eventually in the Jewish past. Time destroys everyone's illusions of a life better than the one they have. Only the dingy grocery with its endless human obligations is timeless, for it is society itself. In essence Morris escapes time by surrendering to his obligations, including the obligation to die.

Besides living in the here and now, identity requires freedom. The novel continually asks what freedom means, and it answers that freedom is suffering done for love. Malamud's favorite paradox is the free man in prison, a paradox that becomes overt in *The Fixer*. In *The Assistant* he makes identity depend on a tortuous winning of freedom. The final paradox in this novel is Frankie's identity as St. Francis the Jew, modern man freely choosing the burden of a double tradition.

Frankie's conversion to Judaism is the last in a long series of painful choices. The physical pain of circumcision at the end ("For a couple of days he dragged himself around with a pain between his legs") is simply the final expiation for his wrongs against Morris Bober. Furthermore, if we think of identity as a continuum, we see the assistant moving from hoodlum to saint, gradually replacing the teacher, who then dies. Having endured his novitiate, the novice is doubly professed as Franciscan and as Jew. Significantly, his admission to spiritual maturity occurs in March, at the time of Easter and Passover.

Malamud makes four references to St. Francis in the novel, each of which reveals a stage in Frankie's spiritual development. The first is in Sam Pearl's lunch room, across the street from Morris's grocery. Frankie feels uneasy at robbing the old Jew with Ward Minogue. At this point, early in the novel, he sees a picture of St. Francis in a magazine and feels his uneasiness turn to remorse. St. Francis is preaching to the birds—and throughout Malamud's fiction, birds signify the spiritual level of life. Frankie relates the bird anecdote to Sam Pearl and says, "Every time I read about somebody like him I get a feeling inside of me I have to keep from crying. He was born good, which is a talent if you have it" (p. 31).

Like the first mention of St. Francis, the second is also an anecdote. By this time Frankie has become the assistant in the grocery and is in love with Helen, Bober's lovely daughter. He walks her home from the library one night and tells her about St. Francis.

> In the park the moon was smaller, a wanderer in the white sky. He was talking about winter. "It's funny you mentioned snow before," Frank said. "I was reading about the life of St. Francis in the library, and when you mentioned the snow it made me think about this story where he wakes up one winter night, asking himself did he do the right thing to be a monk. My God, he thought, supposing I met some nice young girl and got married to her and by now I had a wife and family? That made him feel bad so he couldn't sleep. He got outside of his straw bed and went outside of the church or monastery or wherever he was staying. The ground was all covered with snow. Out of it he made this snow woman, and he said, 'There, that's my wife.' Then he made two or three kids out of the snow. After, he kissed them all and went inside and laid down in the straw. He felt a whole lot better and fell asleep." (p. 95)

Love is Frankie's version of the future as illusion—at least, physical love. Though the parable is obviously coy, the import is prophetic: Helen is his snow woman, self-denial his vocation. Later, when he attempts to make a flesh-and-blood woman of the snow image, he reenacts his original crime against Bober and repudiates his vocation. His novitiate as sufferer in the second half of *The Assistant* is thus an atonement for rape as well as robbery.

The third Franciscan moment occurs in the park before Helen's near-rape. This time, instead of telling a story, Frankie is feeding the pigeons. He has begun to take on the exterior identity of the man he resembles. The interior struggle takes longer. "Coming up the block, Helen saw a man squatting by one of the benches, feeding the birds. Otherwise, the island was deserted. When the man rose, the pigeons fluttered up with him, a few landing on his arms and shoulders, one perched on his fingers, pecking peanuts from his cupped palm. Another fat bird sat on his hat. The man clapped his hands when the peanuts were gone and the birds, beating their wings, scattered" (p. 118).

Frankie's Jewish identity keeps pace with his Franciscan one. The very next section of the novel is a dialogue between rabbi and student. Frankie learns what it means to be a Jew. He asks Morris why the Jews suffer so much:

> "I suffer for you," Morris said calmly.
> Frankie laid his knife down on the table. His mouth ached.
> "What do you mean?"
> "I mean you suffer for me." (p. 125)

Frankie's knowledge is experimental, not theoretical. He suffers renewed guilt, now not only for the original robbery, but for his petty thefts from the till. Theft symbolizes spiritual imperfection, a necessary condition for perfecting strength in weakness.

The final vision of St. Francis is one with Frankie's Jewish conversion. He sees St. Francis taking Frankie's wooden rose from the trash can where Helen had thrown it. "He tossed it into the air and it turned into a real flower that he caught in his hand. With a bow he gave it to Helen, who had just come out of the house. 'Little sister, here is your little sister the rose.' From him she took it, although it was with the love and best wishes of Frank Alpine" (pp. 245–246). Yet Malamud is too good a writer for easy resolutions. The rose is only a dream. The point is that Frankie is now worthy of the dream; his love is a blooming rose, despite his shortcomings.

Given such a story, the context for celebration is always limited. Here it is the grocery. Bober is the celebrant of banal mysteries: credit to the Drunk Woman, the three-cent roll before dawn to the Polischer, tea and a sympathetic ear for Breitbart. Bober's suffering transforms the grocery into a secular temple. All who enter are his congregation. They dimly realize that he is their scapegoat, their surrogate. Thus his ritualized work—oiling the floor, dragging the milk cases in, shoveling the sidewalk—is a source of spiritual strength for them as well. Morris's suffering purifies the food he dispenses, making sacred the secular fruits.

The other context for celebration is the library, which represents the secular equivalent of spiritual tradition. Frankie's other mentors are Flaubert, Tolstoi, and Dostoyevsky, whom Helen has forced upon him. But it is love, not literature, which draws him to the library. If work is his principal bond with the father, love is that bond with the daughter. In each case, the shared experience extends and renews personal identity.

The overt acts of celebration in *The Assistant* assume the ritual form of lament. For Malamud, the ritual lament always has a liturgical context. Frank laments his unformed life; Breitbart and Morris, their suffering lot; Helen, her lost youth and love; Ida, their poverty. Theirs are all psalms of lamentation. The final lament is the rabbi's eulogy for Morris. But since it occurs outside the context of the grocery, it seems excessive.

Anti-celebration in *The Assistant* is personified in Ward Minogue. Ward is Frankie's alter ego, the bad son of a brutal father. In almost schematic fashion he offers Frankie demonic alternatives to Jewish sonship. He pistol-whips Bober while Frankie offers him a glass of water; he tries to rape Helen, an act which Frankie completes somewhere between love and rage after beating Ward off; he burns Karp's store while Frankie saves Morris from burning his own. Unquestionably Frankie is part Ward, but in the last instance he out-Bobers Bober by rescuing him from his own weakness. The apprentice sufferer assumes the master's role at this point and begins to endure identical indignities—the Polischer's reproaches, the guilty stares of former customers as they hurry by, Breitbart's light bulbs and complaints. He endures the quiet celebration of his own mortality.

In *The Assistant* the feast of everyday contains and transmutes the violent world. As Sidney Richman suggests, "At the most there is, in Martin Buber's famous depiction of the holy men of Chassidism, the 'hallowing of the everyday.' " [3] But celebration in the novel is a holding action. However complete and redemptive, it is beset by its opposite: Karp's liquor store burns down next to Bober's grocery. Anti-celebration, the spirit of riot, runs amok in the *goyische* world. And Malamud, feeling the necessity to live in that world (or at least to try), comes to grips with it in *A New Life* (1961).

Unfortunately, the attempt is unsuccessful. Theme and genre are at one another's throats. The attempt to redeem the time by forging an identity through suffering is undercut by satiric thrusts at academia. The effect is like watching Stephen Dedalus come of age in Laputa. Stephen in this case is one S. Levin, a protean hero whose boundless dreams exceed his ability to make them real. In expanding his narrow world to meet the demands of pluralistic living, Malamud puffs it up beyond belief.

Critics have seen *The Red and the Black, Anna Karenina,* and *Lady Chatterly's Lover* as analogous works, but such comparisons are misleading. The story of an Eastern Jew in a Pacific Coast college is more like *Tristram Shandy,* abounding in private jokes, burlesques, false starts, and delayed birth. After an academic gestation of nine months, Levin's new life begins. Only then do we catch the authentic Malamudian voice: the hero, at last made vulnerable by the will to love, pits his freedom against his fortunes and welcomes the consequences.

Thus *A New Life* seems to be only a preparation for the novel that Malamud did not write. In trying to connect private life and public world, he must connect Levin's past with his present. That past is merely a gratuitous addition halfway through the book, however. Until he conquers Pauline, Levin has been simply a tool for prying up the rocks to look at the academic slugs underneath. When the tool quickens into life we do not believe it.

Another problem is that character and context change simultaneously in *A New Life.* We start from no fixed psychological or moral point, and we have no perspective for viewing Levin's clash with Cascadia College. Pauline Gilley springs to life out of nowhere; Gilley himself changes from caricature to full-blooded antagonist; the mountains and forests of the first half shrink to the dimensions of Levin's bed in the second half of the book. Such changes are justifiable in themselves, but not if Levin is changing at the same time. Elizabeth Bowen reminds us in her "Notes on Writing a Novel" that simultaneous changes in character and physical scene cancel each other out.[4] And so they do in *A New Life.*

A third problem is the air of contrivance about the novel. The physical scene is curiously detached from the human one. This is all the more puzzling when we remember that Malamud spent twelve years at Oregon State (1949–1961), teaching composition and literature. Somehow his acquired experience is unavailable to him; probably he was too close to it. Though Levin's trip across the mountains and some individual scenes ring true, Cascadia College does not. It is inventive in the worst sense, fabricated out of whole cloth.

The lack of a moral center in the novel gives the illusion of freedom in theme and technique. But the irony is that neither develop freely. Like Wallace Stevens' Crispin, Levin is overwhelmed by these jungles of Yucatán. The world is much larger than the humans who inhabit it. Malamud sets the green and fluent mundo against the human world; inhibited by civilization, Levin can avoid neither colds nor cow-pies.

Technically, the book is constrained by burlesque. All the characters except Pauline, Gilley (at the end), and Levin are caricatures; Levin himself is constantly sacrificed for the isolated pratfall. The style reflects the burlesque in deliberately coarsened diction. Levin skids on wet leaves and lands on his head; he rushes along with the other instructors correcting the d.o. (departmental objective examination), "without pausing to drink or pass water"; while making love to Pauline, "Levin experienced a fiery pain in the butt."

Malamud carries this buffoonery surprisingly far for a serious novelist, which he obviously is. Take the pants bit, for example. On his arrival at the Gilleys, Levin gets "a hot gob of tuna fish and potato in his lap." He changes into Gilley's baggy pants, only to have Erik urinate in his lap. Meanwhile, "Gilley was tying dry flies." Later, when Gilley is about to make love to a waitress in a barn, his Syrian roommate steals their clothes. Laverne walks back to Cascadia wearing his pants, while he goes naked. And still later his students howl with laughter after he has taught his first class with his fly down.

Or consider Malamud's burlesque of literary allusions. He has Bucket (more nearly the real hero of *A New Life*) talk like Tristram Shandy. Or again, Leo Duffy, Levin's alter ego, charges into a tea party while the chairman is upstairs taking a bath; Fairchild emerges like the carpenter-husband in "The Miller's Tale": "Half asleep in my tub I was awakened by the commotion and thought the house was burning down—he was loudly repeating the word 'fired.' Naturally I jumped out of the tub, and before I had thought twice, ran out into the living room in my birthday suit—" (p. 46). Or again, Gerald Gilley surprises Levin about to have intercourse with the department spinster in his office; he wants to borrow some Thomas Hardy to help his wife sleep. He asks for *Far from the Madding Crowd*—a ludicrous irony under the circumstances—and gets *Under the Greenwood Tree,* where Levin will shortly make love to Pauline himself.

In essence, then, *A New Life* is a tour de force of individual effects. The burlesque covers uncertainty of purpose, as though Malamud could win his game by scoring so many points. Clearly, once he shifts from the narrow world of the ghetto he loses authentic celebration. The gulf between personal and group celebration in this novel simply polarizes empty ritual and private daydreams.

He tries to bring off private celebration here, but his feasts are at once too forced and too rhetorical to be convincing. His principal device is the technique of the double. The first doppelganger is Mr. Fairchild, the chairman's father. He has Levin's beard and eyes. The tale of the old drunk, so like one of John Cheever's set pieces of comic misfortune, emphasizes the man's weakness for liquor, his good intentions nonetheless, and his excessive guilt for celebrating life. The burlesque account concludes with Emerson's words to Whitman: "I greet you at the beginning of a great career." It will be a short one.

The second double-figure is Leo Duffy, at first only a vague, terrifying rumor. But as the novel goes along, he appears to be Levin's avatar—an Easterner from Chicago, bearded, a rebel, and Pauline Gilley's lover. Both Duffy and the elder Fairchild are bizarre celebrants whose lives are intended to reinforce Levin's. But since they never appear in the book, the effect is limited.

The first official celebration is the department potluck dinner. Fairchild presides as anti-priest. "His wife, the Anti-Liquor League V.P.," sits beside him. The picnic is an occasion for a sermon directed at the sinners in the department: finish the dissertation, publish the textbook, marry. As a community, Cascadia's English department reflects the American spirit during the McCarthy Era; its celebrations are dismal.

By contrast, Malamud makes sex synonymous with freedom and feast. Levin, eager to begin his new life, is constantly interrupted by its fearful, anti-festive tendencies. Sadek forestalls him with Laverne, Gilley with Avis Fliss, social mores with Nadalee Hammerstad. He tries to repress his natural desires for her in wild fantasies of incest. After he has made love to her, genuine guilt prohibits him from further contacts. A large part of that guilt is the anti-sex, anti-liquor, anti-festive air in which Levin lives.

In his search for love, Levin goes from burlesque celebration with Nadalee (no-haven) to its authentic counterpart with Pauline. The Nadalee affair is set in an out-of-season motel on the foggy Oregon coast. Levin comes on as a bumbling Jewish conquistador (Cortez—no, Balboa) discovering the Pacific for the first time.

> There stood Nadalee in a sheer nightie.
> "Mr. Levin—I mean Seymour."
> "Nadalee—I got lost." Before he could say where or why, she had shucked off her garment and her gloriously young body shed light as he hungrily embraced it. (p. 143)

Levin's Glorious America ends, geographically and morally, in a dingy motel room—an echo of *Lolita*. In addition, Levin has come to Nadalee as the city slicker conned by country bumpkins, a stock butt in American folklore. In sum, the burlesque celebration inverts the international theme. The innocent European is corrupted by the virgin wilderness.

With Pauline in the woods, the glory is accidental. Levin runs into her while bird-watching one warm afternoon in late January (the meaning of the bird motif remains constant in Malamud). Her kisses launch him "in flight, bearded bird, dream figure." Their union on the pine needles is spontaneous and free. "He was throughout conscious of the marvel of it—in the open forest, nothing less, what triumph!" (p. 185). The sexual feast unlocks Levin's heart, and he pours out his history of past humiliations. But his past suffering is manufactured for the occasion. Too late Malamud forges it for his character. The sunlight on his shoes in that distant basement is only a bulb clicked on by the author.

But celebration is dangerous. "Sometimes he silently celebrated his performance in the open—his first married woman, sex uncomplicated in a bed of leaves, short hours, good pay. He was invigorated by the experience, one he would not have predicted for himself. A few minutes later he was soberly conscious of this figure within—an old friend with a broken nose warning him against risking his new identity. The new life was very new" (p. 189).

Yet the suffering is superimposed for thematic purposes on the romantic love story. Malamud manufactures a tension between Levin's identity as lover and his career as instructor. This doesn't work. Of all Malamud's heroes, S. Levin is least likely to confuse his subjective reality and his objective position. Levin develops new identities and celebrates them in dreams, but we do not believe them: Levin the scholar; Levin the department chairman; Levin, the new Duffy; Levin the victim and father. This dizzying sequence of new lives obscures his real rebirth in love.

The plot complications are both gratuitous and harmful. At the end of the novel Levin is less a person than a typical victim. In exile from his society, he sees himself imprisoned by the desire to love: "The prison was really himself, flawed edifice of failures, each locking up tight the one before. He had failed at his best plans, who could say he wouldn't with her? Possibly he already had and would one day take off in the dark as she lay in bed. Unless the true prison was to stick it out chained to her ribs. He would look like a free man but whoever peered into his eyes would see the lines of a brick wall" (pp. 331–332).

Malamud is setting up a contrast between the false view of the self and the true one. But Levin is scarcely the man to accept a role passively, at the expense of his immense vitality, even though that role be so thematically important as victim. Somehow the victimization doesn't really hurt.

The last pages of *A New Life* bring Levin to birth. This moment of doubt is set between two tremendous assertions of faith, one a celebration of freedom, the other of paternity. In the interview with Gilley, Malamud establishes the connection between Levin's fantasy self and his real one. He accepts Gilley's terms for getting the children and promises to leave teaching forever.

"Goodbye to your sweet dreams," Gilley called after him.
"I hope yours are sweet."
"An older woman than yourself and not dependable, plus two adopted kids, no choice of yours, no job or promise of one, and other assorted headaches. Why take that load on yourself?"
"Because I can, you son of a bitch." (p. 330)

The second celebration, of paternity, is probably gratuitous, a final reflection of the narrator's heavy hand in the novel. Pauline confesses that she is two months pregnant. Thus the new life, a rebirth into suffering, is thematically extended by a new pregnancy. And the eastward movement is towards the past, towards roots and intelligible social forms.

Unfortunately this movement is possible only at the expense of the novel as a whole. Celebration does not connect role and identity here, as it did in *The Assistant*. Rather, it separates them. Malamud's engagement with the outside world results in an orderly retreat from the field, a retreat that carries him all the way back to an earlier time and a different place, Tsarist Russia.

The Fixer (1966) is a major novel. It reworks the materials of *The Assistant* on a broader scale. If it does not show forth viable celebrations, it reveals what is wrong with the ones we have. Furthermore, it moves towards a more drastic definition of the split between identity and community. And it defines the role of victim, finally, as avenging angel.

Perhaps the most obvious difference between *The Fixer* and Malamud's previous novels is its scope. Malamud is concerned with the Jew in history—nothing less. He defines Jewish tradition as a continual victimization, an indictment against history. Yakov Bok, the archetypal Jew, turns his identity as victim against his persecutors. Unlike Morris Bober, who originates in the Book of Job, Bok derives from the Book of Macchabees. Suffering arms him to destroy the state: "Let the Tsar jig on his polished floor. I shit my death on him" (*The Fixer*, p. 269).

The militant note is new in Malamud, though the quixotic Levin marks the transition from Bober to Bok. Other qualities are new as well: a more powerful style based on meticulous observation of cruel details, and a concept of celebration as the expression of organized hatred. The suspicion and fear which characterize Cascade College's English department now describe a whole civilization, Tsarist Russia, and its attitude towards the Jews. Public celebration can express only full-throated anti-Semitism. Yakov Bok is thus a mirror reflecting self-hate and a wish for national suicide.

The novel describes Bok's coming to Kiev one cold October day in 1910, a handyman looking for work. The atmosphere is ripe for a pogrom: defeat in the Russo-Japanese War, the Revolution of 1905, and the massacre at the Winter Palace have left the nation looking for a Jewish scapegoat. It finds him in Bok, whose kindness to a drunken old bigot, Lebedev, leads to his vulnerable position as overseer of a brickyard. He alienates the employees when he discovers them stealing bricks. When a twelve-year-old boy is found murdered in a cave, Bok is accused; he is the Jew. Though he has previously denied that identity, events force it upon him through three years of suffering in prison. At the end he turns that suffering against his persecutors.

The connection between identity and celebration is quite close. Bok enters the novel a freethinker; in sheer terror of an anti-Semitic boatman, he drops his bag of prayer things into the Dnieper. He assumes a Russian name and a false identity as overseer, but he becomes unhappy in the role. "Something that unexpectedly bothered him was that he was no longer using his tools. He had built himself a bed, table, and chair, also some shelves on the wall, but this was done in the first few days after he had come to the brickyard. He was afraid that if he didn't go on carpentering he might forget how and thought he had better not" (p. 61). The anxiety results from his half-conscious rejection of a false identity and leads to a true one.

The false feast is the dinner with Zina, Lebedev's daughter. Starved for affection, the poor girl invites him to dine with her "In celebration of the completion of your fine work, and most of all, to your future relationship with Papa, though he has already retired and we shall be alone" (p. 48). Fine food, sad music, and sexual need lead Yakov to Zina's bedroom. But she is unclean. Bok the freethinker will not touch her, however; he will not violate the Law.

Counterpointing this false feast is Passover. Yakov rescues an old Jew who has been stoned by Russian boys. If the rescue of Lebedev has led to a false identity, the rescue of the old Jew leads toward a true one. Like Zina, the old man bleeds at his feast. But this blood and this feast are eucharistic. "He said the blessing for matzos, and sighing, munched a piece. It came as a surprise to the fixer that it was Passover. He was moved by a strong emotion and had to turn away till it was gone" (p. 65).

Henceforth the novel probes the meaning of Yakov's identity

as Jew. He undergoes a process of death and rebirth which is counterpointed by feasts of hate. From innocent peasant to sufferer; from sufferer to indignant citizen; from indignant citizen to orthodox Jew; from orthodox Jew to Christian and back again, now to self-accusations of guilt for Raisl's suffering; from guilt to forgiveness of Raisl and acknowledgement of her bastard son as his own; from reconciled husband, unreconstructed Jew, and defiant victim to would-be regicide and national hero—thus the progress of Yakov Bok, fixer.

Bok's persecutors attack the very basis of Jewish identity, its traditions and rituals. When it finally comes, the indictment attacks the festive traditions of Judaism as criminal. Yakov's freethinking is called a fabrication by the indictment, "in order to hide from the legal authorities that he had committed a vile religious murder of a child for the sole and evil purpose of providing his Hasidic compatriots with the uncorrupted human blood needed to bake the Passover matzos and unleavened cakes" (p. 297). Conviction on such a charge is a mandate for genocide.

True celebration, then, is outlawed, possible only among outlaws. Each communion between Yakov Bok and another is a fatal feast: Bibikov, the inquiring magistrate, shares a Turkish cigarette with Yakov and is driven by the prosecuting attorney to hang himself in the next cell. Fetyukov shares a sausage with Yakov and is shot by a guard while trying to escape; Kogin, Bok's guard, shares his woes with him and is shot by the deputy warden while protesting the inhuman treatment of his prisoner. All those who touch Yakov Bok with human compassion celebrate his suffering with him, and so die.

The authorities, on the other hand, celebrate hate. Father Anastasy, a clerical embezzler unfrocked by the Roman Church, leads the fixer to the cave where the boy's body lies "disinterred from his grave for the occasion, lying naked in death, the wounds of his grey shrunken pitiful body visible in the light of two long thickly dripping white candles burning at his large head and small feet" (p. 137). In the background Marfa Golov, strumpet and real murderer of her son, weeps copiously, "and Father Anastasy, the stink of garlic rising from his head, fell on his knees and with a quiet moan began to pray." The event is a black mass, an appalling parody of Christian ritual.

Slowly Bok turns his cell into a temple appropriate for the celebration of suffering—in this way his action resembles Bober's in
The Assistant. Bok discovers an ancient prayer shawl and phylac-
teries there; one morning he awakens to find pages torn from the
Old Testament littering his cell; again, moved by a desire for
sanity, he composes his own psalm of lamentation and chants it to
his guard. Yet Bok is a Jew without faith—"He thought of himself
pursuing his enemies with God at his side, but when he looked at
God all he saw or heard was a loud Ha Ha. It was his own
imprisoned laughter" (p. 209).

The prison tests his will by offering freedom in exchange for
his identity. He dreams of Marfa Golov spreading her legs for
him; he is offered passage to anywhere in the world; Raisl comes
to him bearing a confession for him to sign. His enemies even offer
amnesty, in a false celebration of the Tsar's mercy: "this was the
year of the three-hundredth anniversary of the rule of the House
of Romanov and . . . the Tsar, in celebration, would issue a ukase
amnestying certain classes of criminals. Yakov's name would be
listed among them. He was to be pardoned and returned to his
village" (p. 294). But Yakov will not accept a pardon; he demands trial by jury.

The whole contest between the state and Yakov Bok rests on
freedom of choice. Malamud asks the question he asked about
Frankie Alpine's conversion, and about Levin's marriage to Pauline: why does a man choose to suffer? In *The Assistant*, the answer is love. In *A New Life*, it is a defiant affirmation of personal
dignity. Here in the fourth novel that defiance becomes more
solemn, even apocalyptic.

> One thing I've learned, he thought, there's no such thing as an un-
> political man, especially a Jew. You can't be one without the other,
> that's clear enough. You can't sit still and see yourself destroyed.
> Afterwards he thought, Where there's no fight for it there's no
> freedom. What is it Spinoza says? If the state acts in ways that are
> abhorrent to human nature it's the lesser evil to destroy it. Death
> to the anti-Semites! Long live revolution! Long live liberty! (p.
> 335)

For Bok the final identity as Macchabee is the only answer.
Like Baldwin, he foretells the fire next time. The cost of this terri-

ble freedom is isolation. Since it is founded on a painfully achieved self, it cannot allow easy feasts. Malamud has divorced feast from identity, finally. The pattern of life is unique; experience is incommunicable.

Yet there remains a spiritual celebration that transcends and organizes political chaos. Bok's defiance is the ultimate witness he can offer to his own experience, an oblation for Zhenia's murder. The final irony is a bracing exhilaration that the broken Jew redeems Gentile sins. Among the crowd who watch his ride to trial are other Jews—weeping, clawing their faces, waving, and shouting his name. Malamud suggests that the only true celebration is after all spiritual, without earthly counterpart. Jew and Gentile, those who extend their hearts to Bok on his ride to judgment share in his death and assert resurrection.

The difference between the stories in *The Magic Barrel* (1958) and in *Idiots First* (1963) is roughly that between the private world and the public one. Predictably, Malamud does better with the earlier collection. The thirteen stories in *The Magic Barrel* are versions of life in the ghetto: three Jewish laments, two Jewish comedies, two Jewish fantasies, two Jewish-Italian comedies, one Italian comedy, and three public stories.[5] The Jewish stories reveal a richness of material and a depth of insight matched only by the later stories of Flannery O'Connor. Two of the three Italian stories are weak, but the best of them, "The Last Mohican" (really a Jewish story in an Italian setting), ranks with the title story as the crowning achievement of the collection. The three public tales are generally grim, manifesting an isolation unrelieved by communal experience.

More specifically, the best stories in *The Magic Barrel* reveal various occasions and forms of celebration. On the whole they point toward *The Assistant* in form, theme, subject matter, and refusal to be evicted from his apartment. The story celebrates the Jew's identity as sufferer, and foreshadows the Bober-Alpine relationship in Kessler and Ignace. At the end of the story Ignace, like Frankie Alpine, assumes the Jew's identity as public mourner. And the ritual lament in the story suggests *The Assistant*.

A similar tale is "The Loan." Here the context is entirely Jewish and traditional. Old friends are reunited in Lieb's bakery after a fifteen-year separation. Kobotsky and the Liebs reveal private grief to each other and celebrate their renewed identities in remembered suffering. The ritual lament is marked by a literal burnt offering: "A cloud of smoke billowed out at her. The loaves in the tray were blackened bricks—charred corpses. . . . Kobotsky and the baker embraced and sighed over their lost youth. They pressed mouths together and parted forever" (*Magic Barrel*, p. 191).

A third story, "A Summer's Reading," is perhaps the most beautifully controlled piece in the collection. George Stoyonovich tries to pass off his unemployment as a summer reading program. The community subtly grants him status as a student, but the lie so crushes him that, after its exposure, he charges to the library, counts off a hundred books at random, and sits down to read. Again, as in *The Assistant*, the library is the context for celebration and renewal.

"The Last Mohican" points beyond *The Assistant* to *The Fixer*. Like Bok, Fidelman finds freedom and identity in Jewish tradition. He comes to Italy to write a study of Giotto. Instead of an artistic past he discovers a personal one, in the fantastic Susskind. Fidelman's illumination comes in the ghetto, where he is seeking Susskind and his stolen first chapter. Ultimately he finds his identity in giving his second suit to Susskind, who has "done him a favor" and burned the chapter. The suit that Fidelman surrenders celebrates his Jewish roots with Susskind. The act prepares him for a rebirth in later stories as lover and painter.

"The Magic Barrel" is doubtless the best of Malamud's stories, even though it has no demonstrable links with the four novels. It unites sacred and secular celebration in the love between a faithless rabbi and a young prostitute. Like Fidelman, Leo Finkle has a position but not an identity. Through the agency of another chimerical teacher, the marriage broker Salzman, Leo learns the emptiness of the Law without the spirit. The story literally celebrates the wedding of flesh and spirit. When Leo meets Stella Salzman, the paradoxical celebration of ecstasy and grief reaches a triumphant climax.

> From afar he saw that her eyes—clearly her father's—were filled with desperate innocence. He pictured, in her, his own redemption.

Violins and lit candles revolved in the sky. Leo ran forward with flowers outthrust.

Around the corner, Salzman, leaning against a wall, chanted prayers for the dead. (p. 214)

In "The Magic Barrel" love and celebration link time and eternity, man and God.

Idiots First reveals Malamud's attempts to cope with the outside world. As in *A New Life*, however, his efforts too often spill over into exaggeration and burlesque. None of the stories develop ghetto experience; all of them reveal either fantastic clowning or an attempt to assimilate Jewish experience into larger public patterns. The collection includes two Jewish melodramas, two Jewish fantasy-burlesques, two Jewish-Italian burlesques, two Italian stories, three public stories, and a scene from a play. In *Idiots First* Malamud has escaped the ghetto, but he has lost the shape which ghetto life gave his fiction. And adequate substitutes are hard to come by.

Take the two Fidelman stories, for example. "Still Life" describes Fidelman's rebirth as a lover, "Naked Nude" his renewal as a painter. But Malamud clowns his way to affirmation; this is a different Fidelman, a goy. The looseness of social forms dissipates identity and freedom. In "Still Life" sexual possession burlesques sacramental confession and the Crucifixion. In "Naked Nude" art is a violent swindle.

Surprisingly, the best of these stories, "Black Is My Favorite Color" and "The German Refugee," connect Jewish experience with the outside world and thus advance Malamud's art. The former describes a Jew's attempts to love Negroes. One might argue that Negroes are simply dark Jews, and that Malamud exchanges one ghetto-prison for another. But the quality of Nat Lime's defeat reveals an acceptance and a worldly wisdom that Malamud's other Jews do not possess.

"The German Refugee" looks ahead to *The Fixer*. The refugee is a critic and journalist who attempts a lecturing career in New York. The time is apocalyptic: like Yakov Bok's 1913, Oskar Gassner's 1939 is the eve of national suicide. The story is even more somber than the novel. Bok finds a new identity in opposition, while Gassner cannot. His lecture on Whitman is a success; for the moment, poetry celebrates the international language of man's hopes for *Brudermensch*.

But the lecture is only a temporary bridge between old life and new. Oskar's wife has been purged by the Nazis; language alone cannot contain personal loss. Confronted with Bok's choice of suicide or martyrdom, Oskar chooses suicide. The private feast of language has been destroyed by brutal public action, rendering his own sundered experience unlivable.

We see a grim, iron quality in these two stories, a quality that anticipates the fourth novel. But Malamud's turn toward pluralism has left him with no viable celebrations. Does the counterturn toward the past in *The Fixer* indicate retreat and withdrawal from contemporary life? So far, Malamud has traced an increasing gulf between private and public celebrations. Unless he can find new vitality in old rites, or discover new ones entirely, he cannot continue to develop.

Yet his achievement to date is impressive. Malamud's reputation is assured in contemporary letters by the best stories in *The Magic Barrel*, by *The Assistant*, and by *The Fixer*. He takes chances with his art and succeeds with remarkable frequency. And no one has been able to make better public use of traditional experience than he has. His celebration of identity as redemptive suffering has given a new direction to contemporary American literature. Together with the more unbuttoned Saul Bellow, Bernard Malamud has shown us that spiritually we are all Jews.[6]

11 &~ Saul Bellow:
Belonging to the World in General

AMONG THESE ten novelists none is more solidly immersed in the American sensibility than Saul Bellow. Marcus Klein concludes his chapter on Bellow in *After Alienation* by calling his fiction crucial. And so it is—crucial, protean, endlessly varied, reflecting the indiscriminate glut of contemporary American experience. The composite Bellow hero is a drifter, part bum and part philosopher; self-obsessed, witty, naïvely optimistic; down on his luck, but always waiting for it to change; half hero and half buffoon; alive. As several critics have observed, vitality informs all the Bellow heroes. Augie, Henderson, and Herzog rise out of these novels to gigantic proportions. Yet strangely enough each man is as much the sum total of current social experience as he is an individual.

Bellow's heroes celebrate reality in festive approval. At the heart of their celebration is the affirmation of life in the face of death. We may read Bellow's novels as the search for an appropriate form to contain the festive spirit; shapeless affirmation is only bravura rhetoric. Character, style, setting, and plot reflect the experience of a talent engaged with reality and determined to make it, or remake it, human. The test of humanity is the extent and the significance of Bellow's ability to celebrate the real.[1]

Dangling Man is on the surface at least an inauspicious beginning. Joseph awaits a draft call that never comes. Jobless, defensive, and out of place in a wartime economy, he withdraws to his room, bickers with his fellow tenants, and transcribes his notes in his journal—the novel itself. Joseph's problem is to join the world; until he does, he and everyone else will question his very right to exist. Joseph lives on the edge, or rather dangles over it.

The root of his problem is his desire to be a whole man. Society is suspicious of whole men; they cannot be pigeonholed. Realizing this, Joseph does his best to fit in: "whether I liked it or not, they were my generation, my society, my world. We were figures in the same plot, eternally fixed together." [2] But he cannot do so. The alienation he suffers (and all of Bellow's heroes are preeminent sufferers) is forced upon him by a society that refuses to allow persons to exist without roles. Yet his estrangement, with its existential overtones, leaves him in a position of great dignity. He is unaccommodated man, an impartial witness in the trial of his world.

Joseph's early attempts to fit into that world on his own terms are comic disasters: he shouts at a former Communist comrade in a restaurant, he is discovered spanking his fifteen-year-old niece in the bedroom. One's own terms will not do, Bellow suggests. One must meet the world halfway. Unlike Malamud, Bellow seeks a pluralistic context for that meeting and its celebrations. If authentic celebration is unavailable in contemporary life, one can at least discover that significant fact.

Two examples of false festivity indicate that wartime feasts are dismal. The first is a party at which the hostess insists on being hypnotized. The party leads him to reflect with Hobbes that life is "nasty, brutish, and short. . . . There were so many treasons; they were a medium, like air, like water; they passed in and out of you, they made themselves your accomplices; nothing was impenetrable to them" (p. 38). Minna's party is a treason against their common need to celebrate the real.

Another false feast involves Joseph's older brother, the rich Amos. Invited to Christmas dinner, Joseph and Iva see how his brother's family despise them as poor relations. He and Iva do not exist; they have no money. Money is real; Amos is real. Thus Bellow initiates the theme of the Faustian double (usually a brother) that runs through his work. The alter ego is almost always rich; he has made a comfortable accommodation with the world.[3] The terms of the struggle with Amos are Beethoven and Cugat, but the issue is fundamental. One must choose either status or isolation. Paradoxically, social status deprives a man of real community. Only the outcast, the grotesque, and the picaro are lucky enough to live in the real world, a world of suffering humanity. (Here Bellow comes closest to the perspective of Flannery O'Connor). Thus Asa Leventhal lives, but Kirby Allbee does not; Augie March lives, but his brother Simon does not; Herzog lives, but Gersbach does not. As Bellow sees it, one chooses either to open himself to experience or to seek refuge in comfortable illusions. All consequences follow upon that crucial choice.

The consequences for Joseph are the army. He chooses to be drafted. And the choice is a liberating one, the last step in a series of decisions about the nature of one's pact with society. These decisions always balance some comfortable illusion against an equivalent reality. For instance, Joseph rejects the illusion of money as a badge of identity when he refuses the $100 Christmas present from Amos. Later, rejecting a liaison with Kitty and the outlook of his friend Alf, Joseph refuses the illusions of lust and irresponsibility.

Obvious choices are no real problem for Joseph. But when he must decide between splendid isolation and involvement with the sordid reality of 1943, the choice is more difficult. Joseph's dialogue with "the Spirit of Alternatives" turns on the issue of a social self versus a separate destiny. If we are integrated by our quest "for pure freedom," how can we be said to have any identity as such? For Joseph and for Bellow, the answer is that the demands placed upon the individual are unique. One achieves freedom in his own way by an individual act. The circumstances requiring that act and one's response to them are one's separate destiny.

Yet this is much too pat and too theoretical. In practice Bellow shows that the comic irony of Joseph's alienation extends even past the moment of surrender. The army will not let him be a victim; when he appears before the draft board to volunteer, the office is closed. He volunteers anyway by leaving a note on the closed door, but the heroism has gone out of the deed. Irony deflates his free choice, thus restoring him to anticlimatic reality. If one acts he only enters a situation where he can be acted upon, as the final journal entry indicates:

April 9

This is my last civilian day. Iva has packed my things. It is plain that she would like to see me show a little more grief at leaving.

For her sake, I would like to. And I am sorry to leave her, but I am not at all sorry to part with the rest of it. I am no longer to be held accountable for myself; I am grateful for that. I am in other hands, relieved of self-determination, freedom canceled.

Hurray for regular hours!
And for the supervision of the spirit!
Long live regimentation! (p. 126)

Irony qualifies Joseph's social integration and merely postpones the difficult choice he will have to make after the army. Of greater significance is Bellow's own uncertainty about the terms of social regeneration. *Dangling Man* is claustrophobic, offering only the qualified promise of release at the end. Thus the festive spirit of Joseph's language is self-mocking and does not reflect his own experience. Whatever celebration permeates this first novel is tentative and skeptical.

If anything *The Victim* (1947) is even more claustrophobic than *Dangling Man*. Asa Leventhal must answer Cain's question for himself; Bellow carefully cuts away any family or social props as Asa struggles to refuse and then to accept responsibility for Kirby Allbee. The symbolic overtones of this spare narrative are extraordinary: the motif of the double embraces the polarities of Jew and Gentile, identity and anonymity, guilt and retribution—in short, of American life. Yet even in his isolation, Leventhal struggles to make a series of commitments, to affirm a web of responsibilities that free him from isolation.

Leventhal's love for his wife is firmer and more fruitful than Joseph's love for Iva: at the end of the novel Mary is expecting. Furthermore Leventhal's family sense is stronger—contrast the farcical spanking of Etta in *Dangling Man* with Asa's effort to get his nephew away from his mother and into the hospital. Asa Leventhal is vitally engaged with Allbee. Isolated by hostility and indifference, he nonetheless can affirm the responsibilities that Allbee (All-Being, Everybody Else) denies.

The Leventhal-Allbee conflict is a distillation of elements in the American experience. Leventhal incarnates the religious, principled, democratic elements in American tradition, despite his Jewish identity and his general air of comic estrangement from society. Allbee, ironically enough a descendant of Governor Winthrop, incarnates the tradition of the New—the American without a past, principles, or freedom—amorphous, opportunistic, cruelly anti-social, anti-Semitic, barbaric.

In a larger sense Allbee threatens more than Leventhal; he threatens society itself. The New, formless and chaotic, threatens to destroy the Old. First Allbee destroys Leventhal's peace of mind; then in successive stages he invades his privacy, his marriage, his home, his bed, and his very life. Leventhal's final break with Allbee comes only when he fills the apartment with oven gas in a futile attempt to destroy himself—and Leventhal. As a principle of self-destruction Allbee brings home to Leventhal the terror of a life without identity. As a symbol of elements inherent in American life he brings home to the reader the terrible consequences of a life without shape.

The brilliance of *The Victim* lives in its balancing of realistic against symbolic elements. Leventhal always responds to Allbee's human suffering, but he cannot respond to his inhuman will to die. Allbee can lay claims on Leventhal because of their common manhood, but he cannot force him to accept suicide, the ultimate irresponsible act.

Allbee educates Leventhal to accept his responsibility for the suffering of others, even though he must be forced into it. Indeed, the whole action of the novel is Leventhal's effort to make vital distinctions, to accept Allbee's humanity while rejecting his cosmology: " 'Hot stars and cold hearts, that's your universe!' " At heart is a radical difference in the nature of being and of human freedom. Allbee takes seriously the ironic dodge that closes *Dangling Man:* he is not responsible—long live regimentation!

Since the struggle to accept one's responsibility is a lonely one, the setting of the novel is appropriately bare. This New York is as empty of props as a Beckett stage, and almost as menacing. The opening paragraph establishes the setting of muffled, gray desolation in which this spiritual struggle takes place: "On some nights New York is as hot as Bangkok. The whole continent seems to have moved from its place and slid nearer the equator, the bitter gray Atlantic to have become green and tropical, and the people, thronging the streets, barbaric fellahin among the stupendous monuments of their mystery, the lights of which, a dazing profusion, climb upward endlessly into the heat of the sky" (p. 1).

These crowds and these lights only underscore Leventhal's problem: to make human, moral decisions in a setting that seemingly denies that possibility.

The other characters in the novel reveal how fragile the social bond really is. Harkavy, Allbee's friend, is willing to blame Leventhal for the loss of Allbee's job, but he refuses to become involved in the consequences of his accusation. Williston, another friend, cannot understand Leventhal's concern for Allbee and tries to buy off his own conscience with ten dollars, a gift that Allbee never receives. Closer to home, Max, Leventhal's brother, is simply a benign version of Allbee. He comes home too late to save his boy from death. What is worse, he cannot see the connection between death and his own irresponsibility. He "doesn't expect much" of life; he feels "half burned out already." To this Leventhal replies, shaken, "Half burned? I'm older than you and I don't say that" (p. 242).

Even the two epigraphs reinforce the theme. The first is an anecdote about personal guilt from the *Thousand and One Nights*; the second describes the ocean of despairing faces that De Quincy sees in *The Pains of Opium*. Individual experience only repeats group experience. If the many, like Allbee, choose to depend on the few and despair, the few must assume their burden as best they can.

Where then is the note of celebration in *The Victim?* Implicitly it is suggested throughout by Leventhal's acceptance of Allbee. Explicitly it appears in the comic coda, chapter 24. Taking place several years later, it reveals Job after his trial, given back twice over all that he had lost. Leventhal and Mary are attending the theatre when Mary sees Yvonne Crane, an aging movie star, arrive. She is with Allbee. Later, with Leventhal, Allbee's affluent mask slips—"Allbee did not look good. . . . [His eyes] had a fabric quality, crumpled and blank. . . . His continued smile gave a touch of cynicism to the sensational, terrible look of pain that rose to his eyes" (pp. 292–293).

As a celebration, the play itself is not very meaningful. It is "sentimental and untrue." But it reveals the chasm that separates true festivity from false. Leventhal goes to the play to please his wife; for them the play is a celebration of the life she will soon bear. For Allbee, public recognition through the movie star is also appropriate. The play is an anti-festival, revealing the emptiness of his heart. He tells Leventhal: "I'm the type that comes to terms with whoever runs things. What do I care? The world wasn't made exactly for me. What am I going to do about it?" (p. 294). Ironically, he says that he is "enjoying life." Yet this surrender of his freedom is only an acting out of his death wish. Leventhal of course does believe the world was made for him. Or more precisely, since Allbee generally parodies belief, Leventhal has made the world over and made it human.

The Victim is a fine, taut novel. It generates considerably more tension than its predecessor, because it reworks the earlier material in more dramatic terms. The stakes are higher here. Commitment to the social self is more difficult but also more necessary. And the effort to live is an obscure, private celebration for Leventhal.

In these severely enclosed novels Bellow explores the individual's ability to find a private celebration in lieu of a public one. *The Adventures of Augie March* (1953) is a reversal of form entirely. Bellow enlarges individual experience to mythic dimensions. Augie is his instrument for celebrating American life at large. Hitherto he has worked outward from the individual to the world. But in *Augie March* Bellow stands on the periphery of an ever-widening circle, looking toward the center of human experience. Indeed, the circle is the dominant metaphor in the novel. People occur almost cyclically in Augie's life. At various points he learns from them and defines himself anew as they recur.

Another important metaphor is plasticity. Like the Invisible Man Augie is a construct of others. "All the influences were lined up waiting for me. I was born, and there they were to form me, which is why I can tell you more of them than of myself" (p. 43). In his plasticity Augie assumes protean shapes. Half-seriously, Bellow develops him as an apotheosis of American experience during the thirties.

Celebrations appear frequently in *Augie March;* Bellow demonstrates a boundless appetite for all forms of social integration. His comic inventiveness is founded in large measure on the relationships he establishes with his society. Manifestly, Augie reflects Bellow's own attempts to give form to the turmoil of American experience in the thirties; if he doesn't emerge as a character in his own right the defect is of secondary importance. Bellow's purpose requires a significant technical shift, however, from the closed to the open form. The constant is the need to accept and to integrate private experience with national experience.

A consequence of the open form is the shift in the background characters from crowds to communities. The faceless mob in *The Victim* is other and unreachable. Note the De Quincy epigraph: "Be that as it may, now it was that upon the rocking waters of the ocean the human face began to reveal itself; the sea appeared paved with innumerable faces, upturned to the heavens; faces, imploring, wrathful, despairing; faces that surged upward by thousands, by myriads, by generations. . . ."

Compare this passage with one of the many crowd passages in *Augie March*: "It was not only for me that being moored wasn't permitted; there was general motion, as of people driven from angles and corners into the open, by places being valueless and inhospitable to them. In the example of the Son of Man having no place to lay His head; or belonging to the world in general; except that the illuminated understanding of this was absent, nobody much guessing what was up on the face of the earth" (p. 160). In *The Victim* Bellow stresses identity versus the crowd; here he suggests identity within it. The identity search is corporate.

Hence the faces in these crowds take form and shape: the poor college students, the chambermaids, the hobos, odd-jobbers, coal dealers, in-laws, and merchant mariners. Augie is their spokesman and their vicar. "I suffered over Joe Gorman, caught and beat," Augie says. The voice is Walt Whitman's.

Whitman, perhaps, is the key to both style and theme in *Augie March*. The epic poem rather than the picaresque novel offers us the proper analogy. Augie's experience is the national experience—his name "Augie" is emblematic. The eye marches through the terrain of American life. Even his initials suggest the identification between man and country. In the Whitman tradition Augie is the free man, the nonspecialist: "Lord, what a runner after good things, servant of love, embarker on schemes, recruit of sublime ideas, and good time Charlie!" At the end Augie becomes Columbus himself: "Why, I am a sort of Columbus of those near-at-hand and believe you can come to them in this immediate *terra incognita* that spreads out in every gaze" (p. 536).

Thus engaged in the national experience, the novel celebrates freedom, hope, and joy. Indeed, it celebrates these feelings more than it demonstrates them, as Ihab Hassan points out in *Radical Innocence*. On the other hand, celebration is basically religious and nonrational. Augie's celebration is thus the product of a basically sacred attitude toward life.

That attitude balances rather evenly between individual and corporate experience. Augie is a Jew, and his ethnic and familial past give his American character a unique stamp. On the level of corporate experience, Augie witnesses death, a birth, an abortion, two marriages, war, several love affairs, labor riots, crime, and countless changes of fortune. The public character of his life defines the growth and development of America from the twenties with its Chicago hoods to the forties with its international swindlers.

On the individual level, *The Adventures of Augie March* is a bildungsroman. Six or seven characters educate Augie to life. He learns something from each of them. In the early chapters Grandma Lausch dominates him. With her Old World ways, her fierce Jewish pride, and her stubborn refusal to accommodate the world, she impresses an indelible mark on his plastic features. Her death marks his initiation into a pluralistic society. Augie must reconcile his Jewish past and the secular present. Yet Grandma Lausch saves him from the complete secularity of his lost brother Simon. He is always "a sucker for family life." At the end experience has prepared him for it: "it's unborn children I pour over far oftener than business deals."

Einhorn, "the first superior man I knew," initiates Augie into that business world. Here too we feel the power of the family in the patriarchal commissioner, Einhorn's father, and in its effect on his weak son Arthur. From Einhorn Augie learns that he has opposition in him. He can resist, he can say no. Periodically Augie returns to this foster father for the support that knowledge of the world can give him. Eventually of course he outgrows his need for it.

But Einhorn has performed a vital function in making Augie aware of his ability to resist. Augie needs that capacity to cope with Renling, the next dominant figure. Renling is a counter-father or false parent. The Renlings' wish to adopt him is an attempt to destroy Augie's familial past. Yet as Augie says, "I had family enough to suit me and history to be loyal to, not as though I had been gotten off of a stock pile" (p. 153). In return for his identity, the Renlings can offer him only money and fancy clothes.

Augie's brother Simon on the other hand has a much greater claim on him, and more persuasive arguments. He offers Augie money, marriage, and social position. The struggle with Simon is Augie's most difficult. Simon's success, like Amos', is bought at the cost of his freedom. To begin with, he has married on the rebound, in a gross parody of celebration. He has locked himself into a family coal dealership with his huge but soulless in-laws; he would have Augie do likewise. But Augie stays loose; he must know love before he can accept marriage. Thus he is ready for the next stage in his education, the amorous.

Mimi and Thea dominate the middle stretches of the book. Their function is to prepare Augie for love. From Mimi, love's restless anarchist, Augie learns "that everyone sees to it his fate is shared. Or tries to see to it" (p. 211). His involvement with Mimi, though nonsexual, is spiritual and liberating. She frees him from the marriage that Simon has planned for him. This freedom enables him to love.

Thea is his first occasion to do so. The episode with her is the longest in the novel, covering six chapters (14–19). What destroys their love is her inflated image of him. Augie has to be someone special and he isn't. On the other hand, her suffering cannot really touch him; and this, Augie realizes, is his own fault.

Caligula, the cowardly eagle, is Augie's comic counterpart. In a passage that reads like a burlesque of *The Plumed Serpent*, Thea (the goddess) reveals Augie's saving human fallibility. The quixotic mate spurs his old jade down a mountain path after a giant iguana and is thrown. Thea is furious: she loves power, and Augie has been deposed. Her vain attempt to drape him in the trappings of a power he never possessed is transparent self-deification.

Stella completes Augie's education in love. Like him she is affable, with a streak of resistance. She tells him, "Oh, you don't have to apologize. We know what the score is here, pretty much. I admit I was often looking, and I have thought of you. But one of the things I thought is that you and I are the kind of people other people are always trying to fit into their schemes. So suppose we didn't play along, then what?" (p. 384). Her problem like Augie's is one of identity. Each has endless possibilities but no direction in choosing among them.

And this is the problem Americans faced in the thirties, when they were coming of age in the twentieth century. Bellow describes that coming of age as an individual and corporate celebration. Augie marries Stella, but the ways of love are perilous. He cannot be certain that he has found his identity at last; like Columbus he can only hope to have shown the way. But hope is an essential mark of celebration—the ritual dance to propitiate the gods.

If *The Adventures of Augie March* is not a complete success, Bellow has at least charted the way for his future development. Curiously enough, however, he reverts to the closed form once more before attempting to build on Augie's experience. The result is *Seize the Day* (1956), certainly his greatest technical achievement and probably his finest work.

Tommy Wilhelm is much closer to Joseph and to Leventhal than he is to Augie. Middle-aged, broke, out of a job, estranged from wife and father, he is another dangling man. Tommy laments his fate to anyone who will listen. He concocts a fantastic set of defenses against a hostile world: colas at breakfast, endless smoking, sedatives, and dramatic explanations of his employer's evil ways. When all these fail, he tells the truth.

Of course no one listens. His father can't be bothered and shrinks from suffering anyway. His wife, whom he regretted marrying even before the ceremony, pursues him grimly for his money. The only sympathetic ear belongs to the charlatan Dr. Tamkin, who assumes the role of spiritual father. If Augie is in the American tradition of Whitman's bard, Dr. Tamkin has roots in Melville's Confidence Man.

Tamkin takes Tommy's last $700 and speculates in the commodities market. The loss of the money, Tamkin's disappearance, and his father's final refusal to help leave Tommy in despair. Desperately he pursues Tamkin into a church, where he loses him in a large funeral crowd. There the novel ends, with Tommy staring down into the gray-haired face of death, weeping bitterly.

On the surface *Seize the Day* simply elaborates the ironic hopelessness of modern life. But a strong counter-pattern asserts itself once we see that Bellow is purifying his hard-luck hero of his illusions. Dr. Tamkin, in his role of father-betrayer, is the chief agent for that purification. He mixes a smooth line with doses of mysticism: "The spiritual compensation is what I look for. Bringing people into the here-and-now. The real universe. That's the present moment. The past is no good to us. The future is full of anxiety. Only the present is real—the here-and-now. Seize the day" (p. 66).

The ambiguity of Dr. Tamkin—more than half fraud, part psychiatrist, part idealist—fittingly reflects the complexity of experience. Himself a dealer in illusions, Tamkin delivers Tommy from the illusions about himself. He teaches Tommy that some few people want to live, and he counts Tommy among them.

The first step in Tommy's rebirth is qualified by irony. All morning he has sat in the broker's office watching market quotations next to Mr. Rappaport, an old, blind financier. At noon the three of them meet on the street. Mr. Rappaport demands to be taken to a cigar store and back to the broker's office. Tamkin leaves him to Tommy, taking the occasion to decamp. The action reflects perfectly the ambiguity of his role as con man and spiritual obstetrician. In helping Mr. Rappaport Tommy unconsciously chooses life over money.

But when he realizes that Tamkin and the commodities market have taken his money, the truth hits him hard. "I was the man beneath; Tamkin was on my back, and I thought I was on his. He made me carry him, too, besides Margaret. Like this they ride on me with hoofs and claws. Tear me to pieces, stamp on me and break my bones" (p. 105). Like Allbee and Simon before him, Tamkin is the double, the alter-ego as death force. But death is necessary before Tommy can live. The celebration of reality, as a consequence, is a celebration of death.

Since death has always been the ultimate horror in Bellow's fiction, he constructs the final scene carefully. The organ is playing, flowers abound, ushers in formal dress conduct the mourners up the aisle. Tommy enters the church in pursuit of Tamkin and finds there—himself. He sees the dead man before him and weeps over the open casket, surrendering himself to his mortality. "The flowers and lights fused ecstatically in Wilhelm's blind, wet eyes; the heavy sea-like music came up to his ears. It poured into him where he had hidden himself in the center of a crowd by the great and happy oblivion of tears. He heard it and sank deeper than sorrow, through torn sobs and cries toward the consummation of his heart's ultimate need" (p. 118). This funeral then is an ultimate celebration. For it reveals Tommy's submission to ultimate reality, to the power that defeats him. Celebration is not always a cry of triumph; here it is a ritual of surrender, a rejoicing in one's infirmities. In that surrender Tommy Wilhelm is reborn.

Through Tommy, Bellow has sounded the depths of contemporary experience and seized upon "the heart's ultimate need"—to die in order to live. If Augie celebrates freedom, hope, and becoming, Tommy celebrates weakness, defeat, and mortality. Taken together the two characters embody the range of American experience.

Seize the Day is an almost necessary prerequisite for *Henderson the Rain King* (1959). Though Tommy Wilhelm is constricted by the bonds of the real world, he can breathe the air of life at the end. The novel frees Bellow, in a sense, from the obligations of reconstructing experience; with *Henderson* he leaps from realism to myth. Yet one has qualms about the book. It may exceed its terms, as Frederick Hoffman suggests. Henderson may lapse into his old ways on his return from Africa, as Robert Gorham Davis indicates. The strength of the novel, though, lies not in a permanent transformation of its gigantic hero, but in his openness to the gigantic possibilities of life once he has seen them. Having demonstrated that celebration is founded on weakness in *Seize the Day*, Bellow transforms that weakness into an obsessive will to live in *Henderson the Rain King*.

Henderson is a restless man whom neither wife nor country can contain. He thirsts for knowledge of his primal origins. That thirst brings him to Africa, where he must relearn how to live. Lacking celebrations, America has never taught him how. His initiation into two African tribes restores his life to a spirit of festivity—first through defeat and then through victory.

The first celebration is ludicrous and splendid. Henderson beats Prince Itelo of the Arnewi tribe in a wrestling contest and thereby wins the hand and the undying devotion of Mtalba, his immense presumptive consort. As she shakes her huge girth in the graceful arabesques of the Arnewi mating dance, we feel with Henderson both the joy of celebration and the impropriety of this celebration for this man. In buffo anticlimax, Henderson is called upon to destroy the frogs that have polluted the Arnewi's water supply. Like any good American he approaches the task with confidence in his technological know-how. Using powder from his .375 magnum cartridges, he overestimates the charge for his bomb and demolishes both frogs and reservoir. He stands defeated amidst falling frogs and sluicing water like a comic Lear. Western technology and Western thought are useless here. In order to be reborn as a man, Henderson must learn to think and feel like a savage.

Henderson learns that the Arnewi can give him a social role, something that no one else has been able to do heretofore. The coat is simply too small for its wearer. So on he goes to the Wariri. Like Tommy Wilhelm's encounter with the corpse, Henderson's encounter with King Dahfu and his lions is an experience of death. Both are shocking. But both carry with them the hint of resurrection. Among the Wariri the stakes are higher, though. Identity becomes a matter of life and death. By comparison with the frog business, the lion hunt is a profound and comprehensive ritual—again, a celebration of man's mortality.

Whereas cattle dominate the Arnewi culture, lions dominate that of the Wariri. Old King Gmilo is dead, but his spirit has reincarnated itself in a lion cub, now fully grown and loose. Tribal ritual calls for King Dahfu to capture the lion-king with his net and to imprison him in the tunnel under his palace as a totem. But Dahfu already has a lion down there, or rather, a lioness. In direct defiance of the tribal imperative he has raised Atti instead of pursuing Gmilo. Yet Dahfu is not evading his task; he is simply reminding himself of his mortality. Once his sexual vigor fails with his harem, for instance, he will be strangled by the Bunam—if he is not killed by Gmilo first. Thus Atti is an appropriate sign of King Dahfu's human condition: power as sex and death.

All this becomes clear to Henderson only gradually; true, he is a willing student. But his education requires a profound reorientation of values. His wish to live, his *"I want, I want, I want,"* must be conditioned by an initiation into death. This begins quite literally when Henderson carries the corpse of the former Rain King out of his hut and into a ditch. This grotesque action is a preliminary trial, though he does not know it. The trial in earnest is also conducted in his ignorance. On a festival day he is seized with the desire to move Mummah, the large statue in the village square. After the tribal strong man fails in the attempt, Henderson tries and succeeds. Only later does King Dahfu tell him that the penalty for failure would have been death.

Shaken by this disclosure, Henderson is now ready for a conscious initiation into the knowledge of death. But first, amidst wild festivity, he is installed as Rain King. The office is the authentic counterpart of his earlier failure among the Arnewi. He possesses the appropriate physical strength; what he now must learn is moral strength. To help him gain it Dahfu takes Henderson down into the tunnel to meet Atti and to conquer his fear of death.

Here again we see the motif of the double. Both Henderson and Dahfu are leaders of the people. They are one in their encounter with fear. Dahfu teaches Henderson to love his lioness, to face the paradox of power as death. With a tremendous effort Henderson overcomes his fear; now he is a fit companion for King Dahfu in the ritual pursuit of the lion.

That pursuit itself is a tragic experience. King Dahfu must drop a net of stone-weighted vines from a rickety perch above the jungle floor over Gmilo, and then descend to inspect the beast for the notched ear of his father. But the plan fails; the net does not ensnare the hindquarters of the lion. Dahfu descends to secure his catch and is instantly castrated and eviscerated. He fully experiences power as sex and death. Ironically the lion is not even Gmilo.

Only now does Henderson realize his inheritance. He is king; Dahfu has educated him not for himself but for the Wariri. But Henderson will not be king in fact. Once his initiation is completed, "the shoe is on the other foot," as Dahfu says. Henderson must now return to the real kingdom of his suburban acres to bear the burden of his newfound nobility as best he can. Yet that nobility is more than simply human. He has not earned it for himself; it has been bestowed upon him by the blood of his friend. Indeed, to live the implications of this festive sacrifice is now Henderson's imperative. As Josef Pieper puts it, "*to celebrate a festival means: to live out for some special occasion and in an uncommon manner, the universal assent to the world as a whole.*" [4]

Henderson's assent to the world dictates his subsequent action.

He returns to his wife and children with his lion cub, Dahfu, and an Iranian orphan. When his plane stops to refuel in Newfoundland, he rushes out into the Arctic cold carrying the little boy in his arms and affirming life against a background of frozen death: "Laps and laps I galloped around the shining and riveted body of the plane, behind the fuel trucks. Dark faces were looking from within. The great, beautiful propellers were still, all four of them. I guess I felt it was my turn now to move, and so went running—leaping, leaping, pounding, and tingling over the pure white lining of the gray Arctic silence" (pp. 340–341). Henderson's celebration of the will to live orders and subdues that Arctic silence.

Henderson the Rain King is the purest distillation of Bellow's affirmation. For all his fantastic excesses, Henderson is the most festive of Bellow's six heroes. Critics have noted that the novel is built on the First Dialogue of *Thus Spake Zarathustra*. Nietzsche might also furnish its epigraph: "To have joy in anything, one must approve everything." [5]

With *Herzog* we come to Bellow's most complex celebration. The novel looks backward both to the closed form of *The Victim* and private celebration, and to the open form of *Augie March* and *Henderson*, with their public celebrations. *Herzog* manages to perform an extraordinary feat: it embodies communal festivity in the experience of one man.

The character of Herzog, first of all, is a composite. The publisher's jacket blurb describes him as "great sufferer, joker and moaner, cuckold, charmer, a man of our time." One might add intellectual, neurotic, compulsive letter-writer, and eccentric. Most of all, however, Herzog is son and father. In these roles he celebrates the rites of life.

Unlike Augie and Henderson, who are still searching, Herzog finds himself. For Augie, life offers endless possibilities. Though he wants to be a father, the problem is to become one: " 'Instead I'm in the bondage of strangeness for a time still. It's only temporary. We'll get out of it' " (*Augie March*, p. 523). And though Henderson returns to his wife and family, the test is yet to come. Each man points toward fatherhood, but only Herzog arrives at it. Herzog's family defines him; in its responsibilities he can mould his protean self into an identity. He discovers his own tradition, without which one dies. The laying hold of tradition and the self is the festive act that restores him. And like all celebrations, Herzog's is an act of love.

In a real sense Herzog does not exist until he makes his commitment to his father and to his daughter. For fully two-thirds of the novel, we hear an immensely cultivated, charming voice, but not a man. Even physically his character lacks definition: Herzog is a handsome, middle-aged Everyman in candy stripes. Bellow manipulates the voice to express the malaise of contemporary life. As John Cheever says in *The Wapshot Scandal,* "The times were venereal."

Herzog then is an urbane, comic, highly literate spokesman for our time. The venereal has destroyed his marriage to Madeleine, nonetheless—just as his own restless desire destroyed his first marriage to Daisy. This is the problem with Herzog, man and book: to achieve personal and structural form.

One means of doing both is Bellow's use of Valentine Gersbach as Herzog's double. Gersbach, Herzog's cuckold, is a Jewish version of Kirby Allbee—the victim with a claim on his benefactor. Like Allbee the victim turns victimizer and parodist.

Gersbach is the buffoon as cultural spokesman, but a buffoon with cynical motives. He is a television "personality" and a burlesque of Herzog the professor. As substitute father to Junie, Gersbach usurps the role Herzog most needs to restore him to life. Herzog describes his rival accurately: "He's a ringmaster, popularizer, liaison for the elites. He grabs up celebrities and brings them before the public. And he makes all sorts of people feel that he has exactly what they've been looking for. Subtlety for the subtle. Warmth for the warm. For the crude, crudity. For the crooks, hypocrisy. Atrocity for the atrocious. Whatever your heart desires. Emotional plasma which can circulate in any system" (p. 215).

Herzog's violent rejection of Gersbach is founded on a sense of recognition. He is part Gersbach himself. He has used Libbie, to whom he escaped in Vineyard Haven, and Ramona, who offers him pleasure and shrimp arnaud. And if Gersbach's burlesque of Herzog evades responsibility, Herzog's dozens of unwritten letters to the great and the obscure are a dodge of his own. They reveal his kind of clowning. More significantly, they reveal his loss of identity without Madeleine and Junie. A man needs to be a father. So long as he is not with Junie, the Herzog voice is disembodied.

The occasion for Herzog's rebirth is a courtroom scene. Quite unintentionally he stumbles onto the trial of a young couple for the murder of their son. The child was beaten repeatedly and died of a hemorrhage. The incident is a sordid burlesque of Herzog's own abandonment of Junie. At first he fails to understand: he is one of those people "who spend their lives in humane studies and therefore imagine once cruelty has been described in books it is ended. Of course he really knew better. . ." (p. 238). But this knowledge, like his life, is uninvolved. The description of the child's death forces the truth upon him: "Reaching the corridor, he said to himself, 'Oh my God!' and in trying to speak discovered an acrid fluid in his mouth that had to be swallowed" (p. 239).

Through the secular ceremony of the trial Herzog comes to a knowledge of his own guilt. It forces him west. New York is the land of estrangement; he must fly to Chicago and Junie. Like Tommy Wilhelm, Herzog finds in a death ceremony "the consummation of his heart's ultimate need"—in this case, to love.

The steps in Herzog's integration are four. Since paternity and filiation are his central task, he must face the familial past, the substitute father, the child herself, and the faithless wife, in that order. The truth about himself requires the admission of guilt and the consequent necessity for purification. But he must stumble through the purification rites without really knowing what he is doing.

He goes to his stepmother's house and without realizing it remembers his father's old nickle-plated pistol. He takes it and some tsarist rubles from his father's desk. His action and his motives here are ambiguous. As an act of piety to his father's memory, taking the pistol serves to restore Herzog to the alienated parent. The pistol and the rubles are a badge of his sonship. But as a sign of his overt intentions, the pistol is an instrument of revenge. Somehow these motives must be resolved by love: "He left by the back door; it made departure simpler. Honeysuckle grew along the rainspout, as in his father's time, and fragrant in the evening— almost too rich. Could any heart become quite petrified?" (p. 253).

The second step in his restoration is a private ceremony. Gersbach is bathing Junie while Herzog looks through the bathroom window. He knows he cannot shoot: "To shoot him! an absurb thought. As soon as Herzog saw the actual person giving an actual bath, the reality of it, the tenderness of such a buffoon to a little child, his intended violence turned into *theater*, into something ludicrous" (p. 258). As a ritual action the bath effectively reverses the courtroom ceremony, blots it out, eradicates it. Witness to both actions, Herzog participates in the second one by restraining himself and is revived by contact with reality.

Step three is his reunion with Junie. Herzog takes her to the Museum of Science in Jackson Park. Here his dual role as son and as father becomes overt. He tells her a story about a boy with freckles like constellations of stars. Hiram Shpitalnik, an "old old old man," takes the boy to his Great-Grandfather Shpitalnik, who lives in a walnut shell. The old man discovers a new star among the freckles. At this point "He held the child on the railing, to his left, so that she would not press against the pistol, wrapped in her great-grandfather's rubles" (p. 276). The two stories are reciprocal. The father in each mediates between child and great-grandfather. Furthermore, Herzog and Junie are looking at the life process itself while he tells her the story: a chicken is about to hatch before their eyes.

The restoration of daughter to father is followed by an anticlimax. Much like Henderson's frog episode, Herzog's wreck, arrest, and arraignment is a corrective action. The pistol incriminates Herzog. But the incrimination liberates him too, for it involves him firmly in the social context. Here again one is free only if he admits his guilt. And the public display of that guilt is the fourth step in his purgation. He must make himself vulnerable to Madeleine's hatred.

Madeleine arrives at the station house to accuse him but incriminates herself instead. Throughout her affair with Gersbach, she has behaved discreetly. Now in her moment of public triumph she goes too far. She sees the two bullets on the sergeant's desk and accuses Herzog of intending them for her and for—she will not say: the sergeant is present. She turns to Herzog, her open hatred for him an admission of defeat. Her eyes "expressed a total will that he should die." The station house incident, the public charge of guilt, works to purify Herzog and to condemn Madeleine. One is saved or condemned by his own heart.

Through such a complex action Herzog becomes a free man. But how will he use his freedom? Neither Ramona nor Madeleine is a viable option for him now; New York and Chicago cancel each other out. There remains Ludeyville. Ludeyville is his personal past, the tradition he has forged for himself. His brother Will is a human equivalent. So he takes Will to Ludeyville to look at the ramshackle house and to help him make up his mind. The final conversation with his brother reveals his determination to keep the old house in the Berkshires and to make it the setting for a new life.

He will not use Ramona any more. He will stop writing letters. Most of all, he will cease wanting: *"My face too blind, my mind too limited, my instincts too narrow. But this intensity, doesn't it mean anything? It is an idiot joy that makes this animal, the most peculiar animal of all, exclaim something? And he thinks this reaction a sign, a proof, of eternity? And he has it in his breast? But I have no argument to make about it. 'Thou movest me' "* (p. 340). Unlike Madeleine, Herzog has been purged of hatred and of self-love. His surrender to the pattern of what is, with all its religious overtones, defines his final, festive state. True freedom for Bellow is active participation in the real, without the "versions of it" that trouble Augie March. No versions now, but the thing itself.

Herzog ends where Joseph began, carrying the weight of his freedom. The development of these six novels indicates that freedom rather than fate determines character. Joseph is willing to surrender his freedom to the army; Herzog is willing to abide in it. Bellow suggests that freedom cannot be programmatic; authentic experience never is. The wonder of Bellow's fiction is the ability to impose fictive pattern on open experience. The shape and direction of his novels suggest what Marcus Klein calls "the jittery act of reaching" that makes Bellow's fiction crucial.[6]

The reaching indicates that the open and the closed form are different versions of the same whole. One cannot predetermine an ideal balance between the individual and his society. The balance shifts with the occasion, contracting and expanding in freeze and thaw. For Saul Bellow the engagement is intermittent, expressed largely in secular celebrations. The quality of life and its very reality rest on the quality of those celebrations.

12 ॐ Postscript

"So WE beat on, boats against the current, borne back ceaselessly into the past." Thus Fitzgerald concludes *The Great Gatsby*. Like the contemporary fiction that we have been considering, Fitzgerald's finest novel brings us to the wellspring of tradition at the end. Gatsby rejected tradition to build his life on an illusion, one which began on Dan Cody's yacht. His eastward movement, like Fitzgerald's, took him away from himself to the fatal consequences of illusion. Nick Carraway, his spokesman and alter ego, makes the westward return trip for him. That trip is an assertion of identity within the context of Nick's personal moral tradition.

But a corollary of Gatsby's illusion is the power of his dream and its wistfulness. One remembers Gatsby staring at the green light on Daisy's dock, and the parties where they danced until three in the morning to "a sad little waltz of that year." *The Great Gatsby* abounds in parties, with at least one in every chapter, but they all define the distance between the dream and the reality. Only the quiet party of two in Gatsby's music room is a genuine celebration:

> "*In the meantime,*
> *In between time—*"
> As I went over to say good-by I saw that the expression of be-wilderment had come back into Gatsby's face, as though a faint doubt had occurred to him as to the quality of his present happi-ness. Almost five years! There must have been moments even that afternoon when Daisy tumbled short of his dreams—not through her own fault, but because of the colossal vitality of his illusion. It

had gone beyond her, beyond everything. He had thrown himself into it with a creative passion, adding to it all the time, decking it out with every bright feather that drifted his way. No amount of fire or freshness can challenge what man will store up in his ghostly heart.[1]

Nick and Gatsby are at odds, really. At this magic moment Fitzgerald turns tradition (Nick) against celebration (Gatsby), so that the festive moment occurs in a world elsewhere, to borrow Richard Poirier's term.

The twenties, of course, were a festive occasion in American literature. For Hemingway Paris was *A Moveable Feast*—one ought not overlook the liturgical pun in that title; for E. E. Cummings, very much a poet of the twenties, poetry is the continuous act of celebrating his lady; Wallace Stevens' *Harmonium* (1923) is his wittiest and most festive volume.

True, the mood of neither the preceding nor the following periods was especially festive. Ideas and protests dominate American fiction from 1930 to World War II. From 1870–1910, American prose style was least poetic; American fiction was least festive. Twain and the realists carefully demythologized American experience. Yet *Life on the Mississippi* and *Huckleberry Finn*, surely Twain's best books, are large-scale celebrations. Each suggests a sense of life larger than the quotidian; each involves the reader vicariously in that life. Henry James is a special case; his concern for shades of awareness, individual and reciprocal, is intensely subjective. His esthetic method forced him away from the communal sharing and praise of life that underlie all celebrations.

We must go all the way back to the American Renaissance to find the first festive moments in American fiction, and we find them in abundance. The final chapters of *The Scarlet Letter* are a sustained feast, turning a political occasion into a marriage liturgy. Some of Hawthorne's best tales, furthermore, abound in festivity: "My Kinsman, Major Molineux," "Young Goodman Brown," "The Maypole of Merrymount," and "The Christmas Banquet."

Melville's fascination with the cannibal rites and the Feast of the Calabashes in *Typee* as well as the heavily symbolic quarterdeck and doubloon chapters in *Moby-Dick* are festive, and so is his attitude toward the American whaling man—the generic hero of *Moby-Dick*. *Walden* strikes many notes of celebration as Thoreau submerges himself in the natural and animal processes around him. Chapter 17, "Spring," is a wholesale celebration of natural life renewed. Who can forget, finally, the famous opening lines in "Song of Myself":

> I celebrate myself,
> And what I assume you shall assume
> For every atom belonging to me as good belongs to you.

Celebration is an ingrained quality in American literature; we may see it as the habit of praise—more frequent during the 1850s, the 1920s, and our own time than at other times, but present in one way or another throughout our literature. The novel gives us the feel of our time, the sense of sharing in it and living it more intensely. Celebration has mythic overtones, then—it is one way of creating a social and national context that defines the aspirations of the group. Thus festive novels tend to express representative desires, as *The Great Gatsby* does.

On a deeper level, celebration is the natural expression of the artist committed to reality (only the best artists are so committed). Reality, of course, is a very different thing from literary realism. It involves the artist's most basic assumptions about life, God, art, and himself. Hence some personal involvement in a spiritual tradition is essential if the artist is to praise the world. America offers examples of many traditions in which the novelist may work. I have tried to identify the major ones—Protestant, southern, Catholic, Negro, and Jewish—and to examine the work of the best novelists currently working within them.

By now it should be obvious that celebration is not a pleasant decoration in a novel, but an essential manifestation of the spiritual element in art and in life. And the ultimate celebration is active worship. For the Catholic, the Jew, and the biblically-oriented Protestant writer, celebration is especially meaningful, then. In an address to the Friends of Sister Mary Corita (an artist who along with Ben Shahn is especially festive) in 1965, the Dutch priest Father Frederic Debuyst put the matter this way:

> The world of the living symbols, of the living gestures, of the living words of the liturgy can only be expressed by a living assembly where all those who participate in it possess a deeply, fully human

and biblical culture. We are much too often purely rational, didactic, sentimental, or nervous beings when participating in a celebration. We are not very often really festive beings. This is probably the principal obstacle to a good adaptation of the liturgy as well as to a good, active, and inspired participation in the liturgy.

We have to watch for sublimity and grace, freedom and harmony, creativity and order. It has never been easy to unite those qualities perfectly in the concrete shape of celebration. Even the Greeks, those masters of festivity, were unable to keep the perfect balance between Apollo and Dionysus.

But we have the living balance of the Bible, the infinite patience of the Church. We should be able to remain, or to become, really what we are: beings created for the perfect jubilation, for the perfect communion of an everlasting feast.[2]

Literature and liturgy are not identical actions, but analogous ones. And so we can take these comments, *mutatis mutandis*, in a literary sense. I am suggesting a very old view of literature now; it is Emerson's notion of correspondence, Dante's anagogical level, and Augustine's polarization of the two cities. All three writers naturally assume that their essential function is the praise of creation and of God.

The contemporary novelist, however, lacks the world view of Emerson, let alone Dante and Augustine. He is confronted with the problem of power, first of all—nuclear, totalitarian, civil, and personal power hangs ominously over the shoulders of Cheever, Ellison, and Baldwin, not to mention Norman Mailer. The problem of freedom, secondly, runs through the work of Bellow, Updike, and R. P. Warren. *The Victim, Herzog, Rabbit, Run, Of the Farm, All the King's Men*, and *World Enough and Time* all project the pressing problem of choice in the creation of the self.

Third, the problem of isolation runs through contemporary fiction. Personal, spiritual, social, and cultural "isolatos" are nothing new in American literature, certainly—Poe and Melville initiated the story of the lone sensibility well over a century ago. Truman Capote's lonely little boys and moronic killers, Carson McCullers' awkward teenagers, deaf-mutes, and loveless loners inhabit a nightmare from which they cannot awaken. Similarly, the best plays of Tennessee Williams and Arthur Miller—*The Glass Menagerie, A Streetcar Named Desire, Death of a Salesman*, and *The Crucible*—are memory plays in which the hero is at best isolated in his own goodness or else trapped by his illusions. Even one of Miller's worst plays, *After the Fall,* reflects the isolation of a man condemned by his memories.

But the breakdown in communication is the major problem with which our novelists must deal at the moment. Our customary, easy assumptions about American life, with its core of Christian, familial, patriotic, liberal-progressive values, have been profoundly shaken by apostasy, divorce, assassinations, ill-considered military adventures, and political extremism. Taken as a whole, these problems reflect a failure of faith. Our novelists are extremely sensitive to such failures, for they bear directly on the writer-to-reader relationship. Writing a novel is an act of faith, and so is reading one.

The breakdown in communication reflects an inability to relate to time and place. The novelist writes from a firm sense of time and place; they are prerequisites for meaningful action. Yet the work of Cheever, Updike, Bellow, and Baldwin reflects rootlessness and the loss of the social context in which the novelist traditionally works. And much of the tension in the plays of Edward Albee and Harold Pinter derives from their unmoored settings.

A third consequence of the breakdown in communication deserves special attention: the treatment of sex in contemporary literature. Pornography is much more prevalent today than it was twenty years ago. But pornography is never art. In pornography, communication among characters is limited to the animal level, on which discrimination of persons, taste, sensitivity, and the higher relationships between people, sexual and otherwise, are impossible.

To put the matter in different terms: in serious fiction choice and the consequences of choice are the chief subjects for fictional development. A substantive or round character can be motivated to choose by the desire for pleasure, for the pursuit of money, for power, for his temporal concerns and his responsibilities in time, or by his response to other people. Pleasure, money, power, time, and people are the chief realities influencing choice. In most serious fiction, significant choice lies in the areas of time and people. In most commercial fiction, it lies in the areas of money and power. Whether the fiction be serious or commercial, however, the most basic motive, pleasure, inheres in the other four. Furthermore, motives are quite often mixed in a given character. For example, Frankie Alpine in *The Assistant* wants to find his place in time and to marry Helen Bober. He takes a certain ascetic or spiritual pleasure in the suffering he endures while pursuing his objectives. By contrast, the protagonist in Budd Schulberg's *What Makes Sammy Run?* (1941), a good piece of commercial fiction, wants power, wealth, and love. He gets them all in the same, acquisitive fashion.

With pornography, however, the pleasure motive is detached from its inherent place among the higher motives and made the total reality. The inevitable consequence is aggression. Brutality is an integral component of pornography. Since the self is the sole reality, all other realities—people, responsibilities, society, love, and God—must be shut out, or violently attacked. De Sade makes this quite clear in *Justine*, and he systematically attacks loyalties to everything except sexual pleasure. A more recent work, Pauline Reage's *Story of O*, is built on the premise that the ultimate sensual experience (if there is one) is the possession of a woman who totally abases herself at all times and in all ways to the sexual appetite of her master. For most adults and serious writers, pornography is boring; it is repetitious, rigidly conventionalized, contrived, meretricious, and unreal in every sense.

What of pornography in serious fiction, then? Apart from his desire to make a financial killing, the contemporary novelist wants to be read. He knows that the general reader will buy books with a sexual repute (on the assumption that the novel is primarily concerned with sex anyway, and that the novelist can get away with more sex than the film-maker can). But unlike the commercial pornographer, the serious novelist—Vladimir Nabokov, Philip Roth, or John Updike—does not endorse sexual fantasies, does not encourage the aggressions resulting from those fantasies, and manifests an allegiance to the more significant motives, time and people. The serious novelist frames the sexual appeal within a wider, more significant context. (*Portnoy's Complaint* is an exception.)

Couples (1968) is a case in point. In pornography, sexual activity occurs in a vacuum. But in *Couples* one is always aware of the social and geographical context (*Time's* cartographer even drew a map of Tarbox for the cover story on Updike). More important, one is always aware of the temporal context—the summer and fall of 1963, with the Kennedy assassination as the pivotal public event on which the private action turns. Implicit here is

Updike's sense of human activity *in* time, with temporal consequences.

Moreover, in pornography the sexual appetite is endless; the sexual act is always refreshing and always climatic for both (or all) parties; bodies and breath are always fragrant; the act is never painful—except by intention. In sexual descriptions the diction is either coy and euphemistic (*Fanny Hill*) or else hyperbolic (*My Life and Loves*). Pornography is quantitative, appealing to the adolescent reader's fervid curiosity—how often? how many ways?, etc. Being quantitative rather than qualitative, pornography does not bear rereading. In *Couples*, on the other hand, Foxy is flat-chested, fearful of discovery, cold (literally and figuratively), frequently uncomfortable during intercourse, and frustrated in her serious attempt to relate an unhappy past to an uncertain future. Piet deceives himself, betrays the integrity of his work, and allows his appetites to destroy his marriage and his peace of mind.

Most important, Updike never lets us take Piet as a reliable spokesman for his own values. Piet's action is multiplied by the infidelities that surround and ultimately corrupt him. *Couples* is aptly titled: it is a novel with a group hero and a group activity (coupling). Updike's narrator brings home the detached, neutral view with his final comment on the willful insignificance with these characters have treated their lives:

> Now, though it has not been many years, the town scarcely remembers Piet, with his rattly pickup truck full of odd lumber, with his red hair and corduroy hat and eye-catching apricot windbreaker, he who sat so often and contentedly in Cogswell's Drug Store nursing a cup of coffee, the stub of a pencil sticking down from under the sweatband of his hat, his windbreaker unzipped to reveal an expensive cashmere sweater ruined by wood dust and shavings, his quick eyes looking as if they had been rubbed too hard the night before, the skin beneath them pouched in a little tucked fold, as if his maker in the last instant had pinched the clay. Angela, who teaches at a girls' school in Braintree, is still around, talking with Freddy Thorne on the street corner, or walking the beach with a well-tailored, wise-smiling small man, her father. She flew to Juárez in July and was divorced in a day. Piet and Foxy were married in September. Her father, pulling strings all the way from San Diego, found a government job for his new son-in-law, as a construction inspector for federal jobs, mostly military barracks, in the Boston-Worcester area. Piet likes the official order and

the regular hours. The Hanemas live in Lexington, where, gradually, among people like themselves, they have been accepted, as
another couple.[3]

Updike's final comment is ironic and detached. He shows that
sex is a metaphor for human freedom; if the characters in Tarbox
abuse their sexual powers and ignore the human responsibilities
that sex entails, they have simply surrendered their freedom to
their passions.

Through narrative detachment, a clinical neutrality in sexual
description, a refusal to accept the mode of fantasy with its assumption that acts do not have consequences, and his insistence
that sex has a corporate dimension, Updike uses sexual material
with artistic integrity. One suspects, however, that like *Lolita*,
Couples has been widely misread. This is not Updike's fault, of
course. Still, one wonders whether *Couples* was worth the effort
for a man of Updike's talents.

Couples is not a great book; it is not even Updike's best book.
It is a book written to prove a point: the serious writer can reach
a mass audience by using the materials of pornography without
the assumptions of pornography. Updike obviously thought the
point was worth making. In *Couples* he connects ceremonial style
with physical scene. But the connection hoped for isn't the one
he made.

Communication still remains the central task for the contemporary novelist, who must compete with television, magazines, and
nonfiction for the contemporary reader's leisure time. For the
minority who can resist the utter passivity of watching television,
nonfiction poses the bigger problem. The reader who is not sex-
obsessed is liable to be fact-obsessed. Certainly Truman Capote
and Norman Mailer have already decided that the novel is an un-
satisfactory form for communicating with the reader and have
chosen reportage instead. One doubts that either man, exhilirated
and enriched in his newly-won public position, will ever return
to the more demanding form in which he began.

In the face of all these contemporary problems the work of our
best novelists demands increasing attention. A study of the quality,
extent, frequency, and significance of celebration in that work

reveals their sense of the possibilities for a full life in modern America. Through meals, weddings, funerals, songs, parties, holiday observances, and riots, they have tried to show the individual's festive encounters with reality.

John Cheever, a New Yorker writing as a New England traditionalist, demonstrates the importance of eccentric, small-town, inherited culture for giving contemporary man a perspective on life. John Updike, through the pieties of the family and the application of various contexts—institutional life, sports, Greek mythology, a Pennsylvania farm, and a Boston suburb—tries in similar fashion to give coherence to modern living. Like his fellow New Englanders, Emerson and Jonathan Edwards, Updike has an almost mystical regard for natural phenomena.

Eudora Welty, writing in the southern context of the Yazoo Delta, is both mystical and mythical. Her milieu is a timeless land whose fertility, variety, and wonder she celebrates. Flannery O'Connor, writing as both southerner and Catholic, dramatizes the encounter between time and eternity. Using the two sources of tradition in which she lived, she elevates the banalities of rural speech into hidden though real celebrations. James Agee, also a southerner, and an Anglo-Catholic, approaches the novel with a background in journalism, film criticism, and scriptwriting. He chooses to ignore that wide experience for a nostalgic evocation of his Tennessee boyhood, in which he celebrates innocence, initiation, and the restorative bonds of familial love.

J. D. Salinger, steadily improvising a myth of eternal innocence and human perfectibility, celebrates the holiness of isolated man, able to surmount the confusion and lovelessness of modern living through mystical union with a dead, saintly brother.

James Baldwin, writing in the context of the Harlem Negro, is the spokesman as compassionate prophet. In his essays he celebrates the ideals of a better life in another country while registering in his fiction the trauma of chaotic life in this one. Ralph Ellison celebrates America through a catharsis of its ills, effected by comedy, parody, and revolution. He contains the violent present by laughing at it. His Harlem riot is an apt secular feast, celebrating victory over self-deception.

Bernard Malamud, writing fables of identity within the context of Jewish tradition, shows that self-denial, humiliation, suffering, and defiance of persecution allow man to celebrate his new identity within ancient Jewish traditions. And Saul Bellow, writing from the juncture of Jewish tradition and secular life, celebrates both the acceptance of isolated suffering and the incorporation of the self in the world at large.

In all ten writers, celebration shows the connection between culture and cultus, or worship. Celebration is an expression of tradition, whatever its shape or origin. The point is that some tradition is essential—some time and place within which the writer can connect secular and spiritual experience. Whether it be Flannery O'Connor's biblical Georgia, James Baldwin's Pentecostal Harlem, Saul Bellow's Ludeyville, or John Cheever's St. Botolphs, that place must suggest life in the fullest sense.

At the same time, the contemporary novelist acknowledges the problems, public and private, which press in upon him. Celebration is a free act founded on the realities of the workaday world but transcending that world. Through celebration the contemporary novelist expresses his faith in the livability of life.

Though the feast be momentary and incomplete, it bears witness to the goodness of reality. Suffering and love are the keys to joy in that reality. But joy is never easy, never assured, and never an end in itself. The ultimate end in much of our fiction now, the ultimate celebration, is a humble assent to the variety, the banality, the beauty, the terror—and the mystery—of existence itself.

Notes

Preface

1. As quoted in Newton Arvin's essay, "The House of Pain: Emerson and the Tragic Sense," reprinted in *American Literature: A Critical Survey*, I, edited by Thomas Daniel Young and Ronald Edward Fine (American Book Company, 1968), pp. 137–138. Arvin's conclusion is also relevant here: "What is there [in Emerson's work], as we have come to recognize when we have cleared our mind of the cant of pessimism, is perhaps the fullest and most authentic expression in modern literature of the more-than-tragic emotion of thankfulness. A member of his family tells us that almost his last word was 'praise.' Unless we have deafened ourselves to any other tones than those of anguish and despair, we should still know how to be inspired by everything in his writings that this word symbolizes" (p. 138).

Chapter 1

1. Ihab Hassan, *Radical Innocence: The Contemporary American Novel* (Princeton: Princeton University Press, 1961); Jonathan Baumbach, *The Landscape of Nightmare* (New York: New York University Press, 1965); Marcus Klein, *After Alienation: American Novels in Mid-Century* (Cleveland: World, 1964).
2. Josef Pieper, *In Tune with the World: A Theory of Festivity*, trans. Richard and Clara Winston (New York: Harcourt, Brace, and World, 1965), p. 23 (italics his).
3. Richard Poirier, *A World Elsewhere: The Place of Style in American Literature* (New York: Oxford University Press, 1966), p. 252.
4. Wallace Stevens, "Sunday Morning," *The Collected Poems of Wallace Stevens* (New York: Alfred A. Knopf, 1957), pp. 69–70.

Chapter 2

1. *The Wapshot Chronicle* (New York: Bantam, 1957), p. 54. Page references in the second novel are to *The Wapshot Scandal* (New York: Bantam, 1963); the dates are those of the original publication, and not of the paperback reprint.
2. George Garrett, "John Cheever and the Charms of Innocence," *Hollins Critic*, I, ii (1964), 10.

Chapter 3

1. "Who Made Yellow Roses Yellow?" in *The Same Door* (New York: Crest, 1959), p. 73. All subsequent references are to paperback Crest editions; dates are those of original publication.
2. John Updike, *"Franny and Zooey," Studies in J. D. Salinger,* ed. Marvin Laser and Norman Fruman (New York: Odyssey Press, 1963), pp. 229–230.
3. "Updike's Quest for Liturgy," *Commonweal*, 78: 192–195. Novak confines his discussion of liturgy to "Packed Dirt."

Chapter 4

1. See Alfred Appel, Jr., *A Season of Dreams: The Fiction of Eudora Welty* (Baton Rouge: Louisiana State University Press, 1965); and Ruth M. Vande Kieft, "The Season of Dreams," chapter 5 of her fine study, *Eudora Welty* (New York: Twayne, 1962).
2. *The Robber Bridegroom* (New York: Atheneum, 1963), pp. 64–65. Other editions cited are as follows: *Delta Wedding* (New York: New American Library, 1963); *The Golden Apples* (New York: Harcourt, Brace and Co.); *The Ponder Heart* (New York: Dell, 1954); and *Thirteen Stories by Eudora Welty,* ed. Ruth M. Vande Kieft (New York: Harvest, 1965).
3. Vande Kieft, *Eudora Welty,* p. 109. There was, however, a serious earthquake in Japan in 1923, producing much loss of life and property.
4. John Crowe Ransom's useful phrase in summary of *Delta Wedding,* cited in Appel, p. 201.
5. Appel, pp. 250–252.
6. Elizabeth Bowen, *The Death of the Heart,* Collected Edition (London: Jonathan Cape, 1948), p. 111.
7. Appel, p. 60.
8. In *Eudora Welty* Miss Vande Kieft applies the epigraph to her discussion of "Music from Spain," p. 133. I see the Scripture passage as an epigraph for her entire body of work.
9. Of particular relevance to my reading of Eudora Welty is Miss Vande Kieft's comment on wonder and celebration in the stories: "Her stories may be viewed, then, as celebrations of so many pieces of life with 'the mysteries rushing unsubmissively through them by the minute': life not so much analyzed and interpreted as rendered and wondered at, perhaps

because what is shown is extraordinary, perhaps because it is simply ordinary" (*Thirteen Stories*, p. 5).

10. Miss Welty is probably remembering Audubon's own statement in the introductory volume of his great work, *Birds in America*, in seven volumes: ". . . The moment a bird was dead, however beautiful it had been in life, the pleasure arising from the possession of it became blunted; and although the greatest care was bestowed on endeavors to preserve the appearance of nature, I looked upon its vesture as more than sullied, as requiring constant attention and repeated mendings, while, after all, it could no longer be said to be fresh from the hands of its Maker. I wished to possess all the productions of nature, but I wished life with them. This was impossible. Then what was to be done? I turned to my father, and made known to him my disappointment and anxiety. He produced a book of *Illustrations*. A new life ran in my veins. I turned over the leaves with avidity; and although what I saw was not what I longed for, it gave me a desire to copy Nature. To Nature I went, and tried to imitate her, as in the days of my childhood I had tried to raise myself from the ground and stand erect, before Time had imparted the vigour necessary for the success of such an undertaking." John James Audubon, *Ornithological Biography: Or An Account of the Habits of the Birds of the United States of America* (Philadelphia, 1831), p. vii. For Audubon's painting of the snowy heron, see *Birds of America*, vol. 6 (Philadelphia, 1840), facing p. 163.

Chapter 5

1. Flannery O'Connor, "The Role of the Catholic Novelist," *Grayfriars*, 7 (1964): 9.
2. O'Connor, "Catholic Novelist," p. 9.
3. Ibid., p. 11.
4. Flannery O'Connor, "A Temple of the Holy Ghost," *Three by Flannery O'Connor* (New York: Signet, 1964), p. 194.
5. Robert Fitzgerald has shown the importance of the giant wife's role in "The Countryside and the True Country," *Sewanee Review*, 70, no. 2 (Summer, 1962): 380–394. I am indebted to him for his fine analysis of the story and for introducing me to Flannery O'Connor's work in his class years ago at Notre Dame.
6. Granville Hicks, "A Writer at Home with Her Heritage," *Saturday Review*, May 12, 1962, pp. 22–23.
7. Flannery O'Connor, "The Lame Shall Enter First," *Everything That Rises Must Converge* (New York: Farrar, Straus and Giroux, 1965), pp. 188–189. All subsequent page references are to this edition.

Chapter 6

1. John Updike, "No Use Talking," *Assorted Prose* (New York: Crest, 1965), p. 215.
2. James Agee and Walker Evans, *Let Us Now Praise Famous Men: Three Tenant Families* (Boston: Houghton Mifflin Co., 1941; 1960), p. 246.

Page references to Agee's novels are to the paperback editions: *The Morning Watch* (New York: Ballantine, 1966); and *A Death in the Family* (New York: Avon, 1959). The letters are collected with an introduction by Robert Phelps in *Letters of James Agee to Father Flye* (New York: Braziller, 1962).

Chapter 7

1. Louis Bouyer, *Liturgical Piety* (Notre Dame, Indiana: University of Notre Dame Press, 1954), pp. 266–267.
2. The complete title of the Pilgrim book is *The Way of a Pilgrim and The Pilgrim Continues His Way*, trans. R. M. French (New York: Seabury, 1965).
3. James E. Miller, Jr., *J. D. Salinger*, [Pamphlets on American Writers, No. 51] (Minneapolis: University of Minnesota Press, 1965), p. 44.

Chapter 8

1. James Baldwin, *The Fire Next Time* (New York: Dell, 1964), p. 124.
2. Baldwin's books are most easily available in paperback. All page references are to the following paperback editions: *Go Tell It on the Mountain* (New York: Signet Books, 1954); *Notes of a Native Son* (Boston, The Beacon Press, 1955); *Giovanni's Room* (New York: The Dial Press Apollo Edition, 1956); *Nobody Knows My Name* (New York: Dell Delta Edition, 1961); *Another Country* (New York: Dell, 1963); *The Fire Next Time* (New York: Dell, 1964); and *Going to Meet the Man* (New York: Dell, 1966).
3. This classification of themes may seem arbitrary and reductive; moreover, some of the essays profess more than one theme. For the sake of convenience and clarity, I have attempted to isolate the dominant theme of each essay. Abbreviations used are: *FNT, The Fire Next Time; NK, Nobody Knows My Name; NN, Notes of a Native Son.*

The Search for Identity
  "Autobiographical Notes" *(NN)*
  "Notes of a Native Son" *(NN)*
  "The Black Boy Looks at the White Boy" *(NK)*
Alienation
  "Everybody's Protest Novel" *(NN)*
  "The Harlem Ghetto" *(NN)*
  "Journey to Atlanta" *(NN)*
  "Equal in Paris" *(NN)*
  "Stranger in the Village" *(NN)*
  "Fifth Avenue, Uptown" *(NK)*
  "East River, Downtown" *(NK)*
  "A Fly in Buttermilk" *(NK)*
  "Nobody Knows My Name" *(NK)*
The Search for a Usable Past
  "Many Thousands Gone" *(NN)*

"Carmen Jones" *(NN)*
"A Question of Identity" *(NN)*
"The Discovery of What It Means to be an American" *(NK)*
"Princes and Powers" *(NK)*
"Faulkner and Desegregation" *(NK)*
The Negro as American
"Encounter on the Seine" *(NN)*
"The Northern Protestant" *(NK)*
"Alas, Poor Richard" *(NK)*
"My Dungeon Shook" *(FNT)*
The Need for Love
"In Search of a Majority" *(NK)*
"Notes for a Hypothetical Novel" *(NK)*
"The Male Prison" *(NK)*
"Down at the Cross" *(FNT)*

Chapter 9

1. Ralph Ellison, *Invisible Man* (New York: New American Library, Signet edition, 1953), pp. 19–20. All subsequent page references are to this edition.
2. *Shadow and Act* (New York: New American Library, 1966), p. 40.

Chapter 10

1. *The Natural* (New York: Farrar, Straus, and Giroux, Noonday edition, 1952), p. 210. Other editions cited are as follows: *The Assistant* (New York: Farrar, Straus, and Giroux, Noonday edition, 1957); *A New Life* (New York: Dell, 1961); *The Fixer* (New York: Farrar, Straus, and Giroux, 1966); *The Magic Barrel* (New York: Random House, Vintage edition, 1958); *Idiots First* (New York: Delta, 1963). The dates are in all cases those of original publication, and not of paperback reprint.
2. A more relevant parallel is *The Great Gatsby*. Memo plays Daisy to Roy's Gatsby. Gus combines the corruptive function of Tom Buchanan with that of Meyer Wolfsheim, the man who fixed the World Series of 1919. A further parallel is Memo's reckless driving on Long Island, where she may or may not have hit a boy in the fog, and Daisy's hitting Myrtle Wilson in Gatsby's car. Robert Shulman relates the two novels to a common source in "Myth, Mr. Eliot, and the Comic Novel," *Modern Fiction Studies*, 12, no. 6 (Winter, 1966–67), 395–404.
3. Sidney Richman, *Bernard Malamud* (Twayne: New York, 1966), p. 70.
4. "Change should not be a factor, at once, in *both* scene and character; either unchanged character should see, or be seen against, changed scene, or changed character should see, or be seen against unchanged scene. *Two* changes obviously cancel each other out, and would cancel each other's contribution to the advance of plot." *Collected Impressions* (London: Longmans Green, 1950), pp. 260–261.
5. My classification of Malamud's stories is arbitrary, but it may help to indicate the principal differences between the stories in the two collections.

Idiots First includes burlesques and melodramas, and it lacks laments and comedies altogether.

Form (or Setting)	The Magic Barrel	Idiots First
Jewish lament	"The First Seven Years" "The Mourners" "The Loan"	
Jewish melodrama		"The Death of Me" "The Cost of Living"
Jewish comedy	"The Girl of My Dreams" "The Magic Barrel"	
Jewish fantasy	"Angel Levine" "Take Pity"	"Idiots First" "The Jewbird"
Jewish-Italian comedy	"The Lady of the Lake" "The Last Mohican"	
Jewish-Italian burlesque		"Still Life" "Naked Nude"
Italian	"Behold the Key"	"Life Is Better Than Death" "The Maid's Shoes"
Public	"The Prison" "A Summer's Reading" "The Bill"	"Black Is My Favorite Color" "A Choice of Profession" "The German Refugee"

6. Cf. Baumbach's chapter on *The Assistant*, "All Men Are Jews," pp. 101–122.

Chapter 11

1. In the best study of Bellow's work to appear so far, John Clayton finds the source of Bellow's festive attitude in the Jewish cultural context which he knows so well:

> Bellow has said of the "Jewish feeling" within him that it resists the claims of twentieth century apocalyptic romanticism; it rejects the belief that man is finished and that the world must be destroyed. The world is, on the contrary, sanctified. Thus we find the struggling householder Tevye (of Sholem Aleichem) celebrating, not cursing, poverty. We find Gimpel ("Gimpel the Fool") humiliated by an extraordinary unfaithful wife but converting his suffering into an acceptance of life and celebration of God. Gimpel comes from a long line of Jewish fools who praise life; there is Bontsha the Silent

(Peretz), who never complains in life and in heaven asks only for a roll and butter each morning; there is also, as we shall see, Moishe Herzog. In Pinski's "And Then He Wept" there is a celebration of endurance in which a poor man accidentally smashes the family's one possession, the bed, and still jokes at misfortune (although his laughter turns to tears when his wife's fury breaks and she cries). In Reisen's stories of poor Jews holding their heads up in poverty, there is again a celebration of common life.

John Clayton, *Saul Bellow: In Defense of Man* (Bloomington: Indiana University Press, 1968), p. 32.

2. *Dangling Man* (New York: New American Library, 1965), p. 18. All subsequent page references except those to *Herzog* are to the paperback Compass editions: *The Victim* (New York, 1964); *The Adventures of Augie March* (New York, 1960); *Seize the Day* (New York, 1961); and *Henderson the Rain King* (New York, 1965). References to *Herzog* are to the original edition (New York: Viking Press, 1964).

3. Marcus Klein sees more dignity in the term than I do: "Accommodation is restoration and love in their ordinary, domestic, painfully contingent instances, and it makes up in plain necessity what it lacks in conscience." *After Alienation: American Novels in Mid-Century* (Cleveland and New York: World, 1964), p. 296. The double figure, who represents a choice of death over life, clearly accommodates the world more than the hero does. But, in fairness to Klein, I must admit to a pejorative use of the term, as opposed to his own neutral use of it.

4. Pieper, p. 23.

5. *Nachgelassene Aufzeichnungen den Jahren 1882 bis 1888,* Gesammelte Werke, 16: 37; cited in Pieper, p. 20.

6. Klein, p. 70.

Chapter 12

1. F. Scott Fitzgerald, *The Great Gatsby* (New York: Scribner Library Paperback, 1925), p. 97. Note that this one genuine celebration occurs midway in the novel, at the end of chapter 5. All the other parties are false feasts, involving ulterior motives of one kind or another.

2. This is the conclusion of Father Debuyst's lecture "The Philosophy of Celebration," and given in July, 1965, at the Immaculate Heart College, Los Angeles, California.

3. John Updike, *Couples* (New York: Crest, 1968), p. 479.

Index